THE ROUGH GUIDE TO CULT FOOTBALL

"There were some good things in the game but I can't remember what they were"

Harry Kampman, Motherwell boss, after a 0-0 draw with Kilmarnock in 1998

Sometime in the autumn of 1990, a Tibetan called **Palden Gyatso** was, with his fellow prisoners in the Drapchi Prison in China, encouraged to watch the **Chinese** national team in the Asian games. As Gyatso notes in his memoir *Fire Under The Snow*, "the Chinese were keen for us to watch these matches as a sign of progress but we turned the occasion into an opportunity to show our resistance. We would all sit in the hall and clap and cheer when China lost. When one of China's opponents scored, we would celebrate with thunderous applause."

Gyatso and his fellow prisoners, some jailed for their beliefs and others for acts of crime, had plenty to cheer about that summer as China lost to **South Korea** in the group stages and went out in the quarter-finals, losing 1-0 to **Thailand**. Football gave them the perfect chance to protest against the conditions they lived in but, as Gyatso notes, the games weren't merely a means by which the prisoners could upset their guards and get away with it. The protest was all the more satisfying because the prisoners loved football so dearly.

All this might seem a long way from the average fan's typical experience on a Saturday afternoon (or, for that matter, with Sky Sports taking over the schedules, a Monday evening) but it isn't really. For every member of the chattering classes who flaunts their allegiance to the beautiful game (**Tony Blair**, **Prince William**, **Norman Cook**, **Salman Rushdie** et al), there are many who are deeply uneasy with football's enduring grip on the popular imagination. For the critics, football is portrayed almost entirely in images of mindless violence, drunkenness, tribalism, bigotry, as though the game (and not the society) was entirely to blame for all these problems. Some, on the left, see football as a natural replacement for religion as the new opiate for the masses. Yet, as the experience of Gyatso shows, football can comfort the afflicted too and, as the experience of countless get-rich-quick chairmen has proved, afflict the comfortably-off.

Of course, football has changed. The days of baggy shorts, paperback books

George Best tries an unusually laid-back approach to dating

for shinguards, and a leather ball so hard only the very brave or the very stupid would dare to head it, are long gone. A certain purity and eccentricity (you must have someone in your local who insists "there are no characters in the game any more") is said to be lacking. And our favourites – unless they're playing in **The Gallpen Press Norwich Business Houses League Norwich Cladding And Steel FJ Potter Cup** (yes, there was such an event) – are likely to take the field wearing some logo or other after a pre-match snack of chicken and pasta, instead of steak and chips. But the hairstyles are as daft as ever, the game remains predictably unpredictable and, crucially, the passion is as strong as it ever was.

This book isn't an excuse for cheap nostalgia – although there's nothing wrong with that (it's certainly preferable to expensive nostalgia) – it's a celebration of a game we have in common. Whether it's Saturday afternoon, or Thursday night, when our teams run out our hearts start beating with an irrational, pathetic pride. That feeling may ebb away in the time it takes us to remember this is the same shower we saw last week. But somehow it never seems to matter.

Brazilian monks enjoy a kickaround in Rio – the Pope, once a keeper, would approve

Sunday morning, Hackney Marshes: a different sort of jumpers for goalposts

Michel Platini, arguably the finest Juventus player of all time and master hurdler

A Belgian defender cowers as Ronaldinho lets fly during the 2002 World Cup

Geoff Hurst and Bobby Moore wonder why they're sitting on a pile of Ford Cortinas

Moore meets Muhammad Ali prior to Pelé's final game for New York Cosmos

Jimmy Greaves makes an unlikely play for gay icon status, years before Beckham

The famous Duncan Edwards memorial window at St Francis Church in Dudley

David Beckham finds the weight of a nation's hopes a little too much to bear

Elton John, unlikely benefactor of Watford, before the club's big day out in the 1984 FA Cup final

Brazil stars (from left to right) Mazinho, Bebeto and Romario rock the baby together

The Czech Republic team don't know where to turn after beating France in Euro '96

Gheorge Hagi, most convincing of the many "New Maradonas" – certainly in terms of talent and temperament

FSV Mainz president Walter Strutz feels the pain as his German side miss promotion

The original Diego Maradona greets the final whistle in a 1986 World Cup game

Valencian players hit new lows after losing the 2001 Champions League Final...

... while victors Bayern Munich go nuts after their penalty shoot-out triumph

Despair for Italian under-16 keeper Francesco Lodi after a defeat against Spain

Alvaro Recoba of Uruguay taunts Australia as his nation reaches the World Cup finals

Diego Maradona helps himself to a hapless victim's shirt after appearing at Wembley

Brazilian Jair comes up with a novel idea for dealing with a snowstorm in Milan

A rare appearance for the orange ball as Tromso of Norway face Chelsea in 1997

Mexican keeper Jorge Campos, famed for short sleeves, Day-Glo tops and the desire to charge from his penalty area

Rene Higuita, celebrated fruitcake and inventor of the scorpion kick

Bruce Grobbelaar, making the maximum possible effort to keep this shot out

1970s Chelsea idol John Dempsey shows it hasn't always been glamorous at Stamford Bridge

Ian Wallace of Coventry, horrific hair rivalled only by notorious brown away kit

Bulgaria's Iordan Letchkov with an earlier version of the Ronaldo triangle

Ruben Ayala of Argentina takes the weight off his hair in the 1974 World Cup

Jason Lee of Nottingham Forest, hounded on national television for his "pineapple"

Chelsea's Ian Britton, often wrongly overlooked in the "worst hair" stakes

Fan worship went too far with Bruno, a Brazilian boy so determined to look like Ronaldo he had dental work

A Senegalese fan models this season's hottest terrace attire

Sid James pops up, inevitably, among the England banners in Japan

Gary Lineker gets into local Sardinian traditions, without realising the joke's on him

Marcello Lippi relaxes with man's best friend

A refugee playing football in a camp in Israel which holds displaced Lebanese

Bob Marley, a keen footballer who wore tights more often than Keith Weller

German striker Fredi Bobic (centre) tries his hand at Europop with his boy band

King Kev pops out for a bite in Germany with a visit to the local Basil Brush

FC St Pauli line up for an unusual photo opportunity – see "The Clubs"

Alan Shearer (left) demonstrates his hilarious sense of japery on an early holiday

Nicolas Anelka finds someone willing to listen while on sulking leave at Real Madrid

Tomas Brolin always did have his own ideas about pre-season training

CONTENTS

CREDITS

Text editors Paul Simpson, Robert Jeffery, Nick Moore
Contributors Helen Rodiss, Richard Pendleton, John Aizlewood, Chris Lepowski, Ulrich Hesse-Lichtenberger, Sam Pilger, Chris Hughes, Damian Hall, Tom O'Sullivan, Robert Matthews, Shaun Campbell, Steve Morgan, Scott Morgan, Lloyd Bradley
Production Sue Weekes, Ian Cranna, Ann Oliver, Caroline Hunt
Picture editors Jenny Quiggin, Lara Richards
Thanks to Cathrine Keen, Michaela Bushell, Mark Ellingham, Julia Bovis, Mat Snow
Picture adjustment Link Hall
Cover design Jon Butterworth
Design Sharon O'Connor, Alex Fanning
Illustrations Karen Bates
Cover photos supplied by Empics, Bob Henriques/ Magnum Photos, Frank Moscate/Mr Bongo Recordings
Other photos supplied by Empics, Corbis, Getty Sport, Science and Society Picture Library, Vinmags, Popperfoto, Hulton Archives, Kobal, Reuters, Magnum Photos, BBC Picture Library, Mirrorpix, urbanimage.tv/ Adrian Boot, James Nachtwey/VII

Printed in Spain by Graphy Cems

Dedicated to Len Glover, Glen Mulcaire and Stevie Nicol

PUBLISHING INFORMATION

This edition published October 2003 was prepared by Haymarket Customer Publishing for Rough Guides Ltd, 80 Strand, London, WC2R ORL

Distributed by the Penguin Group

Penguin Books Ltd, 27 Wrights Lane, London W8 5TZ

A catalogue record for this book is available from the British Library
ISBN 1-84353-228-X

THE ROOTS

How an English invention conquered the world; and the world then conquered England

Berlin police, refusing to recognise English rules, play "horse football" in 1954

"For as much as there is great noise in the city caused by hustling over large balls, from which many evils may arise, which God forbid, we command and forbid on behalf of the King, on pain of imprisonment, such games to be used"

Edward II bans football in London in 1314

When England hosted the European Championship finals in 1996, the Football Association claimed that Britain had "given football to the world." This is at best an exaggeration; at worst, a lie. True, moustachioed young Victorian graduates may have exported the game to many corners of the Empire, but often all they did was present the locals with an organised set of rules for what had hitherto been a random kickaround.

Many races have strong claims to being the first to put boot to leather, yet none is definitive. The earliest is probably the Chinese: ancient documents dated at around 2500BC allude to kicking or handling a spherical object through holes

A German drawing, dated at around 1600, shows early training methods

in a net stretched between two poles. The game was used to keep soldiers fit between battles. By 350BC, this had become *zuqiu*, still the Chinese word for football. Four hundred years later, *zuqiu* had become **tsu chu**, with a leather ball filled with feathers and hair being hoofed between bamboo poles.

But the Italians can also lay claim to the game. **Harpastum**, practised by the Roman armies of around AD 200, bore certain similarities to the modern game in its rules (the field of play, the shape of the ball), but the action was a hybrid of rugby and American football with scrums and crude lineouts when players were tackled. Still, *harpastum* may have influenced football, as records show soldiers undertaking an official world tour, whipping conquered nations in a manner the English would fail to repeat in modern times. History fails to record, however, if the Romans also popularised the sweeper system, the theatrical dive and the alice band.

> ***"Football is all very well as a game for rough girls, but it is hardly suitable for delicate boys"***
>
> *Oscar Wilde*

Across the globe, the **Aztecs** were crossing football with the Eton Wall game, forcing the ball through makeshift portholes. Their major contribution to football history was to tie the leather together with laces, a practice which lasted well into the 20th century. Some form of the game is also recorded before the Middle Ages in Egypt, Greece, Japan, Scandinavia and Central America.

It would be nice, at this point, to imagine the English developing the game around a common set of rules over a civilised cup of tea. Sadly, that didn't happen until the 1800s, and for most of the previous 700 years football was synonymous with riot, mayhem and official disapproval.

Entire towns chased balls – probably imported by the Romans or the Vikings – through streets, people's homes and across fields with little or no ultimate aim. What took place was more steeplechase than football match, with staying power and brute force emphasised over individual skill and proper teams. Matches in the City of London became popular, while games held in Derbyshire, Nottinghamshire and Surrey are still celebrated and re-enacted today.

It was such abandon that first brought "futeball" into confrontation with the authorities. Deaths were not uncommon, and the widespread disorder triggered when hundreds of young men rampaged through urban areas earned the wrath of the church – clashes were often staged on the Sabbath. In 1314, **Edward II** became the first monarch to ban the game officially, citing "great uproar in the city (London), caused by hustling over large balls… from which many evils perchance may arise." Edward III ordered footballers to take up archery. In

Scotland (where games between married and unmarried women took place in several towns) James I proclaimed in 1424: "From this court I debarre all rough and violent exercises, as the foot-ball, meeter [better] for lameing than making able the users thereof." Other monarchs issued stricter edicts against the game (although **Charles II** – if not a convert – did attend a match in 1681). Local councils also banned it in almost every significant town in Britain. Football would be little more than a historical footnote had public schools not popularised it – though they did it for their own gain, not out of altruism.

The likes of Harrow, Eton, Rugby and Blackheath quickly recognised that football fostered team spirit, promoted physical fitness and was remarkably popular among the pupils. But the lack of a unifying code made inter-school competitions impossible and allowed blatant foul play to go unpunished. Even "gentlemen" footballers deemed it acceptable to hack at ankles, punch off the ball or shove viciously, while scorelines were often forgotten amid mass brawls.

Gradually two factions developed: those who favoured handling the ball and those who championed dribbling. Then, in the 1840s, a pair of Cambridge house masters defined rules for use within the university, cutting down on hacking and handling. As graduates weaned on the game spread into positions of influence across the country, new clubs were formed playing a more unified code.

In 1863, a group of Cambridge graduates who were now masters at some of

A glimpse of an early England-Scotland fixture: the chaos hasn't changed that much

the top public schools met to decide matters once and for all. They drew up what were known colloquially as the Cambridge Rules, and in October that year, representatives of various schools and clubs in the London area endorsed the rules and formed the Football Association – the basis of the modern-day body.

The **Cambridge Rules** were still some way from the spectacle we enjoy today. Handling was still allowed in certain circumstances (it was soon banned, though many players had to wear gloves to remind them not to handle). Offside laws were rudimentary, and there was no set pitch size. Hacking, however, was finally consigned to the dustbin, and further refinements over the next 20 years would regulate kit, referees and numbers of players.

Blackheath, poshest of the posh public schools, was the notable dissenter in the whole debate and left the FA within months to embrace a handling code which later became rugby. Though egg-chasers claim the game evolved directly from a pupil at Rugby School picking up the ball and running during a match, this is almost certainly Victorian romanticism.

The organisation of the game of the masses had very little to do with the masses at this point. The strong sense of civic responsibility felt by young do-gooding public-school toffs left them feeling compelled to share the game with the less fortunate when they became clergymen, industrialists or teachers.

Preston North End's famous "Invincibles", the first footballing superpower

The 1850 Factory Act, meanwhile, meant that most workers now had Saturday afternoons off, and given the state of urban housing at the time, they were probably happier kicking a ball around than sitting at home. The government was happy, too. Despite its unruly history, football was seen as less harmful to the social order than drinking, voting or joining a trade union. Early organised competitions were still dominated by the southern schools or teams of former public schoolboys, but the game's popularity spread in northern industrial areas and in Scotland. Disgruntled, many public schools turned their back on their creation and returned to rugby.

Many of the best-known British clubs can be traced back to various good causes of the 1860s and 1870s, such as churches, factories, social welfare projects and even cricket teams. **Notts County**, generally regarded as the oldest club still playing professionally, were formed in 1862, although **Sheffield**, who began life in 1860, were the first northern, working-class side affiliated to the FA and still play in the lower echelons of non-league today. In 1871, player and journalist **Charles Alcock** persuaded 15 English teams, and the leading Scottish side, Queen's Park, to take part in the first **FA Cup**, won at Kennington Oval in London by **The Wanderers**, who beat the **Royal Engineers** 1-0.

Such competition and the arrival, in the form of railways, of cheap mass transportation, increased interest in the game and turned it into a spectator sport, defining geographical allegiances and favoured players. Although only 2,000 saw the first final of football's oldest competition, by the turn of the century all manner of matches were attracting six-figure crowds.

> ***"... I debarre all rough and violent exercises as the foot-ball, meeter for lameing than making able the users thereof"***
> *James I of Scotland*

Media interest was piqued by the first official international fixture between England and Scotland at the West of Scotland cricket ground in Glasgow a year later. It was a goalless draw, but the event soon became an annual one. The Scots were briefly dominant against their neighbours as they realised the English dribbling game was fundamentally flawed and intuitively sensed they might make headway if they actually passed the ball occasionally.

By 1888, there were 12 clubs of sufficient size and stature to form the world's first league, won by **Preston North End**, who also took the FA Cup in the same year to complete the first Double. Professionalism was by now widespread, after the FA sanctioned the payment of "expenses" to key players. Cash transfers followed, and there was a furore when **Alf Common** left **Sunderland** for **Middlesbrough** in 1905 for £1,000, the first-ever four-figure fee.

THEY REWROTE THE RULES

Sam Chedgzoy In 1924 the Everton star dribbled all the way from the corner flag to score, upsetting the Spurs defence and prompting the FA to decree that a player taking a corner could only touch the ball once before another player touched it.

Bill McCracken The Newcastle defender's extraordinary success at managing the offside trap led to 30 free-kicks in one match and a pitch invasion. In 1925, the law was changed to favour strikers who would, henceforth, be onside if there were two opponents between them and the goal.

William Gunn So adept was Notts County and England footballer – and England cricketer – Wiliam Gunn at the one-handed throw that, after Scottish protests over a match in 1882 where both sides threw the ball in whatever manner they liked, the rules were changed to ban single-handed throwing.

Hendry The partially-monikered Notts County defender stuck his hand out to stop Stoke equalising in a game in 1891. Notts County massed on the line to block the free-kick and the FA felt it had no option but to follow Ireland's example and introduce the penalty-kick.

Leigh Richmond Roose The legendarily eccentric keeper ruined the game for goalies, who had been allowed to handle the ball outside the 18-yard-box – until Roose carried the ball in his hands to the other end of the field.

Meanwhile, the game was being exported successfully by British traders, the armed forces and colonials. Australia and America preferred their own handling-based derivatives of the game but by the 1920s, football was known in every country on the planet and played enthusiastically in most. The fact that the British were so zealous in foisting their creation on the rest of the world would, of course, come back to haunt them.

But the early pioneers knew only the joy of introducing the natives to the first organised, enjoyable and – crucially – cheap team game they had been able to take part in. All over the globe, locals set up clubs, formed leagues and introduced a degree of professionalism along British lines.

Europe was conquered first. In the 1890s, football spread through Scandinavia, Holland, Germany and beyond. Italy dropped its foot-based game, *calcio*, when introduced to football, and Brits helped form the great Turin side, **Juventus**, in 1897. **Barcelona**, meanwhile, began life after a game against the Royal Navy.

Argentina had been hooked on football since the British built railways there in the 1860s. The large expat community soon spread the word across the continent, notably to the first world champions Uruguay and, later, Brazil, where the first recorded match also involved the British Navy (tours by teams like **Chelsea** and, er, **Exeter City** helped popularise the beautiful game in Rio and Sao Paolo). Africa and Asia boasted pockets of footballing activity in the 19th century but development proved slower.

Alf Common, who commanded the first £1,000 transfer fee

WHERE IT ALL BEGAN

Some of the world's most famous clubs started in very humble circumstances

Everton (1878) Formed by Methodist churchgoers with the blessing of their Reverend

Liverpool (1892) When the Everton side moved to a new ground, their old landlord decided to start his own team

Manchester United (1878) Railway workers founded Newton Heath; the name changed in 1902

Arsenal (1886) A works team for employees of a munitions factory; began in south London but soon moved north

West Ham United (1895) Known as the Irons, as they began life at an ironworks

AC Milan (1899) Started by expat Alfred Edwards, who insisted on the English spelling of the city

Inter Milan (1908) An Italian breakaway from Milan: Inter players wanted more free-flowing, less rigid play

Benfica (1904) Essentially an import business, the Portuguese giants shipped in Africans to work in local factories and play football

Dynamo Moscow (1887) An entrepreneur's ad in *The Times* asked for engineers who could also play the game to emigrate

River Plate (1901) English residents in Buenos Aires founded this most Argentinian of clubs

In 1904 Fifa was formed in Paris as an overall regulatory body for the many international sides and matches that had by now sprung up. England resisted joining for a year and was still stubbornly refusing to play ball by the time the first **World Cup** was staged in Uruguay in 1930. Romania's King Carol II picked his own World Cup squad and the hosts paid the travelling expenses of the 12 nations involved, but the lengthy sea voyages did for most of visitors. Uruguay triumphed with a 4-2 victory over Argentina.

The fourth World Cup in Brazil in 1950 was England's first and led to one of the greatest international shocks of all-time when the USA beat a team containing the likes of **Tom Finney** and **Billy Wright** 1-0. The result was treated as a fluke back home, but three years later the humiliation deepened when Hungary's "Magical Magyars" arrived at Wembley. Led by **Ferenc Puskas**, Hungary demolished their hosts 6-3, the Magyars' mastery so complete their play seemed, to the marooned British defence, like a form of sorcery. The result, England's first home defeat to a side from outside the British Isles (Ireland had beaten England in 1948 at Goodison Park), symbolised football's rapid development overseas. Television had brought a new audience of armchair spectators in European nations and with it a greater desire for foreign competition.

Top players had begun to move not just between clubs but also countries, and the rise of the "star player" was imminent. George Best is usually credited as the first footballing icon, a claim which ignores the fame of Denis "Brylcreem Boy" Compton but, in the 1950s, Alfredo di Stefano of Spain and his Real team-mate Puskas were the real revolutionaries. Ability had been stifled by rigid tactics and shibboleths about the role of team-work – players like di Stefano defied such categorisation, forcing coaches to change their tactics.

Such talent was showcased with the advent of European competition in 1955. After **Wolverhampton Wanderers** had beaten **Honved** of Hungary in a floodlit friendly match in 1954, their manager **Stan Cullis** proclaimed them champions of the world. Prompted by Gabriel Hanot, editor of *L'Equipe*, the new European football association, Uefa, put the boast to the test. Wolves weren't invited (they weren't champions) but even the might of **Manchester United** was no match for **Real Madrid**, as the Spaniards – inspired by di Stefano – swept all before them. Madrid won the first five **European Cups**; their 7-3 win over **Eintracht Frankfurt** in Glasgow in 1960 is regarded as the greatest match ever played.

> ***"At that time we had forwards and defenders doing separate jobs, but he did everything"***
>
> *Matt Busby on Alfredo di Stefano*

On the world stage, the idea that football could achieve the grace and beauty of an art no longer seemed utterly preposterous. Italy and West Germany had taken the World Cup to Europe after Uruguay's initial victory, but between 1958 and 1970 Brazil took the title three times with breathtaking skill – England's 1966 triumph on home soil, which interrupted the run, was a rare triumph for industry.

The 1970 Brazil side was almost as good as the Hungary team of the 1950s and boasted, in Pelé, the most complete talent the game ever saw. Having finished top scorer in the 1958 tournament in Sweden aged just 17, he had blossomed into a footballing artist who seemed to embody his nation's sporting ethos – to play for sheer enjoyment (although he was not averse to the odd foul). Brazilian coaches prized attacking invention, forcing European tactics and techniques to play catch-up and, perhaps, provoking Total Football. Team-mates such as Didi, Rivelino and Garrincha were sometimes unjustly overshadowed by Pelé's stardom but still take their place in the pantheon of greats.

By the time the next true superstar, Diego Maradona, was stealing the show as Argentina won the 1986 World Cup, the game had changed. Defenders resorted to ever more cynical fouls and the pressure to perform would tell on Maradona, who, by the time Italia 90 came around, would have a waistline to

STAR PLAYERS

King Charles II Given a demonstration of the Italian football hybrid, calcio, at his court and thus gave his blessing to the game, becoming the first monarch for centuries not to immediately ban football.

Oliver Cromwell Was said to have been a "boisterous" player at university, but didn't approve of the working classes indulging in the game, flogging boys caught playing in the street. Ironically, after his (posthumous) execution, his head is said to have been used for a kickaround in Westminster Hall.

Pope John Paul II An accomplished goalkeeper during his youth, yet as a childhood friend recalled: "A couple of minutes before four o'clock, he would just leave the field. Everyone would be angry, but he would just say: 'I'm sorry, but I promised my father I would be home.'"

Julio Iglesias A goalkeeper in Real Madrid's youth team, he was forced to give up football in 1963 after a car crash. While in hospital, a nurse lent him a guitar, thus sparking a musical career.

Albert Camus His time between the sticks for the Algiers University team gave the legendary philosopher and novelist plenty of time to contemplate the nature of existence. "Everything I know about morality, I owe to football," he once wrote.

Rod Stewart Likes to boast of his time on Brentford's books, but his talent must be in question if he couldn't make the grade at Griffin Park.

Sylvester Stallone World champion boxer, celebrated war hero and – without even trying – the greatest goalkeeper in the world during *Escape To Victory*.

match that of Luciano Pavarotti, singer of the tournament theme. Maradona's fate mirrored the game's malaise, as off-the-field violence and hooliganism reached its nadir with the loss of 39 lives in the Heysel disaster of 1985.

Money would save football just as it shaped it in the first place. Industry – and in particular television – woke up to the commercial possibilities of the people's game. Safer stadiums were funded by huge TV revenues, sometimes with satellite broadcasters, and merchandising deals. Twin powers, Italy's **Serie A** and Spain's **La Liga**, emerged, attracting talent from all corners of the globe. Soaring income from TV deals meant that England's **Premiership** would later join them.

Players – previously more tradesmen than celebrity entertainers – reaped the rewards. Transfer records rocketed – from £3m for Maradona in 1982 to £45m for **Zinedine Zidane** 19 years later – and so did wages. The potential merchandising profits drove Western clubs into Asia and the US. Fifa has staged the World Cup in the US (1994) and Japan and South Korea (2002) to exploit these opportunities, while Africa may – if Sepp Blatter sticks to his promises – yet get to stage its first World Cup in 2010, although it has yet to fulfil Pelé's famous prediction that it will produce the tournament's winners.

Football's future depends on balancing the commercial demands driving its expansion with the need to entertain its audience through traditional sporting means. The threats of a potential **European Super League**, rule-tampering, the pestilence of the worst kind of agents, the boom-and-bust economic cycle affecting many clubs (or, in the lower leagues, a more depressing cycle of bust-to-bust) and the alienation of local communities from clubs, are all real but not yet over-riding. Football still stands on its own two feet. Sort of.

TACTICS OR TICTACS: THE GREAT FORMATIONS

In the beginning was the **WM**. Defenders lined up on the points of a W, attackers on the point of an M. The tactical formation, in which the centre-half was reinvented as a "stopper", a term which still describes too many No 5s today, was prompted by the 1925 offside law which said an attacker could not be offside if two opponents were between him and the goal-line.

Before World War Two, tactical innovations in British football were about as rare as an unblinkered FA official. Yet abroad, exiled Scottish coach **Jimmy Hogan** was helping the Austrians perfect a short, passing game which would be known as the **Vienna School** and would give the Austrians the best team in Europe in the 1930s – despite Italy's two World Cup victories.

In the 1950s, Tottenham manager **Arthur Rowe** caused great excitement – in Britain – with the "push and run" school in which short passes and bursts of speed were used to attack; the Vienna School with go-faster stripes. All conventional wisdom about tactics would be overturned by the Hungarian side of the 1950s, who played a precursor of total football in which centre-forwards came so deep they almost ended up down the pit. The speed of their positional changes and passing bewildered slow-footed opponents but had as much to do with the genius of the personnel (and the fact that they played for club and country together) as any revolution in tactics. Yet the Hungarian side still ran off the ball with more imagination than most present-day players.

Brazil won the 1958 World Cup with a flowing **4-2-4** formation which should have ushered in a golden age of attacking football. As the Italians switched to *catenaccio* (the word means doorbolt), the **4-3-3** became a sterile defensive formation, although its pioneer, Helenio Herrera, always insisted it was an attractive system – if only the left-backs could be bothered to join the attack in what today we might call overlapping full-back mode. Still, *catenaccio* gave us the sweeper, the *libero*, which, to the English, still conjures up images of men with flat caps and cigarettes surgically attached to their lower lips trying to keep the roads clean. England won the 1966 World Cup with a wingless 4-3-3 formation but this

THE WOMEN'S GAME

"Women should be in the kitchen, the discotheque and the boutique, but not in football"

Ron Atkinson

Big Ron probably wouldn't last too long if he was thrown to the Millwall Lionesses, but he isn't alone in deriding women's football. The idea of the fairer sex playing it has long sparked curiosity, schoolboy sniggers and outright disgust.

Even in staid Victorian times, pioneers were getting girls into the game – and themselves into trouble. **Nettie Honeyball** took it upon herself to organise both a British Ladies' side and a North versus South exhibition game in London in 1894, "with the fixed resolve of proving to the world that women are not the 'ornamental and useless' creatures men have pictured." The 1890s saw something of a mini-boom for the ladies' game, but the large crowds were mostly flocking to see a "freak show". Meanwhile, doctors were encouraged to explain how football could harm the delicate female physique and even render players infertile.

In the 1920s, the **Dick Kerr** ladies' team came to national prominence – formed at a Preston factory of the same name as a means of raising money for charity, the team made a virtue of male distaste through aggressive poster campaigns and became something of an success. A series of challenge matches against male sides culminated in over 50,000 packing into Everton's Goodison Park to see them play, and they later undertook a US tour.

Dick Kerr Ladies play by floodlight, but they remained a curiosity

The FA didn't see the funny side – even though one player performed cartwheels when she scored – and in December 1921, ruled: "The Council feel impelled to express their strong opinion that the game of football is quite unsuitable for females. The Council request the clubs belonging to the Association to refuse the use of their grounds for such matches." Since almost every club, professional or amateur, has to belong to the FA or use FA-affiliated facilities, this edict starved the women's game of resources. As a direct result, however, the English Ladies FA was formed, matches were played on rugby pitches, and the women's game developed its own ethos and ideals. The Women's FA was formed in 1962, and had nearly 200 member clubs by the time the FA finally deigned to recognise them in 1973.

Other European nations had embraced the game in the 1960s, with Italy boasting the world's first, short-lived, professional league and Scandinavian countries actively encouraging the game. Yet an unofficial World Cup held in Mexico in 1971 illustrates the difficulties still facing female players at the time – many players found themselves shooting at pink goals and being asked to wear hot pants and blouses.

Fifa woke up to the need for parity in the 1990s, staging the first official **World Championship** in 1991 and women's football became an Olympic sport in 1996. (England, incidentally, are just as consistently disappointing as their male counterparts.) **Fulham** became the first British club to run a full-time professional ladies' side, but when cost-cutting was needed, the idea was rapidly abandoned. The best hope for the future lies in the US, where girls have picked up on the game faster than boys (without the inbuilt prejudices of the public school system, for example, it is not seen as a "male" sport) and the national team enjoys enthusiastic support. Even so, the days when the sexes compete on a level playing field remain the stuff of sub-standard ITV drama series...

soon fell into disrepute as the Germans and the Dutch dominated the 1970s with **Total Football**, which meant that any player could play anywhere; not a style you could play if your defenders were as mobile as **Steve Foster**.

Total football, like tank tops, fell out of fashion and the world fell back on **4-4-2** and 3-5-2 (4-3-2-1, **Terry Venables**' Christmas tree formation, lasted as long as a real Christmas tree does). Variations on the theme include the pressing game – Milan coach **Arrigo Saachi**'s 4-4-2 but with added bite in the tackle further up the pitch, split strikers (or the striker in the hole – ie just behind the centre-forward), and **10-0-0**, the approved formation whenever a team gets a player sent off. If the term wing-half can make a comeback, there's still hope for the revival of the **inside forward**, as rare these days as a good word for football agents. We haven't mentioned the **long ball game** for obvious reasons.

TROPHY BITTER: THE CUPS THAT TIME FORGOT

In 1969 **Swindon Town** won the **League Cup** but, due to some obscure footballing by-law, because they were in Division Three, they weren't allowed to play in Europe. To prevent a mob of torch-wielding Wiltshiremen bearing down on Lancaster Gate and ritually sacrificing Bert Millichip, the FA hurriedly invented the **Anglo-Italian Cup** as a consolation prize – and in the process unleashed a barrage of extraneous football tournaments on the fans.

In the inaugural Anglo-Italian final, the Robins beat **Roma** 5-2 on aggregate, not a result we expect to see repeated any time soon. That said, Swindon returned to the final a year later and beat **Napoli** 3-0. Italian fans, enraged, started hurling their seats in the direction of John Trollope and his Swindon colleagues.

Newcastle and **Blackpool** were the only other clubs to bring the cup back to Blighty before it was left to swim with the fishes in 1975. It was, though, revived in the 1990s when, after another four seasons of games watched by minuscule crowds, Notts County added their name to the Anglo-Italian roll of honour.

By now, however, a mania for meaningless competitions had set in. In 1970 the **Watney Cup**, a pre-season festival of fun for the two top-scoring clubs from each division, was introduced. Innovations included – gasp! – penalty shoot-outs

and an offside rule only applicable in the penalty box. **Derby County** thrashed

Manchester United display their grim northern credentials in a 1907 match

Uruguay in training for the 1930 World Cup, which they won as hosts

Manchester United 4-1 in the first final, each player presumably receiving a commemorative Party Seven with their medal. The barrel was finally drained after four seasons, with **Stoke City** the last winners.

Texaco clambered on the bandwagon in 1971, gathering together teams from England, Scotland and Ireland who weren't otherwise heading for Europe. **Wolves** defeated **Hibs** to become the first winners of the Texaco Cup, taking home a set of tumblers, a *Motoring Atlas of Great Britain* and a hundredweight of Green Shield stamps. The Irish clubs then pulled out due to the Troubles and, in 1976, it was replaced by the Anglo-Scottish Cup. Like its forerunner, it never managed to get itself taken very seriously, though Newcastle were once kicked out for scandalously fielding a weakened team against **Ayr United**. It lasted five seasons before the Scots took their ball home in a huff at the declining status of the English teams – they probably had a point: the ultimate final was a mouthwatering affair that saw **Chesterfield** beat Notts County.

The competition lumbered on as a contest for lower-division English clubs as the Football League Group Cup (1981-82) and then the Football League Trophy (1982-83) – heady days for **Grimsby** and **Wimbledon**, the two winners. Then, semi-interestingly, it was relaunched again as The Associate Members' Cup, a competition still very much with us, despite having undergone more makeovers in the 1980s and 1990s than Madonna – incarnations include the Freight Rover Trophy, the Sherpa Van Trophy, the Leyland DAF Cup, the Autoglass Trophy, the Auto Windscreens Shield and now the LDV Vans Trophy. Do we detect a theme here? Perhaps the most pointless tournament of the lot (though maybe not to **Chester City** fans) was the Debenhams Cup, involving the two lower-division teams who had gone furthest in the FA Cup. Chester won it in 1977 and it remains their sole honour to this day. A year later, **Blyth Spartans** extracted some kind of revenge on their fifth-round FA Cup conquerors **Wrexham** by beating them in the Debenhams.

Trying to fill the void left by the post-Heysel European ban in 1985, the Screen Sport Super Cup provided the six English teams who might otherwise have been heading for the Bernabéu or San Siro with the consolation of a jaunt to Carrow Road. Liverpool beat Everton in the first final – played more than 12 months after the tournament began.

That season also saw the launch of the **Full Members' Cup**, devised by then **Crystal Palace** chairman Ron Noades on the notion that a crunch Southern Area group match against **Reading** would lure back all those missing punters. Ignored by the big clubs, terrestrial television and most sane fans, it was won twice by **Chelsea** and **Nottingham Forest**, and sponsored by Simod and Zenith Data Systems. The high point was a titanic 6-6 draw involving **Tranmere** and Newcastle in 1991-92, which saw hat-tricks from moustachioed Scouse poachers **John Aldridge** and **Mick Quinn**, a penalty for each team in the first minute of extra time, Newcastle coming from 5-3 down to 6-5 up, and Tranmere winning the shoot-out. The tournament was still axed at the end of the season.

In 1988, the Football League marked its 100th birthday with a whole banquet of meaningless events These kicked off with the **Mercantile Credit Centenary Classic**, an all-star friendly match at Wembley – what better way to celebrate than bringing together Diego Maradona and **Steve Ogrizovic**? This was followed by the **Centenary Festival**, a surreal two-day knockout event at Wembley involving 10-minute games featuring 16 teams from all divisions – the kind of "innovation" for which we have known and loved Jimmy Hill for decades. Nottingham Forest, acquiring a worrying taste for this sort of thing, won, although Cloughie didn't turn up. The **Centenary Trophy**, which rounded off the celebrations, saw Arsenal defeat Manchester United at a semi-deserted Villa Park.

> ***"I just opened the trophy cabinet. Two Japanese soldiers fell out"***
>
> *Tommy Docherty*

Just to prove England doesn't have a monopoly on this kind of thing, the 2000 **Fifa World Club Championship** in Brazil, Sepp Blatter's attempt to launch a global alternative to Uefa's Champions League, is as spectacularly pointless as, say, the Watneys Cup or, indeed, the **Confederations Cup**. Manchester United famously pulled out of the FA Cup to play against the likes of **Real Madrid**, **Al-Nassr** and **South Melbourne**, but the 2001 event, slated to include **Hearts Of Oak**, **Woollongong Wolves** and **Los Angeles Galaxy**, was cancelled for assorted reasons, none of which was lack of interest. Honest.

A KICK IN THE GRASS: THE NASL REMEMBERED

Despite the success of USA '94 and a creditable performance by the US team in the 2002 World Cup, America's view of "soccer" is still best encapsulated by an episode of *The Simpsons*. In it, Homer and family are enticed by a TV commercial ("It's all here – fast-kicking, low-scoring... and ties? You bet!") to watch a football match so boring it sparks a riot. But it could have all been so different. In the 1970s the **North American Soccer League** (NASL) had it all – big names, full houses and super-sized helpings of razzmatazz from sea to shining sea. Alas, the NASL over-reached itself and collapsed in 1984, but it left behind a legacy of ridiculous club names, audacious rule changes and memories of an era when Tommy Smith could grace the same Astroturf as Teofilo Cubillas...

The 10 most memorable NASL club names

1. New York Cosmos (1971-84)
Pelé, Franz Beckenbauer and Shep Messing; the Cosmos were the NASL's superpower. Inspired by Carl Sagan's blockbusting 1970s intergalactic space opus. Or not.
2. Team Hawaii (1977)
The most glamourous away trip in history. Statistics don't record whether they ever won 5-0, or indeed if fans advised referees to "book him, Danno!"
3. The Caribous of Colorado (1978)
Never Colorado Caribous, oh no. Named themselves after a type of stag, and wore a brown kit with Wild West-style fringing on the chest. Yes, really.
4. Chicago Sting (1975-1984)
In no way related to the box office hit of the time (part one). But no doubt teams ran out to a rousing selection of Scott Joplin rags.
5. San Diego Jaws (1976)
In no way related to the box office hit of the time (part two). Just when you thought it was safe to go back to the soccer stadium…
6. Las Vegas Quicksilver (1977)
If there's a lesson from this list, it's that the teams with the best names lasted the shortest. Cashed in their chips after finishing bottom, below Team Hawaii.
7. New England/Jacksonville Tea Men (1978-80)
Let soccer flood out! OK, so New England has a solid connection with tea, but Florida? The team was owned by the Lipton Tea Company, amazingly.
8. Detroit Express (1978-80)
Sounded a bit like a 1970s soul group and were the product of a transatlantic "Motown" link-up with Coventry City as part of Jimmy Hill's brief foray into the NASL.
9. Tampa Bay Rowdies (1975-84)
Once the summertime home of Frank Worthington and Rodney Marsh. Still can't work out why they called themselves rowdy, mind…
10. Washington Diplomats (1974-81)
They used to be the Diplomats; now they're down the laundromat. Easily the dreariest name in NASL history. Probably carried their boots in briefcases.

Those NASL rule changes in full

The Offside Line

In 1972 the nascent NASL introduced a rule seemingly nicked from Subbuteo which stated that players could only be offside beyond a line marked 35 yards from the goal-line. Intended to generate more goals, the change's major impact was to bring the NASL into conflict with Fifa, and it was eventually dropped.

The shoot-out

Because it was assumed that Joe American couldn't cope with draws, the NASL simply scrapped them. If a match was drawn it went into "overtime", before being settled by a shoot-out – but not from the penalty spot. Instead, five players from each team were given five seconds to run from the 35-yard line and score by either dribbling round, chipping over, or blasting the ball past, the outrushing keeper.

The mini-game

In the two-legged playoffs, ties weren't settled on aggregate score. If both teams had won one match each, the outcome was settled by a 30-minute mini-game played straight after the second leg. In 1979, **Vancouver Whitecaps** beat **New York Cosmos** in their first meeting, but the second match was tied at 90 minutes. Americans don't do tied games, remember, so it was on to overtime which still couldn't separate the teams. New York won the shoot-out, so after two hours of football in 80-degree heat, the teams now faced a 30-minute mini-game... which was drawn. Cue another shoot-out – which Vancouver won to take them into the Soccer Bowl where, fully rested, they beat Tampa Bay.

The points

The NASL continually fiddled around with the points system, awarding bonus points for goals to encourage attacking play. During the League's glory years, teams were awarded six points for a win, one point for a shoot-out win, and up to three more points if they scored three goals…

"Beckenbauer... Pelé... Hector!" Six unlikely NASL pairings

1. Gerd Müller and Keith Weller (Fort Lauderdale Strikers 1980-81)

Der Bomber is best remembered for netting 14 goals in the World Cup. Keith Weller is best remembered for wearing tights one chilly afternoon at Filbert Street.

2. Carlos Alberto and Charlie Cooke (California Surf 1981)

The 1970 legends of the Copacabana and the Kings Road briefly teamed up for a creaky Indian summer in sunny Anaheim.

3. Franz Beckenbauer and Dennis Tueart (New York Cosmos 1978-79)

Der Kaiser and, erm, Der Dennis were both delegates at the Cosmos' United Nations of soccer in the late 1970s. And Tueart scored two in the 1978 Soccer Bowl.

Gordon Banks gives in trying to convert Americans and does it their way instead

4. Roberto Bettega and Phil Parkes (Toronto Blizzard 1983)
Roberto Bettega was a sort of goalscoring Don Corleone, while Phil Parkes was a sort of goalkeeping Donkey Kong.

5. Johan Cruyff and Bobby Stokes (Washington Diplomats 1980)
Yes, Johan might have pulled off the odd Cruyff turn in his time, but he never ran a greasy spoon "caff" like the late Bobby Stokes.

6. Ruud Krol and Kevin Hector (Vancouver Whitecaps 1980)
In the shadow of the Rocky mountains, Ruud supplied the total football while a great, big, goalscoring old Hector from Derby added the finishing touches.

Ten unlikely stars of the NASL

1. **Sam Allardyce** (Tampa Bay 1983)
2. **Alan Birchenall** (San Jose 1977)
3. **Len Cantello** (Dallas 1978)
4. **Mick Coop** (Detroit 1978)
5. **Mike Flanagan** (New England 1978)
6. **Alan Foggon** (Rochester 1976)
7. **Trevor Hockey** (San Diego-Las Vegas 1976-77)
8. **Terry Mancini** (Los Angeles 1977)
9. **Jim McCalliog** (Chicago 1977)
10. **Harry Redknapp** (Seattle 1976-79)

Ten genuine superstars of the NASL

1. **Pelé** (New York 1975-77)
2. **Peter Beardsley** (Vancouver 1981-83)
3. **George Best** (Los Angeles, Fort Lauderdale, San José 1976-81)
4. **Teofilo Cubillas** (Fort Lauderdale 1979-83)
5. **Kazimierz Deyna** (San Diego 1981-84)
6. **Eusebio** (Boston, Toronto, Las Vegas 1975-77)
7. **Geoff Hurst** (Seattle 1976)
8. **Bobby Moore** (San Antonio 1976, Seattle 1978)
9. **Johan Neeskens** (New York 1979-84)
10. **Hugo Sanchez** (San Diego 1979-80)

THE LEGENDS

An unashamed celebration of the men who made the game what it is, from George Best to Segar Bastard

Bob Paisley keeps busy in pre-season

"In my private life I do what I like. The night is my friend. If I don't go out, I don't score"

Romario explains to Valencia's coach why he won't stop disco dancing

What makes a footballing legend? The highest levels of achievement in the game are a useful pre-requisite, but not the only criteria: equally important, if not more so, are charisma, style and the common touch. Not everyone in this selection has made it at the highest level. Many never even came close. Yet they all endeared themselves to the sporting public by standing out from the crowd. Some, like **Tony Adams**, are celebrated for their ordinariness despite being quietly remarkable; others, like **Garrincha** or **George Best**, took the game to a new level. And then there's **Segar Bastard**...

GEORGE BEST

"One day people might say I was another Ryan Giggs"

George Best is watching his own ghost, in a rerun of a 1971 League game against Southampton when he grabbed a hat-trick. On the screen in his hotel suite, he watches as he beats John McGrath – the Saints defender who had told him before kick-off: "If you put the ball through my legs I will kill you" – waits for McGrath to catch up, and then beats him again. Even Best is elated by this reminder of his prowess. Jumping from the sofa, he mumbles hoarsely: "God, I was f***ing quick. I'd forgotten I was that f***ing quick."

It's easy to forget, whenever he goes into a pub and orders a drink which will be emblazoned across the nation's front pages, that before the "where did it all go wrong, George?" talk, Best was a player of outrageous natural talent. This was a player who, having scored six in an 8-2 thrashing of Northampton Town, decided to give his marker a break: "It was getting embarrassing. I didn't want to score any more, so I spent the last 20 minutes at left-back."

The idea of Best as the fifth Beatle may seem strange now but he was on a par with the Fab Four. With his natural gifts, Beatle-ish haircut (later he sported a fetching Ché Guevara beard) and the kind of unbridled hedonism celebrated in actors or musicians, but frowned upon in athletes, Best was as much a rebel as John Lennon. **Denis Law** may have been as vital to United, but he never bedded Miss World(s) or ran a boutique; **Kevin Keegan** might have bossed a European Cup run, but he never went to prison, got nicknamed "El Beatle" or made your parents shake their heads in disapproval. After the Beatles split, El Beatle was almost more of an icon than Lennon and McCartney.

Best stood out by being more interesting than anyone else in the game. He is a man of many faces, from the eight-stone Belfast boy dancing round hospital tackles from gnarled defenders, to the drunken loon embarrassing himself on *Wogan*. A player with the finesse, speed, vision, control and ability to score from impossible angles, now a shambling, yellow figure getting stomach implants.

Best will remember himself above all as the European Player of the Year and European Cup winner, hailed "the best in the world" by **Pelé**. He'd also point out that his career lasted longer than many assume. He was called up to play for his country at 35, and left **Manchester United** – where he was top scorer for five seasons in a row (from 1965-66 to 1968-69 he only missed two league games) – because he was tired of carrying the side himself. He left Old Trafford the same season as Bobby Charlton and Law.

Ultimately, it seems that professional football cannot cope with stars like Best. Sadly, it doesn't seem that George Best can cope with himself, either.

Best wasn't just a surname; for six seasons that's what George was

ARTHUR WHARTON

The hidden gem of history

He was a syphilitic alcoholic with numerous illegitimate children, but **Arthur Wharton** was one heck of a footballer. He was also the first black professional in England, if not the whole of Britain. Born the son of a missionary in 1865 in Ghana, Wharton moved to Durham in the 1880s to complete his education and was soon appearing as a goalkeeper for **Darlington**. He quickly forgot his studies and signed for **William Suddell**'s dominant **Preston North End** team – where his appearances were limited – before moving on to **Rotherham Town**.

By all accounts, Wharton was a graduate of the **Bruce Grobbelaar** school of keeping, regularly using his crossbar to propel himself across the box, venturing out of his area to tackle oncoming forwards and exchanging jokes with the crowd. He was also an all-round athlete (an AAA 100-yard dash win made him briefly the fastest man on the planet) and he was touted for an England cap.

Wharton: nice moustache, too

While Wharton may have endeared himself to the northern fans whom he entertained, the FA and the London media (who referred to him as a "real nigger" and a "darkie" and questioned his flamboyance and easy banter with the supporters) were less impressed, and Wharton ended up omitted from both national selection and – even less excusably – the record books of the time. He flitted around various northern clubs before finally retiring while on the books of **Stockport County** in 1902. He died penniless in 1930, the result of an extravagant off-field lifestyle which included a lengthy affair with his sister-in-law.

Wharton's story was unearthed only in the 1990s by author Phil Vasili and shattered the myth that black players first appeared in the 1960s. In fact, researchers now believe **Andrew Watson**, who appeared for **Queen's Park** and Scotland in the 1880s, was the first black league player, though he would not have been professional. For romantics, however, Arthur's tale takes some beating.

LADISLAO KUBALA

Franco's second-favourite footballer

When **Barcelona** celebrated their centenary in 1999, they held a vote for the greatest player of those 100 glorious years. The winner wasn't a Catalan, or even Spanish. Slovakian Ladislao Kubala has a place in the hearts of the **Nou Camp** faithful that even Johan Cruyff would envy. This is nothing short of remarkable when you consider he was regarded as a traitor in his homeland, received a one-year ban from Fifa and was once followed by a private detective hired by his club to observe his drunken antics. Kubala was a player of such intelligence and elegance, he would be forgiven almost anything.

Born in Hungary in 1927 to Slovak parents, Kubala was a Czech international at the age of 17 but also went on to play for Hungary and Spain, winning 28 caps in all. He fled communism in 1949, pitching up in Italy, but the Hungarian regime was furious and saw him successfully banned for 12 months. Kubala ended up in a refugee camp where he formed a team of exiles to tour Europe. His talent saw him courted by both Barça and **Real Madrid**; legend has it he signed for the former because their president got him so half-cut he no longer knew where he was or who he was joining. It has a ring of truth.

Soon, however, he was a legend, adored by the crowd whose love was christened *Kubilismo.* Like Real's Gento, he was a favourite of General Franco, who had him star in a popular anti-communist film. Though he was viewed with suspicion by non-Catalans, nobody could deny his ability and he fired Barcelona to three titles, two Spanish Cups and two Fairs Cups before he left in 1961. He trained longer and became fitter than his team-mates, a remarkable feat considering his fabled bouts of drunkenness. However, the club finally saw red and slapped a tail on him after he led the squad into a red-light district on the eve of a crucial European tie.

In Jimmy Burns' book on the club, *Barca, A People's Passion,* fellow player Angel Mur recalled nipping round to Kubala's place on the morning of a match to find the star paralytic: "I put him in a cold shower, gave him a massage with pure alcohol and made him drink a cup of black coffee before putting him to bed for a few hours. Later he got up and went and played as if nothing had happened."

> *"I put him in a cold shower, gave him a massage of pure alcohol and made him drink black coffee... later he got up and played like nothing had happened"*
>
> *Angel Mur on Ladislao Kubala*

Paisley (right) with fellow managerial icon Sir Matt Busby at the 1983 Milk Cup Final

BOB PAISLEY

Everyone's favourite uncle

At first glance, Bob Paisley didn't seem cut from the right cloth to become the most successful British manager of all time. For a start, he lacked ambition. Following the shock resignation of Bill Shankly, the Liverpool board had to gang up on Paisley to get him to take the job. Even when finally bullied into it, Paisley's speech to his players the next day consisted of: "I never wanted this bloody job. But it looks like you're stuck with me."

A shy, avuncular figure, Paisley was the yin to the Shankly's blustering yang. While the eminently quotable Scot talked about wanting to "conquer the bloody world", the quiet Geordie seemed barely able to express himself. "The team meetings with Bob would be hilarious because he'd struggle to string two sentences together," remembers Alan Hansen. "He was always getting names wrong. The laughter was unbelievable."

Paisley picked up the affectionate moniker of "Dougie Doins" as a result of his habit of referring to opposition players as "doins" rather than their real names. Dressing-room comic Terry McDermott even did an uncanny impression of Paisley's bumbling – sometimes getting caught out by the manager in mid-flow. It's hard to imagine Alex Ferguson putting up with that.

But the cold, hard facts speak for themselves. Paisley masterminded six League Championship wins, three League Cups, one Uefa Cup, five Charity Shields and – truly amazingly – three European Cups. So how did he pull it off?

For one thing, Paisley knew the club inside out. He'd been there as a player, and then a coach, since 1939. Under Shankly he was renowned for his tactical acumen, and his judgement of players was better than the Scot's. Paisley also had a no-nonsense canniness learned during World War II, where he was a Desert Rat: rolling down a boulevard in Rome prior to their 1977 European Cup triumph, Paisley told his players: "The last time I drove down here, I was in a tank liberating Italy." (Appropriately, "Gunner" was his other nickname.)

His straightforward style worked wonders. "Paisley's philosophy was simple – we played to our strengths and exploited their weaknesses," says Hansen. Paisley had an astounding knowledge of how the game worked, was a marvellous man-manager and was also a first-class physio, able to diagnose what was wrong with a player just from the way they walked.

Paisley remains loved not just for his achievements, but for the humble manner in which they were made. "Bob's the only man I know who had no ego," says **Kevin Keegan** of a man whose great pleasure was a tinkle on the electric organ on Sunday afternoons. But the anecdote that sums up Paisley perfectly comes from **Graeme Souness**. "After the 1981 European Cup final in Paris, Alan Hansen and I decided to stay in the hotel," he says. "We went to Bob's room. He's sitting there in a jersey with soup stains on it. He's got his slippers on because he had problems with his ankles. It's like a night in watching *Coronation Street*." It was that kind of ordinary greatness that would bond Bob Paisley with the Liverpool fans forever.

ROMARIO and EDMUNDO

Brazil nuts

Romario and Edmundo fit squarely within the category of flawless players who are flawed human beings. Yet even by football's standards, the pair are in a class of their own. Between them, **Edmundo Alaves de Souza** and **Romario de Souza Faria** have turned the soap opera of Brazilian football into full-scale tabloid opera involving nightclubs, carnivals and a monkey called Pedrinho.

Known as "the Animal", and labelled "a liability to mankind" by one journalist, Edmundo has been named as defendant in a paternity suit by a Brazilian TV presenter, been sent off seven times in one season, brawled on the beaches of Rio and once spent a week under arrest in an Ecuadorian hotel after destroying a TV camera. And in December 1995, a car that he was driving was involved in an accident that left three pedestrians dead. Edmundo was found guilty. His lawyers launched the first of a series of appeals, but **Vasco da Gama** sacked him, and he left for Italy two years later. He signed for **Fiorentina** and the club briefly had a chance of winning Serie A, but with striker **Gabriel Batistuta** injured, they needed Edmundo badly. His response was to go and party at the carnival in Rio.

A similar error of judgement cost Romario his job at **Flamengo**. The night before they lost against **Gremio**, he had been seen in a nightclub. Unimpressed by Romario's claims that he was suffering from insomnia, Flamengo sacked him. Romario's response was to launch a £1.5 million lawsuit for unfair dismissal. Not to be outdone, Edmundo got himself into trouble again, this time with animal rights organisations. He'd hired a circus to perform in his garden to celebrate his son's birthday, including Pedrinho the chimpanzee. Edmundo wasted no time getting Pedrinho drunk on beer and whisky.

Both players ended up with **Vasco da Gama** again (but not before Edmundo had been sacked by **Cruzeira** for deliberately missing a penalty against Vasco). The pair soon fell out when Edmundo saw a crude cartoon of himself on a toilet door in a nightclub owned by Romario. When it was suggested that Romario be captain of Vasco, Edmundo refused to play. It wasn't the first time that a toilet had got Romario into trouble. National team manager **Mario Zagallo** had already sued him after seeing similarly crude graffiti about himself in the same toilet.

If there's one thing Romario loves more than partying, it's sex. He told one journalist that "Good strikers can only score goals when they have had good sex on the night before a match" and one Brazilian priest is worried that Romario has had so much sex that he might pass on "bad spirits'" to **Ronaldo** just by playing in the same team. Time, and the appeals process, finally ran out for Edmundo in June 2003. The Brazilian Supreme Court confirmed his earlier conviction, and he now faces four-and-a-half years in an open prison, although he'll be allowed out during the day so he can play for Vasco.

But Romario and Edmundo did manage to hold it together long enough to annihilate Manchester United in the inaugural World Club Championship in 2000. It was a game that reminded the world why so many managers have indulged both players, and suggested that even "the Animal" might have a different side. Edmundo celebrated scoring by raising his shirt to reveal a picture of Rafael Barcelar, a five-year-old boy who had died from meningitis the week before. "The boy's wish before he died was for Vasco to beat Manchester United," he said. "The beauty of the goal was dedicated to him."

BEST OF TIMES

George Best was discovered by Manchester United scout Bob Bishop, playing schools football in Northern Ireland. He immediately sent Matt Busby a telegram which read: "I believe I've found you a genius."

Ferenc Puskas (left) provides girth and mirth for England skipper Billy Wright in 1953

FERENC PUSKAS

"Look at that fat chap over there... we'll murder this lot"

"I came away wondering to myself what we had been doing all these years." Tom Finney's stark assessment of England's 6-3 drubbing by Hungary at Wembley in 1953 heralded the end of England's era as a footballing superpower as the baton passed to foreign fields. Yet while we deify the Brazilians, Italians and Argentinians who have since risen to prominence, the protagonist of that epoch-defining defeat – a short, squat, former Army officer from behind the Iron Curtain – is often overlooked.

It may be because so little footage of **Ferenc Puskas** exists that we forget what talents he possessed, but he was the first player to impose his individuality on the game to the extent that he overshadowed the rest of his team. While **Nandor Hidegkuti**'s role in "the hole" was credited with destroying England that day, it was the fact they couldn't get the ball off Puskas which had most to do with the outcome. Puskas won every domestic honour and scored 83 goals in 84 internationals, though his equalising strike in the 1954 World Cup final was disallowed as West German industry overcame eastern European flair. He also unwittingly became a symbol of resistance when he defected to first Austria and then Spain following the failed Hungarian uprising of 1956.

With Real Madrid, Puskas defied age and an ever-expanding waistline – one Wolves player described how Puskas amazed onlookers by demolishing countless helpings at a post-match dinner when **Honved** played at Molineux – to win three European Cups and score four goals in the thrilling 7-3 defeat of **Eintracht Frankfurt** in the 1960 final. When he finally went home in 1993 to manage the national side, he was mobbed in Budapest by fans to whom he represented not just outstanding artistry but hope.

BILLY MEREDITH

Boy from the black stuff

When **Billy Meredith** made his debut for **Manchester City** in 1894, the game was in Newcastle. The problem for Meredith was that he was employed full-time as a miner in his home town of Chirk, North Wales. After slaving in the pit throughout the Friday, he caught a train at 2am, arriving on Tyneside at 11am. He played the game, losing 5-4, then took a return train and went straight back down the pit. It may sound like a "When I were a lad..." sketch from Monty Python, but such were the realities of football shortly after the formation of the league. Billy Meredith went on to become its unlikely first superstar. Deeply religious and family-orientated, he didn't want to be a footballer – he was quite content in the mines (where he'd started straight from school, aged 12). But his talents and fate conspired to push him into the game. He was already recognised as Wales' most talented player from his amateur heroics with Chirk, and a miners' strike meant he needed to supplement his income. Manchester City were ready to pounce.

Meredith refused to move to Manchester, instead commuting from north Wales. It didn't harm his career: the nippy right winger was nicknamed the Welsh Wizard and was bamboozling defenders over 90 years before **Ryan Giggs**. Meredith, who played with a toothpick in his mouth, was feted for his strength and skill. He was a key player as City lifted Manchester's first FA Cup in 1904, and by the age of 30 he was club captain.

But in 1909 disaster struck: Meredith was accused of bribing an **Aston Villa** player before an important match. He denied the charges strenuously, but was suspended by the FA for eight months. Many felt Meredith was being punished for his role in attempting to set up a players' union and campaigning for the abolition of the maximum wage. Meredith nearly got his way in 1910 when the amount was raised (total abolition would not come until the days of **Jimmy Hill**), and the union victory meant he left a lasting mark on the game.

Meredith was also remarkable for his endurance. He transferred to Manchester United in 1909, winning two league titles and another FA Cup, before re-signing for City in 1915. A health-conscious teetotaller, Meredith played until he was 49, picking up the last of his 48 Welsh caps at 45. Still the oldest player ever to appear for City, he played a total of 1,568 games, scoring 470 goals. And he was still fit for doing some real work down the pit at the end of the day.

GIL HERON

Celtic's greatest soloist

Jazz poet Gil Scott-Heron's record sales have always been disproportionately good in Glasgow, and noticeable numbers show up at his concerts there wearing green-and-white hooped **Celtic** shirts. This is no surprise given that his father, **Gil Heron**, played for the Bhoys in 1950-51 and left such an impression on the city – on both sides of the divide – that few Glaswegians over a certain age do not respect The Black Arrow.

So-called for his phenomenal speed, the centre-forward was born in Jamaica in 1922 and began playing football when he joined the Canadian Air Force towards the end of World War II. Having become a regular in the Jamaican national side, he moved to Detroit in 1947, playing for **Detroit Corinthians** and **Detroit Wolverines**. Celtic spotted Heron playing for the latter when they came to the Motor City to play Chicago Polish Eagles in the summer of 1951; they invited him for trials in Glasgow that August and promptly signed him up. He made his debut that month against Morton in the Scottish League Cup, scoring once and having another goal disallowed.

Heron was the first black player to join the club and was an immediate hit with the crowd. As a big music fan he was also well known in Glasgow at the jazz and folk clubs and concert halls – hence the lasting affection from his adoptive city. Unfortunately his treatment by his fellow professionals and even the club's management wasn't always so warm. His ability in the air and with the ball at his feet was unquestioned, but his blistering acceleration frequently found him victim to dodgy offside decisions and the idea of this talented, popular black man waltzing into the team caused a fair amount of resentment in many quarters

BEST OF TIMES

United signed George Best as a 15-year old in 1961. He and four other 1961 apprentices went on to make it into the United first team – Willie Anderson, David Sadler, John Aston Junior and Francis Burns. This was an incredibly high intake for one year and would not be matched until Giggs, Beckham, Scholes and the Neville brothers shared a youth side in the early 1990s.

On at least one occasion he got embroiled in fist fights with his own team-mates, but despite having boxed professionally in Jamaica, he found it hard to adapt to the physical nature of the Scottish game, "lacking resource when challenged" as one local paper put it.

In fact, the Black Arrow only played five first-team games, scoring twice. Relegated to the reserves he netted 15 in as many appearances and drew the kind of crowds previously unimagined at that level, but he was "let go" by Celtic at the end of that first season. He joined **Third Lanark** and then **Kidderminster Harriers** before returning to Detroit and the Corinthians. He refereed in America until the end of the 1960s, then returned to the profession he had abandoned to come to Scotland: photography. Heron still lives in Detroit and has published two volumes of poetry.

The reason most frequently offered by his former colleagues for his apparent under-performing is the old chestnut that "black players don't like the cold." But this is a man who had lived in Detroit for years and begun his professional career in Canada, two locations where snow is not exactly uncommon. Maybe his son should write a song about that.

FAUSTINO ASPRILLA

Shooting from the hip

It's a fine line between genius and insanity. In the case of **Faustino Asprilla**, the line was obliterated a long time ago. Madness has followed the Colombian around

Asprilla: never minded the cold, particularly enjoying his time in the north-east the globe and self-destruction has reduced what should have been a glorious career to a few wonderful bursts of sun-kissed football and a cuttings file crammed with the wrong type of headlines. Colombians don't go in for half-measures (which may be why crime, drugs and poverty are their major claims to fame), so it's fitting that their country's most gifted player blew his talent not with alcohol and models but guns, porn stars and the persistent whiff of hard drugs.

> ***" By the end he was knackered-o. I think that's the Spanish for it"***
> *Kevin Keegan on Faustino Asprilla's first game for Newcastle*

The Black Panther rose to fame after joining **Parma** in 1992 and lit up Serie A for four years. With the ball at his feet, he was peerless: able to shift his balance in an instant and glide past defenders. He also had a knack for delivering the goods, inspiring the team to the Italian Cup, Uefa Cup and Cup Winners' Cup as the Tanzi family's massive investment began to pay off in style. **Kevin Keegan** then signed him for Newcastle United in 1996 and he seemed perfect for the gung-ho St James' Park mentality of the time – the most flamboyant, and best-loved, of a recklessly forward-looking side. Like Asprilla, Newcastle never captured the biggest prizes, but it didn't seem to matter: a sublime hat-trick that saw the Magpies come from two-down to beat Barcelona 3-2 is still talked about in wonder to this day. Particularly memorable was Asprilla's late "injury", which spared the knackered star the inconvenience of having to walk off the pitch – instead, he was stretchered the length of the stadium, waving to the crowd like royalty.

With a guiding hand, perhaps, Asprilla might have become the outstanding talent of his generation, yet he was left to his own devices and spent his time in the north-east chasing mini-skirted Geordie girls in the Bigg Market. He left for a short-lived return to Parma in January 1998 after being quizzed by police keen to know where a Colombian man found with four pounds of cocaine strapped to his leg in Newcastle city centre had got the money to make this not-insubstantial purchase. It remains a mystery.

At that year's World Cup, when Asprilla should have shone, he was sent home for unspecified "ill-discipline" and his career soon became a bad parody of **Diego Maradona**'s. Guns, always an obsession, landed him in trouble with the authorities in Colombia on several occasions as he drifted through Brazil, Chile (where he was disciplined for firing near team-mates to make them work harder in training), Mexico and his homeland, showing sporadic brilliance and more general indifference. A bizarre return to the north-east with ambitious **Darlington** was mooted but, not surprisingly, never came off. Perhaps it's just as well…

TONY ADAMS *Ass you like it*

To call **Tony Adams** a cult – yes, Spurs fans, that says "cult" – seems, at first glance, somewhat ridiculous. After all, he's not some little-known midfielder with a disgraceful barnet or a suspect goal celebration. He was one of the most reliable English centre backs of modern times, the greatest captain Arsenal have ever had (twice winning the Double) and one of England's most rousing skippers. But this most effective and inspirational defender is also a donkey, and for that he remains all the more loved by the Highbury crowd.

It was always reciprocated irony, too. When Adams' name was announced over the tannoy, 20,000 fans would bray in unison and the "ass" himself would beam delightedly from the centre circle, pumping his fist in the air in time, then giving a double thumbs-up to each of the ground's four stands. To the outside world Adams was the archetypal, resolute **George Graham** player, getting the job done in a manner that valued efficiency over elegance. True enough, he used to turn like an oil tanker and run with the ball like a Keystone Cop. But while he might have been a donkey, to Arsenal fans he was their donkey. For a brief period, cardboard donkey ears were even worn at matches in a slightly surreal show of solidarity.

The whole donkey business stemmed from the 1988-89 season when, after an undistinguished European Championship for England in West Germany, Adams began to take regular flak for lack of pace and mobility. Opposing fans began making donkey noises whenever he got the ball and, following a 1-1 draw at Old Trafford, in which he scored both goals, a waggish sports editor at the *Daily Mirror* had donkey ears drawn on his picture.

After that it wasn't uncommon for him to get pelted with carrots, but after a particularly veg-tastic 90 minutes at Middlesbrough the Arsenal fans stepped in and took control of the hee-hawing rights. With the insult thus muted, Adams' swift collusion turned it into an in-joke love-fest as he orchestrated the braying.

For the Arsenal crowd to latch on to it this way had far more resonance than simply being a bit of a laugh. The constant criticism in the press, which he felt was undeserved, was starting to sting and though any stick from opposing fans tended to spur him on, the donkey noises and carrots were getting through. Especially the carrots. To have it spontaneously turned around to cement the bond between the fans and the captain – who had never played for another club – did a huge amount for Adams' sense of self-worth.

There was no question that it was enormously appreciated – and was a big part of what made his time at Highbury so special – but it did have a downside. As he revealed after Arsenal's 1997-98 Double win, it could be a bit of a pain when over-refreshed Gooners sustained the mantra across restaurants – restaurants where, you could bet, the new model Old Vic-attending, art gallery visiting, piano-playing, degree-doing, Shakespeare-studying, Sunday paper columnist donkey was eating anything but carrots.

PONGO WARING

The sweet smell of success

There must have been something in the water in 1900s Birkenhead. Within four months of each other, two men were born in the town who'd single-handedly contest the country's record for goals scored in a single season. One was **Everton**'s maestro Dixie Dean, the other was **Aston Villa** legend Tom "Pongo" Waring. Pongo still figures large in Midlands football mythology, and was recently voted the second-best player in Villa history. A giant forward with speed, power, strength and guts, he scored goals for fun in his first professional season at local side **Tranmere Rovers** (24 in 27 games), prompting a nationwide scramble for his signature. Villa won, paying a then-incredible sum of £4,700 for the Merseysider. They were amply repaid: Waring banged in two goals every three games. It's a ratio unheard of in the modern English game, and only Dean could match him through history: Pongo's 49 goals in one season has only been beaten by Dean's staggering tally of 60.

> ***"He kept chickens in the front room of his house in Nelson Road"***
>
> *Villa fans remember Pongo Waring on the Internet*

Even Waring's debut for the Villans was something special – an incredible 23,000 spectators turned up to watch him score a hat-trick for the reserves against local rivals Birmingham City – always a good way to endear yourself to Villa fans. He ended up scoring 167 in a total of 226 appearances, although the management did have some trouble with Waring. Billy Walker remembered him as "a funny lad. There were no rules for Pongo, and nobody on the staff could do anything with him."

The King of the Holte End, also known in those more innocent times as "the Gay Cavalier", was such a maverick that he even managed to get his own dressing room. (We can only speculate as to whether this was due to petulance, status or team-mates' desire to avoid the smell from the chickens he kept in his front room.) Still, he earned five England call-ups, a remarkably small number considering his mercurial talents and eye for goal, scoring four times, and fired Villa to second place in the League in 1931. He found it hard giving up the game, playing for New Brighton during the War, and turning out for amateur sides well into his fifties. When he finally did retire, Waring gave away all his medals, awards and caps, although he remained interested in the game. He was often seen back on the Wirral supporting Tranmere. He apparently stood in the Paddock wearing wellies and – still known as Pongo – bantering with the fans.

HRISTO STOICHKOV

Holy cow

"There are only two Christs," said **Hristo Stoichkov** in 1992. "One plays for Barcelona and the other is in heaven." Given the fact that Hristo is Bulgarian for Christ, you might suspect that this was an amusing play on words. But not to Stoichkov: only the Almighty could rival an ego of his magnitude.

Stoichkov was a ridiculously talented player, yet he boasted a temperament so volatile few could bear to deal with him. Coaches, friends and team-mates all came and went, but the fans – those in Barça and Bulgaria, at least – saw the celestial comparisons as spot-on. Stoichkov was technically excellent and could take a game by the scruff of its neck, wringing victories from otherwise mediocre teams with his mesmerising skills. When he blew up, however, Stoichkov did it in style. At various times he has been known to his countrymen as the Dog, the Bitch, the Fool and the Dagger.

> ***"Van Basten is an incredible player but I deserved the Golden Ball and Van Basten recognised that "***
> *Hristo Stoichkov*

Born in Plovdiv in 1966, Stoichkov was the star striker of army club **CSKA Sofia** and Bulgaria's most celebrated player by the age of 19. Controversy first reared its head in the 1986 Bulgarian Cup final, when Stoichkov's part in a mass brawl earned him a lifetime ban – rescinded a year later after he had been working as an electrician. **Johan Cruyff** took him to the Nou Camp, but even the Dutchman – Stoichkov's boyhood hero – could not calm him, and the pair clashed frequently. Stoichkov, it seemed, hated everyone – he told the press during pre-season training: "I am not talking to any of you bastards until November." He argued with referees as a matter of course and was banned for two months in 1992 for stamping on an official's foot. He questioned the parentage of Barça's directors on live television. Yet each time he was forgiven, having fired his club to four Spanish titles and taken his country to the semi-finals of the 1994 World Cup.

Off the pitch, he paid for the 1992 Cup Winners' Cup Final to be beamed back to his homeland, and his acts of benevolence became legendary. What Hristo Stoichkov wanted most, however, was for everyone to know he was the best. Pipped to the 1992 European Player of the Year title by **Marco Van Basten** (Stoichkov would win it two years later), he was typically modest: "Silvio Berlusconi used his influence to have Van Basten win. Van Basten is an incredible player, but I deserved the Golden Ball and Van Basten recognised that."

Stoichkov: had a knack for lifting average teams, in particular his homeland Bulgaria

BEST OF TIMES

Best's first game for United reserves, in 1962, was against West Brom reserves, where he was marked by Welsh international left-back Graham Williams. When he came to make his first senior appearance in 1963, it was again versus the Baggies – and once again Williams. Inevitably, when Best received his first international call-up, it was against Wales. Williams once again marked Best in this historic game, which Northern Ireland won 3-2. After the game Williams grabbed his face and said: "So that's what you look like – I've played against you three times and all I've ever seen is your arse."

FRANCIS BENALI

Saint and sinner

To **Nick Hornby**, Arsenal's former centre-half **Gus Caesar** was the epitome of football's everyman, the clogging defender. That, however, displays a certain paucity of experience – to most Premiership watchers of the past decade, Southampton full-back **Francis Benali** is almost certainly the least talented player to grace the pitch (and on more than 300 separate occasions, no less). The *Guardian* hinted as much in 1997, when one of its writers questioned Benali's right to appear on the same turf as Dennis Bergkamp.

They missed the point. In an age where standards are pushed ever higher by gifted stars commanding spiralling transfer fees, Benali represents a link to a bygone era when players were not supreme athletes but ordinary men who got lucky, who grasped a rare opportunity and cherished it. Benali is a cult among Saints fans for his 15 years with his hometown club. He has rewarded them with consistent determination (he once played on with a broken arm), good humour, and just occasionally casual violence (11 sendings-off, most notably when he tackled **West Ham**'s **Paulo Futre** so hard he was thrown over the hoardings – Benali walked without waiting for the inevitable red card).

Every club boasts a journeyman or a local cult hero, but few have fitted the mould quite as well. Benali refuses to set foot in Portsmouth, so dedicated is he to the red-and-white cause, and his curry house in Southampton city centre has become *the* place to be seen post-match. For a while, he had his own fan club, who all turned up in Benali t-shirts.

In 1997 loyalties and patience were rewarded when, after 287 games, Benali scored his first (and almost certainly only) first-team goal. A looping, slightly fortunate header against **Leicester City**, it was greeted at The Dell as if it had won the World Cup. For now Benali (34) limps on, appearing mainly in emergencies or Worthington Cup games, but his eventual retirement will be the South Coast equivalent of the ravens leaving the Tower of London.

GORDON HILL

The original wing Wizard

Left foot cocked, head held snootily upright, **Gordon Hill** was an unmistakable sight; and with a nickname like "Merlin The Wizard", there was no forgetting him. This was not Hill's universal nickname. His Manchester United team-mates, not all of whom warmed to Hill's blimp–sized ego and laissez-faire approach to defending, had a variety of alternative monikers for him, "Flash London Bastard" apparently being the most popular. But between 1975 and 1978, the cocksure Cockney, signed by **Tommy Docherty** from **Millwall** for £70,000, held worshippers at the Theatre of Dreams in thrall: shimmies, back-heels, overhead kicks, breathtaking goals… Hill was the archetypal crowd-pleaser.

He was also a pathological show-off, a player for whom the easy option was always rejected in favour of the miracle ball or impossible shot, usually a volley from 30 yards. Hill's volleying technique was sheer perfection. His party piece was to loiter at the edge of the box at corners, wait for a half-hit clearance, then return the ball, on the full, into the top corner. His accuracy was startling and, for a winger, his scoring record phenomenal (51 goals in 130 appearances).

Hill's best performance came in the 1976 FA Cup semi-final against **Derby**

Gordon Hill livens up the 1977 Cup Final with Liverpool by roping in a policeman

County at Hillsborough, his two blinding strikes securing a Wembley appearance for Docherty's team. But, as is often the way with wide men, Hill could be maddeningly inconsistent. Overawed, he was substituted in both the 1976 and 1977 FA Cup finals and, following the sacking of Docherty, was quickly shown the door by new boss **Dave Sexton**. His departure created a gaping hole in the United forward line – one which took a long time to fill.

> ***"You need an O-level or a degree to understand the tactics at Old Trafford"***
> *Gordon Hill*

SEGAR RICHARD BASTARD

Who's your father, referee?

These days you can't go to a game without somebody questioning whether the referee's parents were married. But in the 1878 FA Cup final the referee really was a Bastard: **Segar Richard Bastard** to be precise.

Segar (or Segal as some reference books refer to him) wasn't a full-time referee. As was quite common in those days, he had two simultaneous careers as a player and an official, but he made his international debut as a referee before he made his international debut as a player. In 1879, at the tender age of 25, he refereed the first-ever England vs Wales game.

A year later he won his one and only cap, against Scotland in Glasgow. The Scots won 5-4 and Bastard's international career was over almost before it had begun. But then Bastard wasn't the kind of chap to let a small setback like this get him down. He carried on playing for his club, Upton Park, and he carried on refereeing. He also played cricket for Essex between 1881 and 1885, and was one of the first footballers to explore the synergy between football and racing – ie being on the racecourse is a fine and enjoyable way to spend the money you earn playing football. Bastard went beyond the odd flutter, though – he is almost certainly the first footballer in history to be recorded as owning his own racehorse.

The surname, by the way, doesn't necessarily imply that Segar's family had illegitimate ancestors. The word "bastard" is Middle English and is believed to derive from the Old French term *fils de bast*, which means "packsaddle son". In other words, Segar's ancestors may just have worked with pack animals. So the next time you hear someone abusing the man in black (or flaming vermilion), try and throw in something about working with packhorses…

Sadly, none of Segar's descendants have been tempted to follow his choice of profession. Thus he remains the one, undisputable Bastard to have refereed a game of professional football.

DIEGO MARADONA *Hands up*

Eric Cantona once said:"In the course of time it will be said that Maradona was to football what Rimbaud was to poetry and Mozart to music."That rather depends which Maradona we choose to recall – and the jury is still out on that one.

For those of us outside Buenos Aires and Naples, **Diego Armando Maradona**'s life is characterised by World Cups, his dramatic rise and tragic fall can be viewed through moments that range from the fleet-footed youngster of 1982 to the cocaine-fuelled, bloated sham of 1994.

Maradona is a child of the television age, and a victim of it. There is much discussion of whether he was the architect of his own downfall or deserves some sympathy, but in truth the only time since he was a small child that he has been truly alone is on the football pitch. There, he can express himself and there he must face the consequences of his own actions; off it, things are a lot murkier.

As a boy, Maradona was paraded on television, juggling a ball like a circus act and hailed as his country's footballing saviour. And how Argentines love a saviour, especially one as arrogant as Diego. When, in 1994, Maradona shot four journalists with an air rifle, the public practically demanded the hacks apologise for daring to be injured. Growing up in poverty and with uneducated parents, Maradona was always going to be exploited. This was a country where the 1978 World Cup victory, which Maradona missed, was billed as a chance "to show these men from the Commission on Human Rights what is the real Argentina." The controlling junta took a special interest in their prodigal son, encouraging him to pass comment on politics and hiding behind him when difficult questions needed answering. "He was the teat on which everyone sucked," says his former Argentinos Juniors president.

Maradona never escaped his troubles abroad. Unhappy with his football in Barcelona, his transfer to Napoli was tainted by rumours of Mafia connections and the devotion of the public – who had never seen such a star in their midst – forced Maradona to retreat into a mansion filled with pornography, prostitutes and cocaine. Managers and advisors never dared advise Maradona that class A drugs and women of ill-repute might affect his football.

The public perception remains, however, that the man himself should shoulder the blame: "My main doubt is whether he has the sufficient greatness as a person to justify being honoured by a worldwide audience," was fellow football icon **Pelé**'s view, which lead to a decade of silence between the pair.

Yet Maradona has now found happiness of a sort, living in semi-seclusion with friends and family, and focusing on his health (though his fitness regime, as shown on a recent television documentary, seems to extend no further than being hosed down by bikini-clad young women). It is perhaps what he wanted all along and had he got it in the 1980s and early 1990s, it is terrifying to consider just how colossal his undisputed talent might have become. We can only hope that the next Maradona, if there ever is one, is dealt a better hand.

ARTHUR FRIEDENREICH

The old Pelé

Arthur Friedenreich was probably the greatest goalscorer that football has ever seen. He is reckoned to have scored an astounding 1,329 goals (45 more than Pelé) but sadly the statistical records – which his father Oscar and, later, Arthur's **Paulistano** team-mate **Mario de Andrade** lovingly compiled – vanished after Andrade's death in the mid-1960s.

Friedenreich's life story is like something out of a South American novel. He was born on 18 July, 1892 on the corner of Vitoria (victory) and Triunfo (triumph) streets, names so heavily symbolic they seem like the invention of a hack novelist. His father Oscar was a German businessman, his mother an Afro-Brazilian. His parentage was important because football was then the preserve of the white upper classes. Because Friedenreich was a mulatto he could play, as *Placar* magazine said, if he pretended to be a white man with an all-year tan. Another famous mulatto player of that era, **Carlos Alberto** of **Fluminense**, whitened his face with rice powder before a match.

The need to maintain this masquerade explains why Friedenreich took 30 minutes before a game to sort his hair out. It was naturally crinkly and he would plaster it with brilliantine and stretch it flat onto his scalp under a hot, wet towel. He made his debut at the age of 17 for **Germania** but enjoyed his football most at the (now defunct) Paulistano in Sao Paulo. His impact was immediate: in 1912 he was top scorer in the Sao Paulo League with 16 goals. He won that honour again in 1914, 1917, 1918, 1919, 1921, 1927 and 1929. Nobody, not even Pelé, has finished top scorer in that league over a span of 17 years.

But it wasn't just the goals which made him unique, it was his style. Literal translations of descriptions of his play often describe him, in rather florid terms, as a "green-eyed mulatto dancer" but he was, by most accounts, an elegant player who, although only 5ft 7in tall and weighing eight stone for most of his career, was never intimidated. The Uruguayans nicknamed him El Tigre ("The Tiger") while elsewhere he was known, bizarrely, as "[Latin] America's sweetheart".

He was the first true Brazilian football superstar and the first to exemplify a new native style of play. After he had scored the only goal against Uruguay in the final of the 1919 Copa America, the Sao Paulo magazine, *Sports*, contrasted the

BEST OF TIMES

Best's first wage at United was £4 1s 9d, of which he sent back £3 to his family. He was allowed to keep the equivalent of £1.09 himself. "It felt like a lot to a schoolboy from Belfast," George recalled later.

British school "which dictates that the ball be taken by all the forwards right up to the opposition's goal" with the Brazilian approach which said that "shots be taken from any distance… and the collective advance of the whole forward line is not necessary, it's enough for two or three players to break away with the ball, which, by its devastating speed, disorientates the entire defence."

That Copa America tournament was the peak of Friedenreich's career and, quite probably, his life. After the final, the streets of Rio were flooded with crowds and raised above them, like a flag, was one of his muddy football boots and a sign which said simply "The glorious foot of Friedenreich". The next day, the boot, which had scored the winning goal, was displayed in a downtown jewellers. His fame spread in 1927 when Paulistano became the first Brazilian side to tour Europe and he scored 11 goals in eight games. But by then Friedenreich had already begun to succumb to the pressures which, even in the 1920s, preyed on a footballer of his immense fame.

Two years after his personal triumph in the Copa America, his international career was interrupted by presidential decree. The 1921 Copa America was to be played in Argentina, a country held to be the whitest (and hence most civilised) country in Latin America. Worried that black players would somehow shame Brazil, president Epitacio Pessoa decreed that only white players could represent their country. Shockingly, and shamefully, Friedenreich's name is indeed absent from the team sheets for that Copa America.

The episode must have left the player wounded, reminding him, in his 29th year, how fragile his career and his fame was. Nor was discrimination the only load he had to bear. Brazilian football had clung to its amateur status until 1918, which left players like Friedenreich having to play an endless round of lucrative friendlies. At the same time, the amalgam of legend and fact which has survived about his private life suggests that he didn't rush down to the bank and put his hard-earned cash into a super savings account.

He is reported to have owned 120 Irish linen suits, drank Sul-America beer and classy French brandy and smoked Pour la Noblesse cigarettes as he cut a swathe through the night clubs of Sao Paulo, often waking up very late the following day, making his way to the dressing room and downing a quick pick-me-up while waiting for the brilliantine on his hair to dry.

After his long career ended, Friedenreich's family may have junked his goal-scoring records, which were reported lost on a Sao Paulo rubbish heap. In an attempt to solve the mystery, Friedenreich was tracked down by reporters but he could not answer any questions, preferring to rub his hands through his hair which had finally gone straight after all those years of treatment.

By the time that he passed away, on 6th February 1969, Friedenreich had forgotten both his name and his incredible fame as a footballer.

WILLIAM FOULKE

Room for a little one?

In Edwardian England, if you were of a mind to go to Blackpool on a sunny summer's day, you might find yourself playing "Beat the Goalie" on the golden sands. And the goalie you were trying to beat in the penalty shoot-out would have been none other than former England and **Chelsea** keeper **William Henry Foulke**. He was known to his friends as Fatty.

It was an odd, slightly sad end to a career which had seen Foulke blaze a glorious trail as a bon viveur, persecutor of centre-forwards and referees, and general man mountain. It's often said that goalkeepers fill the goal. At 24 stone, Foulke genuinely did. Born in 1874, he enjoyed a league career which took him to **Sheffield United, Chelsea** and **Bradford**… wherever there was a good breakfast, really. At Chelsea he popped into the club canteen one match day before the rest of the team and ate all eleven breakfasts – and those of the opposition too. When his understandably outraged team-mates took him to task, Foulke told them: "You can call me anything but don't call me late for dinner". This was more than slightly disingenuous in that nobody had ever had to call Foulke to dinner in his life. He would always be there at the head of the queue hoping that someone wouldn't turn up so he could have their serving too.

Foulke: a nightmare for club caterers

But Fatty wasn't simply famous for being fat. He once kept goal for England and won two FA Cup finals with Sheffield United, so he must have been halfway decent at his job. Of course he would have been even more at home in the modern game where he would have had one hell of an advantage in all those penalty shoot-outs which now seem to loom large in every team's season.

But it was Foulke's attitude towards referees and centre-forwards – whom he regarded with the same single-mindedness as a square meal – that loom large in his reputation. After his beloved Blades had lost the 1901 FA Cup final to non-league **Tottenham**, an enraged Foulke chased the referee

Tony Kirkham into a boot cupboard. He was only prevented from causing the referee actual bodily harm by the presence of the FA secretary. Apparently Foulke sat in the team bath after the game plotting his revenge on the referee. (History doesn't record how many team-mates managed squeeze into the bath with him.)

Centre-forwards were frightened of him for several very good reasons. He was not the kind of keeper you would relish competing with for a cross and he had been known, when enraged, to take the law into his own hands. When, one day, **Liverpool** striker George Allan was deemed to be going about his work with undue enthusiasm, Foulke strode towards him, picked him up and stuck the amazed forward, head first, in the mud. The Reds got a penalty out of it but the lesson was not lost on other strikers, or on referees. Against **Port Vale**, in 1905, Foulke picked up an opposing forward and threw him into the net; the referee pointed to the spot and later noted: "I kept a reasonable distance from Foulke for the rest of the game." When he wasn't turning strikers into sticks in the mud, he was snapping crossbars (imagine 24 stone of flesh dangling from a slender beam of Douglas fir) and breaking stretchers (once when he was injured, six men had to carry him off because the stretcher couldn't bear the load).

Foulke wasn't really the kind of man who worried what anyone thought about him, as long as they thought to bring him some food. All of this made his end as the custodian of a joke goal on Blackpool beach that much sadder. He caught a chill on the beach one day and died of pneumonia in 1916, but he left behind an enduring legend.

"You can call me anything, but don't call me late for dinner"
William "Fatty" Foulke

He was the first goalkeeper really to convince the rest of the world that you had to be crazy to do that job. It's hard to see him fitting into today's game. While an industrial crane could always be on hand to pull him off the pitch if he got injured (thus sparing his team-mates the burden), he'd never get used to eating just chicken and pasta. Still, you'd always know where to find him on the morning of a match – at the nearest purveyor of cholesterol-based food.

LEN SHACKLETON

The original maverick

What is it with the north-east and footballing clowns? Forty years before Paul Gascoigne burped, joked and swore his way into the public consciousness, there was the original gifted joker, Len Shackleton.

The parallels with Gazza are numerous. On the pitch, Shackleton was one of the most entertaining players of the 1940s and 1950s, wowing the huge post-war crowds with his flamboyant skills and spectacular goals. Off it, he was a comedian, and like Gazza, his approach sometimes got him into trouble with the authorities and meant his talents often went unrecognised. When one selector was asked why Shackleton had been left out of the England team again, he answered: "because we play at Wembley Stadium, not the London Palladium."

A Yorkshireman, Shackleton started his career at **Bradford Park Avenue**, often cheekily moonlighting as a player for **Bradford City**, whom he supported as a boy. He went on to play for **Newcastle United**, but really made his name at **Sunderland**, scoring 101 goals in 348 appearances – still a post-war club record. Via two FA Cup semis and a second place in the Championship, Shackleton soon earned his crown as football's "clown prince".

On one occasion, as Sunderland led **Arsenal** with five minutes to go, he dribbled into the opposition penalty area, stood on the ball and pretended to comb his hair while looking at his watch. Shackleton regularly bamboozled opposing full-backs by playing one-twos off the corner flag, and once deliberately lost a ball at Bramall Lane by booting it into a massive snowdrift. He could even kick the ball 15 yards ahead of him with so much spin on it that it would screw back to him.

> ***"We play at Wembley Stadium, not the London Palladium"***
>
> *FA selector on omitting Len Shackleton from the England team*

Shackleton further enraged the establishment when he published his autobiography, which contained a page headed The Average Director's Knowledge of Football. It was blank. He was capped only five times for England, scoring a memorable goal in a 3-1 defeat of West Germany, but frustrated manager **Walter Winterbottom**. "If only Len would come half-way to meet the needs of the team, there wouldn't be many to touch him," sighed the boss.

Retiring from the game in 1957, Shackleton went on to work as an outspoken journalist. He's now as much admired as an anti-establishment figure as he was as a player – even capturing the attentions of anarchist rockers Chumbawumba, who included Song For Len Shackleton on their 2002 album, *Readymades*. Shackleton died in 2000, aged 78.

WLODZIMIERZ LUBANSKI

Poles apart

What if **Paul Gascoigne** hadn't made that suicidal lunge at **Gary Charles**? What if **Diego Maradona**'s handball goal had been disallowed? And what if

Lubanski: his country's outstanding talent, but probably not a fan of Roy McFarland

Wlodzimierz Lubanski had been fit for the 1974 World Cup? The last question is probably the biggest lingering imponderable in Polish football.

Poland came third in that World Cup – losing to West Germany in the semi-finals on a sodden pitch that suited the more physical host nation and disrupted the fluent passing game of the underdogs. Had Lubanski played, however, many feel Poland might well have had enough to win their first World Cup. But while the Polish players were doing a lap of honour with their bronze medals, their nation's greatest-ever goalscorer was under the surgeon's knife, getting his knee mended.

> ***"He was a revelation to play with... it would be hard to pick out any weaknesses"***
>
> *Grzegorz Lato on Wlodzimierz Lubanski*

Rewind nearly 12 months to 6th June, 1973. The game in progress was Poland v England and the host nation were cruising to a 2-0 win – Lubanski having scored one of the goals – when a crunching challenge by England defender **Roy McFarland** ended the Polish striker's World Cup hopes. The damage was a serious knee injury and three years in the international wilderness.

It's worth pointing out here that Polish football in the 1970s was in its pomp, boasting such fantastic players as Grzegorz Lato, **Kazimierz Deyna**, Jan Tomaszewski, Andrzej Szarmach, Jerzy Gorgon and **Zbigniew Boniek**. Apart from **Michel Platini**, Boniek was perhaps the greatest European player of the 1980s. Deyna enjoyed a glittering career, but of Lubanski – one of a kind even among so many greats – little is remembered.

Having captained the Polish national team to the gold medal in the 1972 Olympic Games, he was pencilled in as a challenger for the Golden Boot two years later – little surprise given his staggering 40 goals in 52 internationals (in many of which he was also skipper). He was strong, quick and a terrific header of the ball. His goals for **Gornik Zabrze** helped them win League titles galore and he just missed out on a European Cup Winners' Cup medal – his team losing 2-1, to Manchester City, in the 1970 final – before he moved to **Lokeren** in Belgium.

In his first season (1975-76) he scored 17 times, and helped the Belgian side to six top-four finishes in seven seasons, including the runners-up spot in 1980-81. That was Lokeren's best ever season: they also got to the quarter-final of the UEFA Cup and the final of the Belgian Cup.

Lubanski's international career resumed in 1976 and he scored a further four goals in 13 appearances. He played in the 1978 World Cup in Argentina and, in the eyes of team-mate **Lato** (who, in his absence, had won the 1974 Golden Boot), was quite simply the greatest goalscorer of his time. "He was a revelation to play with," said the little Pole. "He knew exactly where you would be and we had almost a telepathic relationship. He was quick, technically excellent and knew where the goal was.

"As a person he was terrific to have around. He had the respect of the team – as every great captain should – and was unique in terms of being a superb all-rounder. It would be hard to pick out any weaknesses."

DAVE BEASANT

He could have been a contender

Pity poor David Beasant. With a chin to rival Jimmy Hill's and a perm to put Southampton-era Kevin Keegan to shame, this gangling colossus of a goalkeeper seemed built for comedic value. He didn't help his cause by committing some of the most celebrated blunders in recent footballing memory, and yet Beasant was – and still is – an outstanding custodian, perhaps among the finest of his time. "Lurch", as he is affectionately known, began his career with customary inelegance, making an unexpected debut for **Wimbledon** in the old Third Division in 1980. Having anticipated not playing, he'd spent the previous night on the sauce and duly fumbled the winning goal into his own net. It mattered not: the head-in-hands moments of disaster (the ball through the legs was a Beasant speciality; **Chelsea** fans hounded him out of Stamford Bridge after he performed it live on television) were always overshadowed by the outstanding reflexes and effortless command of the penalty area which were the true Beasant trademarks.

In the twilight of his career, Beasant has taken his travelling freak show to a clutch of clubs including **Nottingham Forest**, **Wigan**, **Portsmouth** and **Brighton**, but will always be one of the Crazy Gang at heart – though he was actually the quiet, sensible rock upon which their madness was built. That reflex penalty save in the 1988 Cup Final against Liverpool was just one of many spot-kicks he kept out in his heyday – and yet Beasant missed out on what should have been his greatest moment, when Bobby Robson kept him on the bench during England's World Cup semi-final with West Germany in 1990. A last-minute substitution could have seen Lurch facing the penalty shoot-out rather than Peter Shilton, who was never comfortable from the spot, and might have led to another 1966. But somehow that wouldn't have been right, would it?

BEST OF TIMES

At United's 1966 match against Benfica at the Stadium of Light, a man ran onto the pitch with a butcher's knife, heading straight for Best. He was wrestled aside by Denis Law and goalkeeper Harry Gregg, but it later emerged that the man was not a homicidal maniac – he was simply a fan who wanted to cut off a lock of Best's hair to keep as a memento of "El Beatle's" visit to Portugal.

PIET KEIZER

Temper, temper

There's no doubt that Johan Cruyff is the most famous Dutch football figure of all time, with good reason. Everyone remembers his grace, goals and turns as a player, and successes as a manager and pundit. But was he the best player Holland has ever produced? And was he even the best player in the great early 1970s **Ajax** and Holland sides? It's a question still debated in the Netherlands, and it's always one name that rivals Cruyff: **Piet Keizer**.

Four years older than Cruyff, Keizer was already an established star when the youngster debuted for **Rinus Michel**'s Ajax side in 1965. Both had initially excelled on the left wing but could switch between midfield and up front, and both became crucial cogs in the total football machine that won three European cups from 1971 to 1973, and came so close to winning the World Cup for Holland in 1974. While Cruyff was a willing pioneer of the exciting new system of football, Keizer was not. A moody, prima donna-ish figure who worked part-time as a newsagent ("the boys know if they don't do well they'll have to go back to their lousy jobs," said Michels), Keizer knew what he liked – and it wasn't taking part in defensive duties. When Michels left for Barcelona, Keizer danced on a table with glee. But his creative genius guaranteed his place in the side, and his popularity. An upright, long-striding player, Keizer could easily beat men, and split defences with precise and accurate passes, often while looking the other way

> ***"He wanted to leave Ajax. It was over for him at that moment"***
>
> *Johan Cruyff loses the captaincy to Piet Keizer*

He was a less elegant player than Cruyff, but their similarity was always going to lead to rivalry. In the end, it was Keizer who inadvertently forced Cruyff out of Ajax. It was club tradition for players to hold a secret ballot to elect their captain. Keizer had willingly surrendered the captaincy to Cruyff after lifting the European Cup in 1972, happily watching his colleague raise the trophy in 1973.

When Keizer won back the captaincy the following year, however, Cruyff was mortally offended. "I saw it in his face: he didn't know this was coming," remembers fellow player **Jan Mulder** on Cruyff's reaction. "It was a deep insult. He wanted to leave Ajax. It was over for him at that moment." Cruyff was later overheard telling his father-in-law: "Call Barcelona immediately. I'm leaving."

Keizer battled on at Ajax. A highly superstitious man, he required a pat on the bottom and the words "Piet, do your best" from a teammate before every game. His moodiness continued to get him in trouble, however. He hated the media and never gave interviews, and in 1974 had another falling out with his coach, this time **Hans Kraay**. Keizer retired in protest and refused to kick a ball for the next 30 years. On one famous occasion, he even stepped away from a ball as it rolled towards him at a game where he was watching his son play. This amazed many onlookers who remembered Keizer as the best player ever to kick a ball in Amsterdam, but the side-step was typical of the man.

CHARLIE MITTEN

International man of mystery

If there's one story that sums up the difference between football today and 50 years ago, it's that of **Charlie Mitten**. It beggars belief now as players move freely between clubs for vast sums, but back in 1950 Mitten was pilloried as a "soccer outlaw" by press and public for transferring abroad to make some money. The "biggest scandal of 1950s football" ruined Mitten's career, and highlighted the way that clubs "owned" their players. All for a year in Bogota.

Raised in Glasgow, Mitten signed for **Manchester United** in the late 1930s. His debut was delayed by the War, when he served as an RAF physical training instructor. He eventually made it on to the pitch in 1946, aged 25, a decade after joining the club. His patience paid off and he established himself as left winger in Matt Busby's side. Renowned for his speed and the accuracy of his shooting, Mitten helped the Reds lift the 1948 FA Cup.

So far, so straightforward, until United embarked on a summer tour of the US in 1950. On the final day Mitten received an unusual call from England defender **Neil Franklin**. The former Stoke man had recently signed for **Sante Fé** in Bogota for astronomical money, and Mitten was invited to do the same. Mitten was out of contract, but in those days, players were prevented from jumping ship by the fact that clubs owned their registrations in all Fifa countries. The catch was, Colombia had left Fifa, and Santa Fé's ambitious chairman was assembling a team of all-stars by paying more than any European club could dream of.

Mitten was offered £10,000 for a year's work – compared to £10 a week at Old Trafford. Not surprisingly, he succumbed. Matt Busby was furious but powerless, and the press crucified Mitten. Life in Colombia proved to be worth the indignity, however. Living in a palatial family residence, Mitten combined well with **Alfredo di Stefano** and won favour with the fans. "The people treated me like a hero, the weather was superb and I improved as a player," he said.

Unfortunately, within a year Colombia rejoined Fifa, and Mitten was forced back to Manchester to face his critics. The FA fined him £250 and suspended him for six

Clough: a kiss was always round the corner, particularly when authority was involved months; Busby then sold him to **Fulham**. Mitten continued to thrive there, but was denied a justified England call-up as he was seen as having a "lack of discipline".

It was an unfortunate note in a fascinating career. Mitten (who died in 2001) later became manager of Newcastle United, but will always be best known for his Bogota adventure. His case was cited in the abolition of the maximum wage, and was one step in the long road to giving players their freedom of movement, leading to the millionaire superstars of today.

BRIAN CLOUGH

"Now listen to me, young man"

Brian Clough's reputation is proof that football will forgive a demagogue anything, provided he keeps the common touch. Clough's managerial reputation is based on the two consecutive European Cups won with **Nottingham Forest** and a gift for turning mundane players into great ones (see **John Robertson**), but it was his idiosyncrasies as much as his successes that made him a hero.

Clough delighted supporters – and bewildered **Terry Venables** – by holding hands with the Spurs manager as they led their teams on to the pitch for the 1991 FA Cup final. He insisted on referring to **Teddy Sheringham** as Edward Sheringham and confidently told the people of Nottingham he could walk on water. The fans, used to well-worn homilies about boys who'd done well and games of two halves, loved it.

> ***"I wouldn't say I was the best manager in the business. But I was in the top one"***
>
> *Brian Clough*

Just how much they would tolerate was demonstrated when two of them invaded the pitch after the team beat **QPR** in the Littlewoods Cup. Clough clouted them as they passed by his dugout but neither pressed charges; one reportedly turned down thousands of pounds offered by Robert Maxwell to tell his story, and both apologised on a memorable edition of the local news. "Sorry, Brian," they mumbled. "That's alright, lads," Clough replied… and kissed them.

Clough was just as popular as a pundit. Commenting on the World Cup, he listened while another member of the panel praised the sweeper system, ending with the words "the Germans do it". Clough added "even educated fleas do it" and the studio descended into a nervous silence.

He was equally willing to get involved in politics. Described by former Labour leader Michael Foot as "one of the best socialists I've ever met," Clough signed the founding statement of the Anti-Nazi League, stood for parliament as a Labour candidate in Derby, and when the miners' strike divided the Nottingham miners, openly supported the strikers. But the abrasive egotism that elevated him to folk hero in Nottingham hadn't always worked so well. In fact, by the time Cloughie arrived at the City Ground in 1975, he needed Forest as much as they needed him.

He had been the youngest manager in the League in 1965 when, aged just 30, he took charge at **Hartlepool**. He took over struggling **Derby County** two years later and managed them to the First Division championship, becoming so popular that the Derby players threatened to strike when he left to join **Brighton** after an argument with the board over his work as a TV pundit. But he had a disastrous time at the Goldstone Ground – an 8-2 defeat by **Bristol Rovers** one of the lowlights – lasting just nine months. Next stop was **Leeds United**, where he replaced Don Revie, who had stepped up to the England job. But his first, calamitous move was to tell Revie's players, respected and reviled in equal measure as the toughest and most successful team in the country, that they were cheats. He left, perhaps unsurprisingly under the circumstances, after 44 days.

After months in the wilderness, Clough joined Forest. He turned an average Second Division club with an average following into European champions, with an air of inspired lunacy that often disguised his genius for creating teams that were greater than the sum of their parts. He gave his son Nigel the job of handing out Kit-Kats on the team bus – and disciplined one player for asking for a Crunchie. He berated his players, punched them and sang to them (normally *Fly Me To The Moon*). He bewildered interviewers with kisses and bon mots prefixed with the famous words: "Now listen to me, young man…"

As long as he was successful it all held together, but it couldn't last. Clough had been fighting a private battle with drink and, as he lost, he surrendered his grip on the club. In his final season – and by now clearly unwell – Clough saw Forest relegated. He resigned and bade the supporters an emotional farewell.

His health has since improved, and with that, has come a renewed appetite for causing controversy by declaiming on everything from Posh Spice's shoes (too many) to foreigners in the Premiership (too much garlic). And he's also provided a suitably humble epitaph to his managerial career: "I wouldn't say I was the best manager in the business. But I was in the top one."

PAUL BREITNER

Be here Mao

Only three men have scored in two separate World Cup finals: Brazil legends **Vava** and **Pelé**, and a big-haired Maoist German defender called **Paul Breitner**. Nicknamed "Der Afro" for his extraordinary barnet (still celebrated on certain websites), Breitner was a classic 1970s German defender, seemingly involved in

> ***"These Scots had nothing to do with the British football we've feared for decades – they are footballing dwarves"***
> *Paul Breitner*

every great side of the era. By the age of 22, the fearsome left-back, noted for his raids down the wing and his powerful shot, had won all the biggest prizes in football.

Breitner took the European Championship with Germany in 1972, starred in the legendary European Cup-winning **Bayern Munich** side of 1974 (also scooping four Bundesliga titles), and a few months later bagged the World Cup. It was no ordinary performance: Breitner coolly slipped home a penalty in the final, putting Germany level after they'd gone a goal down against the Cruyff-inspired Dutch without touching the ball. Breitner then went to **Real Madrid**, winning La Liga four times, and resurfacing in the German international side of 1982 as a midfielder, scoring a consolation goal in their 3-1 loss to Italy.

A millionaire with extreme left-wing views and an unfashionable (for a Bavarian millionaire) admiration of Mao, Breitner was unusually outspoken for a German, clashing regularly with team-mates and coaches. Like **Eric Cantona**, he used his striking physical presence to good effect as an actor as well as a player, starring in "action crime" films like *Kunyonga*, and switching from midfield general to army sergeant for a role in the 1976 flick *Montana Trap* – a German "comedy Western" (now there is a thought).

Breitner is now established as a German football pundit, and is not exactly reticent in this arena either. "I am actually sorry for my mate Berti," he said when his former colleague Vogts struggled as Scotland's new coach, "because the way his players are punishing the ball will give him a gastric ulcer. Those Scots had nothing to do with the British football that we've feared for decades. There is no technical quality at all…[they are] footballing dwarves." Don't beat about the bush, Paul – tell us what you really think.

ROBIN FRIDAY

Fun, fun, fun

Everybody knows about football's disastrous underachievers: the Gascoignes, Bests and Worthingtons who should have produced so much more than they did. Few have heard of **Robin Friday**, because his underachievement was so spectacular, and ultimately tragic, that he never fulfilled anything close to his potential. His ludicrous antics – drugs, booze, women, fights, prison and even being impaled on a spike – meant he never had a chance. But find a **Reading** or

Cardiff City fan who saw Friday play in the mid-1970s and they'll soon be trying to convince you he was Acton's very own answer to Pelé.

Born in 1952, Friday spent a chaotic London youth in and out of borstal. But his talent for football was God-given and, despite a disdain for training, he soon stood out as the best forward in the capital's non-league game. He was signed by Reading aged 21, became a cult hero at Elm Park within weeks, and had journalists enthusing over the "sheer magic" which turned an average Royals team into an awesome one. His skill and vision were beyond doubt. He could beat players with ease and his 53 goals are widely considered among the best Reading have ever seen. Even experienced referee Clive Thomas was reduced to applauding one strike in 1976, telling the player that "even up against Pelé or Cruyff, it rates as the best goal I've ever seen."

As Friday fired Reading to promotion in 1976, managers like **Bertie Mee** and **Bob Paisley** queued up to court the mercurial talent. But just as his star was rising, Friday's hellraising was beginning to get him in serious trouble. A notorious boozer, he was soon barred from virtually every pub in Reading for fighting, often while naked. The list of his misdemeanours is endless. He terrorised his elderly neighbours with loud heavy metal at 3am. He stole shirts from markets, posed as a guard on trains to get free tickets and removed statues from graveyards. He used huge amounts of dope and LSD – on one away day he was caught naked on a hotel snooker table flinging balls around the room; on another, he paraded around a team meeting with a swan under his arm, procured from a nearby lake.

> ***"Yes, but I've had a much better time than you've ever had"***
>
> *Robin Friday answers his critics*

Friday wasn't much better on the pitch. He drank before games, kissed policemen after scoring, kicked players in the face and grabbed them by the testicles. His disciplinary record was appalling, and only his stellar performances ensured that his managers kept patience. By 1977, though, his career was already on a downward spiral and, after a mysterious bout of dysentery, he was transferred to Cardiff City.

There he produced a number of performances that still make Bluebirds fans misty-eyed, but he would go missing for days at a time and the club finally lost faith in him. He returned to London to work as an asphalter, but never managed to turn his life around. Divorced twice in acrimonious circumstances, he reportedly lived in squalor out of plastic bags until he died in 1990, aged just 38.

Ultimately, it's hard to gauge how much Friday deserves to be put up on a pedestal. His story grows with each telling, and in many ways it's sad that such a tragic figure has been painted as a hero for the *Loaded* generation (his story inspired the Super Furry Animals' Top 20 hit, *The Man Don't Give A F****). But it sure makes for a better yarn than an anodyne **Michael Owen** autobiography.

Reading coach Maurice Evans once told the forward: "If you'd just settle down for three or four years, you could play for England." The reply: "Yeah, but I've had a far better time than you've ever had," is a fair summation of Robin Friday's life.

LEIGH RICHMOND ROOSE

"A hero to every boy in the land"

Leigh Richmond Roose didn't have to be a goalkeeper. The boy from Holt, near Wrexham, had qualified as a doctor of bacteriology and was rich enough to hire his own train to get him to an away game on time. But in the 39 years of his life (he was born in October 1877 and died on the Somme in 1916) he created a footballing legend which endures to this day.

During a game he could usually be found leaning casually against the goalpost as if he were standing on the corner watching all the girls go by. Occasionally he would lean against the post for so long that he fell asleep. Later, when his team-mates complained, he tried to stave off sleep by talking to the crowd. Nor was he averse to the odd practical joke – he once turned up for a game with his hands encased in bandages vowing, defiantly, that he would still play; he did play and when the bandages came off, there proved to be nothing wrong with his hands. Roose's hands also played a part in shaping the modern game. Until Roose came along, goalkeepers had been allowed to handle the ball outside the 18-yard box but his "persistent antics in carrying the ball" persuaded the authorities to change the law.

Roose: changed rules, but not shirts

Roose's jersey was also the stuff of legend. He swore that he could only keep goal in one particular jersey made by one particular person in one particular way. He also insisted the vest he wore under it should never be washed because it might bring him bad luck. As he kept goal for 17 years (for a string of clubs from **Ruabon Druids** to **Aston Villa** and **Celtic**) and

24 times for Wales, it must have been quite an item by the end of his career. When he wasn't leaning against a post, Roose could be pretty athletic. Contemporary records show that his "daring gymnastics in goal" made him "a hero to every boy in the land", with youngsters also warming to his sporting approach to the game. When he made his debut for Celtic in the Scottish Cup semi-final in 1910, he let in three goals; after he'd retrieved the ball from the net for the third time, he ran up the pitch and shook the scorer, Chalmers, by the hand. History doesn't record what his team-mates made of this gesture…

Young lads also had to admire the ease with which Roose addressed the problem of arriving late for an away game. He just hired his own personal train. But then, with 13 clubs in 17 years, he was an experienced traveller.

Boredom was Roose's greatest enemy and only constant change could keep him stimulated. In one way, Roose was a spiritual ancestor of **Bruce Grobbelaar** – brilliant, but with the capacity to have you wondering if he was actually paying attention to the game. Unlike another famously reticent Welsh goalkeeper, **Neville Southall**, Leigh Richmond Roose was proof that you didn't have to be miserable to be a goalkeeper. And as one of a tiny handful of players who have been directly responsible for a change in the laws of the game, his own personal legend is not his only legacy to the game.

RODNEY MARSH and STAN BOWLES

Super hoops

Lots of fans go misty-eyed for the 1970s, the supposed "golden era" of English football, but few more so than supporters of **Queens Park Rangers**. The west Londoners can look back to a brief period spent as the best club in the capital, inspired by two flash players who made the rest of the league envious: **Rodney Marsh** and **Stan Bowles.**

The English forwards shared curious parallels beyond wearing the famous QPR number 10 shirt. One was a Mancunian who ended up in London; the other was a Cockney who eventually escaped to Manchester. Marsh and Bowles were both flamboyant entertainers on the pitch and boozed-up rascals off it; they both had run-ins with their managers; neither won as many England caps

BEST OF TIMES

In 1970 Best had a brief fling with a girl from a rich family, who started sending exotic gifts to him at Old Trafford. Best sought advice from his manager Wilf McGuinness, who asked what sort of gifts were being sent through. "A Bush record player," said Best. "Gucci shoes, an Italian suit, a gold Rolex. And today a car was delivered. A bloody MG Sports car! What should I do?" McGuinness replied: "Send the record player back."

or trophies as their talents merited; and they both became controversial pundits.

Both started out with immense promise. Eastender Marsh played as an amateur with **West Ham United** before finding his feet at Loftus Road. He was a rare English creative magician, and knew it: when asked what he thought of being called "the white Pelé", he answered: "Nah, Pelé's the black Rodney Marsh." His career highlight came in 1967, when he scored the winner for QPR in the League Cup final against **West Bromwich Albion** before 100,000 fans.

It was an amazing feat for a Third Division club, and Marsh was instrumental in taking the Hoops up to the top flight – scoring every other game. Marsh soon found out he was very famous, recalling: "I went to a restaurant and the owner walked up to me and cut off my tie. Apparently it was the custom of the house for celebrities, but nobody asked me."

> ***"I stopped training, except for running to the bookmaker's for the two o'clock "***
>
> *Stan Bowles on his time at Queens Park Rangers*

Unfortunately, his move to **Manchester City** in 1972 was the start of his downfall. Although still a magnificent player recognised with nine England caps, Marsh did not blend in well with City's direct style, and many fans blamed him for their failure to win the league in 1972. "I slowed down their pattern of play," he admitted. Marsh's difficulties led to alcoholism and depression, and by the time he signed for Tampa Bay in 1976, he was drinking a bottle of vodka a day. And teaming up with George Best at **Fulham** 12 months later didn't help.

On the pitch, Fulham's "showbiz 11" entertained the crowd by mucking about tackling each other: off it the duo terrorised the fashionable Kings Road in Chelsea. Marsh finally got the wake-up call he needed when his doctor told him that his liver was almost twice the size it should have been.

QPR fans may have worried that they couldn't replace Rod, but then they didn't reckon on Stan Bowles, the forward with a left foot "as good as a hand" according to **Terry Venables**. Bowles was at the centre of QPR's best ever team in 1976-77, which made the quarter finals of the UEFA Cup. Mancunian Bowles also had difficulties off the pitch, particularly with gambling. "If only Stan could pass a betting shop like he could pass a ball," his manager famously lamented. Bowles fell in with Mancunian crime syndicate the Quality Street Gang, enraging his Manchester City assistant manager and noted bon viveur **Malcolm Allison**, who he ended up punching outside a nightclub.

He almost gave up the game after that, admitting: "I stopped training, except for running to the bookmaker's for the two o'clock race." He eventually started playing again, winding up at QPR. Bowles' dazzling artistry inspired Rangers even more than Marsh had, the highlight being their second-place league finish in 1976. He soon adapted to big city life too, losing huge sums playing big-money cards with notorious hoodlums (he was a terrible card player).

Unfortunately, it caught up with him. Bowles blew £250,000 gambling, became addicted to valium and was arrested in a stolen van loaned to him by a dodgy mate. He even got drunk the night before appearing on *Superstars*, where he registered the lowest score in the show's history. He was sold to **Nottingham Forest** in 1979 where he fell out with Brian Clough, then went to **Leyton Orient** and **Brentford** before retiring in 1984.

Inevitably, like Marsh, Bowles ended up as a pundit, the two of them still managing to wind up the public to this day, much as they did to opposition players years before. In a corner of west London, the pair will never be forgotten.

CHIC BRODIE

Luck be a lady

"...and so I had to ask the physio for a new pair of shorts!" Such is the typical anecdote recounted by professional footballers when asked by the club programme for an "amusing incident" that took place on the pitch. Then there was Chic Brodie, an otherwise-unremarkable journeyman goalkeeper who was drawn inexorably to the slapstick. Brodie had enjoyed a deeply ordinary career with **Manchester City**, **Gillingham**, **Aldershot**, **Wolves** and **Northampton Town** when he signed for **Brentford** in 1963.

The misfortunes began in his first season, when our hero swung from his crossbar while seeing out a dangerous cross against **Lincoln City** and managed to bring it crashing down around him, causing the postponement of the game. In November 1964, while between the sticks in a game at **Millwall**, a hand grenade was lobbed by the ever-friendly home support into the goalmouth: Brodie picked it up, examined it and, in his own words, "bloody scarpered", leaving it to a policeman to retrieve and dispose of the item, which turned out not to be live.

Brodie entered the all-time annals of outrageous misfortune six years later, when a small black-and-white terrier ran onto the pitch to intercept a backpass in a game between the Bees and **Colchester** at Layer Road. Keeper collided with canine and the result was a shattered kneecap: "The dog might have been a small one, but it happened to be a solid one," Brodie said later. The injury ended his professional career and he became a cabbie in Kent, yet still he hadn't learned his lesson.

In 1971, he was tempted out of a short-lived retirement by non-league **Margate** and he led the seasiders to an FA Cup meeting with **Bournemouth**. The result was an 11-0 defeat, in which Ted MacDougall stuck nine goals past the unfortunate Scot to set a competition record.

Trautmann: escaped whole armies, but still couldn't get out of Manchester City

BERT TRAUTMANN

Keeping with the enemy

Many would say that **Bert Trautmann** had endured enough suffering by the time he turned up at **Manchester City**. During World War II he was captured by the French, Americans and Russians but escaped every time. He was buried in a cellar for three days while fighting as a paratrooper, and was later court-martialled for sabotage. After being taken prisoner by the British, he was shipped to a POW camp in Ashton-in-Makerfield in Lancashire, where his displays between the sticks began to catch the eye (though he had only performed as an outfield player in amateur games in Germany).

Somehow – and sadly the details are decidedly sketchy – he ended up playing the 1948-49 season for **St Helens Town** in the Liverpool County Combination and was poached by City to become the first German to play in the Football League. And what a player – Trautmann's raw talent electrified Maine Road and he is regarded by many as the greatest-ever keeper to play in this country. The fans who threatened a boycott at the prospect of one of the enemy turning out at Maine Road soon saw him as a hero, and his status as a legend was sealed when he played on with a broken neck to win the 1956 FA Cup final.

When he retired, 60,000 turned out for his testimonial. But there was also a sadder side to Trautmann that few ever saw – the death of his son in a car crash led to the end of his marriage and he cast a lonely figure towards the end of his City career, playing football in the streets with kids after training rather than returning home alone to face an empty house.

Truly, it's all a very long way from *Escape To Victory*.

"BIG" RON ATKINSON

Boy lollipop

Used to be a decent defender at **Oxford United**, Ron Atkinson. Managed a few clubs too: **Kettering Town**, **Cambridge**, **West Brom**, **Manchester United**, **Athletico Madrid**, **Aston Villa**, **Coventry City, Sheffield Wednesday** and **Nottingham Forest**. But who cares, when he says things – on live telly, obviously unaware the cameras are still rolling – like: "He's a little twat, that Totti. I can't see what all the fuss is about. Are there any sandwiches? I'm starving."

However respectable his achievements as a manager were, Big Ron will always be best remembered as an analyst, fashion icon ("Mr Bojangles"), bon viveur and wit. His unique linguistic magic in the commentary box has inspired a huge cult following, and his addition of several gobbledegook phrases to the national vocabulary has led to the creation of "Ronglish".

Favourite Ronisms include: early doors; amusement arcade forwards with tricks in the locker; the little lollipop (a deceptive jink); sticking the big ugly whip on it (a fearsomely powerful cross); spotter's badges and the Wide Awake Club (membership awarded for defensive perceptiveness); giving it the full gun (a high-powered shot); the little eyebrows (a subtle, glancing header); and doing the ugly, old-fashioned things (tackling and giving). In Ron's world, a player will come out and "go bang" and some lads can throw a ball further than he goes on holiday. He's also seen the odd shot saved because a forward has hit it too well. And, I'll tell you what, that boy has got to be reading comics if he thinks he can score from there.

> ***"I never comment on referees and I'm not going to break the habit of a lifetime for that prat"***
>
> *Ron Atkinson*

Ron's cheek has sometimes got him into trouble. "You won't see that again now the Scouser's got it," he quipped as Liverpudlian **Steve McManaman** raised the European Champions Cup for Real Madrid. To be fair, Ron himself was born in Liverpool's Old Swan, and has had some trouble with Scousers. "Going to

WHAT'S IN A NAME ?

It doesn't say anything particularly positive about the footballing imagination that players' nicknames are generally formulaic. The simple substitution of a name's last three or four letters for an 'o' – as in Thommo or Deano – or an 'a' – **Gazza** or **Macca** – is usually deemed enough. If inventors of such things are having an especially creative day they might come up with Psycho or Tank for the midfield hatchet man. In recent years there have been numerous Tanks, Rocks and Walls, plus at least one Rocket (**Boudewijn Zenden**), Cannon (**Ronald Koeman**), Axe (**John Jensen**), Hammer (**Jorg Albertz**), Nail (**Wim Jonk**), Lamppost (**John van Loen**), and even a Computer (South African **Jan Lechaba**) too.

Then there are the vocations: the Professor (**Arsène Wenger**), the Philosopher (**Lilian Thuram**), the Doctor (**Socrates**), El Matador (**Marcelo Salas**), the President (Laurent Blanc), the General (**Rinus Michels**), the Butcher (**Rene Trost**), the Assassin (**Ole Solskjaer**, albeit baby-faced), and there are hordes of Princes and Kings.

But professions and DIY boys' toys come a poor (joint) second in the world football sobriquet league. The indisputable champions are animals. Indeed football has so many – including of course *the* Animal, **Edmundo** (actually meant as a compliment rather than a reference to his violent streak) – it's surprising no manager to date has earned the nickname Noah. There's the Black Cat/Spider/Octopus (according to who you believe, **Lev Yashin** and any half-decent keeper since), the Dutch Swan (**Marco van Basten**), the Vulture (**Emilio Butragueño**), the Black Panther of Mozambique (**Eusebio**), the Giraffe (**Jack Charlton**), the Goat (**Shaun Goater**), the Fox (various), the Horse (**Oleg Luzhny**), the Snake (**Kanu**), the Pit Bull (**Edgar Davids**), the Bat (**Cle Kooiman**), the Bald Eagle (various), the Gazelle (**Faustino Asprilla**), the Magpie (**Winston Bogarde**), the Buffalo (various), the Mosquito (**Erik Mykland**), the Flea (**Jesper Olsen**) and the Llama (**Frank Rijkaard**). All apparently are complimentary.

In Europe, the Italians and the Dutch show more imagination, boasting the Little Soldier (**Angelo di Livio**), the White Feather (**Fabrizio Ravanelli**), the Divine Ponytail (**Roberto Baggio**), the Snowflake (**Ronald Koeman,** again) and the Black Tulip (**Ruud Gullit**). Curiously, the not-particularly-squirtish **Marco Tardelli** is the Squirt. The Brazilians surpass that, however, with such pearls as the Encyclopaedia, the Possessed, the Phenomenon (**Ronaldo**), the Human Bullet (**Roberto Carlos**), the Helmet, the Hurricane, the Old Wolf, the Village Cannon, Tom Thumb, the Atomic Kick (**Rivelino**), Cry Baby and Mister Sadness. But even those don't compare in grandeur with the Bomber of Borovo (Yugoslav **Sinisa Mihajlovic**), the Emperor of Cameroon (**Roger Milla**) or the Prince of the Red Square (Russian **Igor Korneev**).

Cartoon characters are popular monikers too. There's Mighty Mouse (**Marc Overmars**), Dumbo (**Edwin van der Sar**), Goofy (**Dejan Govedarica**), Shaggy (**Darren Anderton, Steve McManaman**), Tin Tin (**Ronald Koeman** – again), Spiderman (**Walter Zenga**), Batman (**Marco Simone**) and two Icemen (**Dennis Bergkamp** and **Rudi Peter**). Football, you'll be pleased to know, even has a Smurf (MLS' **Antony De Avila**).

Anfield was like Vietnam," he said of his visits as Manchester United manager. He was once tear-gassed on a trip there, and had to put up with baffling Kop banners reading "Big Ron's Leather" and "Ron's Tart Is A Slag."

Still, not much bothered him. "I thought we might scrape a draw when it was only 7-1," he said after his Forest side had been hammered by Manchester United. "I'll be down to my last 37 suits," he quipped after United sacked him. It led to accusations that he cared more about wiseguy gags than his job, but this was wide of the mark. Beneath the mahogany tan lies a remarkable knowledge of football – ask him to name the **Honved** team of the mid 1950s and he can discuss their strengths and weaknesses – and a real love of the game, as he shows weekly in his excellent tactical columns in *The Guardian*.

But Big Ron's real problem as a manager was that he was always too damned quotable. How could it be otherwise when he keeps coming out with statements like: "I never comment on referees, and I'm not going to break the habit of a lifetime for that prat." Long live the King…

LORD KINNAIRD

Toff at the top

70 Many footballers try to write their names into the game's history books. **Lord Alfred Kinnaird** simply tried to rewrite history. In 1877 Kinnaird was keeping goal for **Wanderers** against **Oxford University** in the FA Cup final when, in trying to deal with an awkward back-pass, he carried the ball over the goal-line and the referee correctly gave a goal. It didn't have any bearing on the result – Wanderers still won 2-1 – but Kinnaird's pride had been hurt and after the game he pleaded with officials, swearing that the ball had not crossed the line. His persistence paid off: the own goal was cancelled and, for a century or so, the official FA version of that day's scoreline was Wanderers 2 Oxford University 0.

Finally, however, the score was amended (by most but not all statisticians) and Kinnaird's shame was recorded in the history books. No doubt his team-mates in the great stadium in the sky now refer to him as "Kinnaird og".

But Kinnaird's contribution to football history doesn't end there. He was probably the very first utility player. He could play anywhere: in goal, at the back, up front. Once, when Scotland were short of a few players, he even played for the Tartan Army (although Kensington born and bred, he qualified as a Scot by dint of owning a considerable part of Perthshire).

Kinnaird was known to most of his team-mates at Wanderers and **Old Etonians** as the Harde Fellow, making him sound like Norman Hunter in an earlier stage of the evolutionary cycle. Not to put too fine a point on it, Kinnaird would have found the tackling of **Peter Storey** and **Norman Hunter** to be effete. Here was a man for all those who bemoan the lack of hard men in the game. His mother, after watching a particularly violent game, once confided to a rival that she feared one day her son would come home with a broken leg. "Don't worry, ma'am," the rival replied, "it won't be his own."

> **"The Luther Blissetts don't exist; only Luther Blissett exists"**
> *Italian anarchist manifesto*

FA Cup finals were Kinnaird's forte. He appeared in nine of them, winning four. He got on the scoresheet three times – once with his terribly embarrassing own goal and twice at the right end – and it could have been even better. In 1883 he "scored" with a free-kick but it didn't count because scoring direct from a free-kick was illegal at that time. The disappointment was exacerbated by the fact that his Old Etonians side went down 2-1 to **Blackburn Olympic**. The previous season they had beaten **Blackburn Rovers** 1-0, a victory the peer celebrated by standing on his head in front of the Kennington Oval pavilion. In 1911, in recognition of such stunts – and the fact that he'd been president of the FA for longer than anyone could remember – he was given the FA Cup to keep.

Twelve years later Kinnaird died (it's to be hoped his last words were "It was never a goal"), having earned himself a unique niche in football history: as a role model for both tough-tackling defenders and mouthy goalkeepers.

LUTHER BLISSETT

Now we are one

It's just as well **Luther Blissett** isn't of a particularly nervous disposition, or he might begin to feel someone is out to get him. Blissett was a reasonably gifted striker who was simply out of his depth in Italy. When he returned home, somewhat deflated, he found he had given rise to a cult which shows no signs of stopping. When Blissett left Vicarage Road, **Watford**, for Milan, the common perception was that the Italians, in true **John Motson** style, had got their black players mixed up and had meant to sign **John Barnes**. Either way, Blissett was back in Hertfordshire just a year later having scored only five goals, but he went on to earn his place in Watford legend.

Then, in 1998, four Italians were arrested for fare-dodging on a train and all four of them gave their names in court as Luther Blissett – their "collective identity". It seems that they had chosen our hero because he was "just a nice guy who had problems with the Italian way of playing football" and may have suffered because of his skin colour. Fellow anarchists picked up the Blissett ball and ran with it, publishing books as a collective on the Renaissance and papal history and a highly acclaimed novel, *Q*, about 16th-century Lutherians.

Apparently, "the 'Luther Blissetts' don't exist, only Luther Blissett exists." The Internet has spread the idea across Europe and South America. Blissett has even become a byword for anarchism in several countries, with Blissett manifestos and philosophies cropping up, particularly in Germany. Some suspect the author Umberto Eco to be behind it all. Blissett himself, having initially described the occurences as "strange", now prefers not to discuss them.

PERRY GROVES

The future's orange

Even **Perry Groves**' song had a whiff of hallucinogenics about it. To the tune of *Yellow Submarine* and with cheerful disregard for poetic structure, the crowd would croon: "We all live in a Perry Groves world, a Perry Groves world, a Perry Groves world." This normally happened while Groves was warming up in front of Highbury's East Stand, something he seemed to do regularly (if not actually best) as a perennial bench-warmer for **Arsenal** for the second half of the 1980s and early 1990s. Manager **George Graham**'s logic seemed to be, "Twenty minutes to go – get the ginger kid on to run at their knackered defence." The thing was, it often worked, too.

Whereas many cult heroes have their status established by a single act or event, Perry Groves had just so much to endear him to the amiably sardonic section of the Arsenal faithful. Most of it was as trippy as his song. He was George Graham's first signing (£75,000 from **Colchester United** in 1986), a winger in a midfield where silky skills were the least of anybody's worries. He was the nephew of 1950s Arsenal legend **Vic Groves**. He once scored against Spurs (as did Uncle Vic). He had hair so orange it could surely be seen from space, and his approach to styling owed more to dramatic licence than sound judgement. And he frequently bamboozled himself in his mazy dribbles.

Groves spent so much time sprinting up and down the cinder track he must have got to know most of the residents of the East Stand Lower by name. Yet it's widely recognised that Groves' energetic appearance as substitute in the 1987 League Cup final was Arsenal's turning point against the strongly fancied Liverpool – with the scores at 1-1, it was his run and cross that set up **Charlie Nicholas**' deciding goal. And remarkably, for a player of such unremarkable talents, Groves has more Championship winners' medals than Paul Gascoigne, Gary Lineker, Alan Shearer and Michael Owen have between them.

Groves left Arsenal in 1992 and retired in 1995. When last seen, he was playing (or was that warming up?) for Arsenal in the London Masters tournament.

Peter Storey (right) displays his "combative" tackling style

PETER STOREY

Bang to rights

Though a Double winner with **Arsenal**, **Peter Storey** only really started to excel once he'd hung up his boots. Storey was a Del Boy before Del Boy was invented, only much, much seedier and with a far greater appetite for breaking the law. The Highbury legend, whose swansong also included 17 games for **Fulham**, trailblazed a career in crime that even the likes of celebrity football rogues **Frank McAvennie** and **Mickey Thomas** have failed to emulate.

Between 1962 and 1977, Storey appeared 494 times for the Gunners midfield in all competitions, scoring 17 goals. Despite having Edwin as a middle name (he and team-mate **Bob "Primrose" Wilson** probably resented their parents equally), Storey won the 1970 European Fairs' (now Uefa) Cup. He was also instrumental as Arsenal won the dramatic League and FA Cup Double in 1970-71 – he scored eight of his 17 goals that season with his critical, last-gasp penalty equaliser against **Stoke City**'s **Gordon Banks** in the FA Cup semi-final arguably his apogee. "Snout" also earned 19 England caps. But his footballing exploits paled beside his off-field antics, with a litany of misdemeanours starting when he was still kicking balls about.

> ***"It's about the drunken parties that go on for days – the orgies, the birds and the fabulous money"***
>
> *Peter Storey on life as a footballer*

As was almost obligatory for any 1970s footballer, he lived a life of birds and booze. However, his hobby became his day job when he retired to concentrate on running a brothel. Unfortunately east London's Calypso Massage Parlour was busted in 1979. Storey was fined £700 and handed a six-month suspended prison sentence.

With typical commitment, Storey next flung himself fully into the counterfeit money trade, getting jailed for three years in 1980 for financing a fake gold coins scam. Two years later he was awarded another six months at Her Majesty's pleasure for automobile theft. He then managed to keep his head down for a few years but in 1990 he was caught smuggling 20 illicit pornographic videos from Europe in his car's spare tyre. For this, he received another spell in the nick, this time just 28 days. Almost as soon as he was out, however, he was back in for another 28 days, for the not-really-a-crime crime of verbally abusing a traffic warden. Disappointingly, Storey was last seen as a law-abiding chauffeur/driver somewhere in south-west London....

Gunter Netzer (left) makes a point in typically diplomatic style to Franz Beckenbauer

GUNTER NETZER

Breaking the mould

When German football fans think of the 1970s, they think of Bayern Munich ruling Europe and of the best national team they've ever had. When they're asked to come up with images defining this era, one player invariably springs to mind – despite neither playing at Bayern Munich or ever truly becoming a West German regular. That man is **Gunter Netzer**.

One typical Netzer image has him leaping in the air on a June day in 1973. It was his last game for **Borussia Mönchengladbach**, the Cup final against Cologne. Netzer had been benched, mainly because he'd already signed with **Real Madrid** at that point, but during the interval before the beginning of extra time he brought himself into the match without asking for the coach's permission. Four minutes later he scored the winner.

Another image has Netzer surging through midfield, his blond mane illuminated by the Wembley floodlights. It was 29 April 1972, and Germany were in the process of winning for the first time on English soil. Netzer was only playing because Cologne's **Wolfgang Overath** was injured, but it was largely his performance that has bestowed the match with near-mythic status in German football lore.

BEST OF TIMES

Best's final bust-up with Tommy Docherty came in January 1974, when he was dropped after showing up "pissed out of his mind" on match day "with a girl in tow," according to the United manager. Best admits he missed training that week "because I'd been out the night before," but is still bitter at The Doc about the matchday allegations. "He said that I turned up in no fit state to play," says Best, "but that's rubbish. I was fit. I walked out... I knew I would never go back to United as a player."

There are plenty more images though – some of which might explain why Overath, the reliable team player, won 81 caps to the 37 collected by the unfathomable and unpredictable genius. There are the pictures of Netzer in the bar he owned, Lover's Lane. Pictures that show him behind the wheel of a fast car (in June 1970, he almost died in a Ferrari). Pictures taken with his beautiful and mysterious girlfriend, a goldsmith. It could be an all-too-familiar story of a footballer going off the rails – but Netzer was not the average football player or typical 1970s maverick. He owned a bar but he didn't drink. He loved cars but he wasn't reckless. He was a sex idol but never a womaniser. He was an icon for all those who hated Bayern's clinical efficiency, yet he was a man with a keen business sense – he was Hamburg's commercial manager from 1978 to 1986, moulding the great side led by **Kevin Keegan**.

Today, Netzer is mainly known as an acclaimed TV analyst, popular for his acumen and honesty. But at the same time, he led the group that bought the broadcasting rights to the 2006 World Cup from the bankrupt Kirch Media company. Some 30 years since his heyday, he still defies the stereotypes.

BARRY FRY

The ego has landed

When he signed for **Manchester United** as a schoolboy in 1962, **Barry Fry** thought he had it made. Matt Busby – rarely prone to exaggeration – said he could be the new **Jimmy Greaves**. He was right, but unfortunately the side of Greaves that Fry emulated was the egotistical, lard-loving pundit rather than the free-scoring striker. He freely admits himself that: "the only reason Barry Fry failed as a player was Barry Fry."

But playing's loss was management's gain. Fry may be a larger-than-life self-publicist but he's a shrewd coach, too. He took over as Dunstable gaffer at the age of just 28, and his early career was dominated by a pair of implausible chairmen. At Dunstable there was the charismatic, Lamborghini-driving **Keith Cheeseman**. Fry remembers him as being amazingly generous and "the greatest conman I've ever known". The naïve young Fry unwittingly got involved in transporting suitcases of embezzled cash around the country, and Cheeseman's dodgy dealings often forced him to go on the run to Miami, where he'd claim to be hanging out with Frank Sinatra and Gloria Estefan.

After Cheeseman came **Stan Flashman** at Barnet. An odious "self-made" ticket tout – or, as Fry had it, "a complete and utter shit" – Flashman sacked his manager on more than 20 occasions, with the result that Fry simply ignored dismissals and turned up the next day as if nothing had happened. "One minute Stan was the most generous person in the world, the next he was a monster," remembers Fry. Highlights included threatening to entomb Fry in concrete because of his team selections ("you'll be under the M25") and asking players to get rid of counterfeit money at the bookie's.

After a spell at **Southend** (where Fry was perhaps the only manager never to be on the receiving end of any grief from **Stan Collymore**) and two pressure-related heart attacks, he finally hit the semi-big time with **Birmingham City**.

Signing 61 players in 29 months, Fry had run-ins with the chief executive, Karren Brady, over her relationship with striker **Paul Peschisolido**, and with the club's owner – porn baron David Sullivan – over the side's results. After Fry announced that Sullivan "didn't know a goal-line from a clothes line" on TV, his days were numbered, despite some successes. He then wound up at Peterborough, where he bought the club, then lost it again due to £3 million worth of debts, only to be saved by a pizza millionaire.

He's still manager of the Posh, and on past record it's impossible to guess what Fry will do next. Two things are bound to stay the same, however: his legendary temper (Fry has thrown teapots, plates of sandwiches and even his shoes at underperforming players) and his love of transfers. His favourite signing ever? "My wife." Awww...

JESUS GIL

Not the Messiah – just a very naughty boy

Your opinion of **Jesus Gil** will almost certainly hinge on your feelings towards **Athletico Madrid**, the club of which he was president, owner and supreme overlord for 17 years. Since most of us don't pledge our allegiance at the Vicente Calderon Stadium, it seems safe to say Gil is the most corrupt, barking despot ever to set

> ***"Carreas, Santi and Otero are no good. They can die. I mean it: some of the players don't deserve to live"***
>
> *Jesus Gil*

foot in a boardroom. Club officials don't often enter the annals of a sport's history, but Gil – who finally retired in 2003 – has been the dominant personality in the Primera Liga for a decade, keeping quote-hungry football hacks in business with his increasingly bizarre antics.

Thirty-nine managers passed through Athletico during Gil's reign, 26 of them sacked and the other 13 jumping before they were pushed. **Cesar Menotti** likened his axing to being "taken for a drive in a Ferrari and being thrown out at 100mph." **Ron Atkinson** left after three months, despite taking the club to second in the league. But that was only the half of it – Gil was first jailed in 1969 when a building he put up collapsed, killing 58 people.

Corruption investigations became an annual event – as mayor of Marbella, he faced 80 court cases. But the mud only really stuck in 2002 when he was found guilty of siphoning public funds into Athletico (the council's sponsoring of the club's shirts was a fairly obvious example) and was banned from public office for 28 years.

It was Gil's passion which captivated fans and catapulted unfashionable Atletico into the upper echelons of the Spanish league, but his passion frequently turned to rage. He memorably described striker **Hugo Sanchez** as being "as welcome as a piranha in a bidet" and once threatened to "machine gun" his entire team. The rant which hastened his demise came after a 1-0 defeat in February

2003, when Gil singled three players out for particular ire: "There's too many passengers in the team. They're not going to laugh at the shirt any longer. Carreras, Santi and Otero are no good. They can die… I mean it, some of the players don't deserve to live… and anyone who doesn't like it can die."

Gil hasn't retired completely, however – he still has his local television show, in which he harangues public prosecutors and other officials from a paddling pool, dressed in swimming trunks.

NEVILLE SOUTHALL

Another fine mess

Wembley Stadium, 1995. **Everton** have beaten Manchester United 1-0 to lift the FA Cup. As Alex Ferguson is turning a whole new shade of purple in the losers' dressing room, the Blues players are heading upstairs for a sumptuous banquet to toast their victory. It soon becomes clear, however, that one figure is missing. The hulking, unkempt goalkeeper more responsible for their win than anyone else has crept out of the Venue of Legends. In fact, **Neville Southall** is back home in north Wales before the aperitifs have been ordered. Such was the nature of Big Nev, a man so famously grumpy he rarely spoke to team-mates, let alone reporters, but who went from Llandudno binman to greatest goalkeeper in the world with such quiet majesty.

Southall: a stranger to the hairbrush and the iron, not to mention the razor

Worthington: looked like Elvis Presley's elder brother , played football like a Brazilian

Southall's agility would not have been out of place in a Roy of the Rovers strip. Even before pies had become the staple of his diet, he cut a comically heavy figure between the posts, yet he seemed to hang in the air like a ballet dancer. The upturned collar, bedraggled hair, un-ironed shirt and unruly 'tache all seemed calculated to lure the opposition into believing he had wandered straight out of bed and onto the pitch. But a record 93 Welsh caps and 750 games in the top flight for Everton tell their own tale of this colossus of the 1980s and '90s, unique among keepers in having no discernible weaknesses.

Any Evertonian will struggle to recall a single Southall mistake during his legendary tenure between the sticks at Goodison Park – his command of the aerial ball was matched only by his shot-stopping, and he was unbeatable one-on-one. Earlier in that Cup-winning season, he had dealt with a pitch invader by lifting him by his collar and simply glaring at him, and it's that steely, unyielding Southall that we'll cherish, as opposed to the almost-immobile chubster who was turning out in the lower divisions (not to mention managing conference strugglers **Dover Athletic** for little more than a couple of months) well into his forties. We won't see his like again.

FRANK WORTHINGTON

Northern star

Such is the romantic mist which now enshrouds such 1970s mavericks as **Frank Worthington** that he seems, in memory, to have exhibited Brazilian ball skills. In reality, Frankie was far more unusual than that. The hairstyle was pure Elvis, and the knee-manipulating comedy routine with which he started many matches was right out of Norman Wisdom. But just as you had begun reluctantly to conclude that he was just a music hall entertainer, he would show a touch of real Brazilian artistry, albeit not quite of the 1970 vintage. **Bolton** fans still talk in hushed tones of a legendary goal he scored against **Ipswich**. Back to goal, on the edge of the 18-yard box, Worthington controlled the ball with his knee, flicked it up and volleyed it over his head into the net.

In the 1970s, as George Best changed clubs faster than he changed pubs, Frankie was a blessed relief. A footballer who seemed to genuinely enjoy himself on the pitch, he even put on a brave face when his once-in-a-lifetime move to Bill Shankly's Liverpool fell through because – well, for all the rumours, only Frank really knows why. He played for a lot of northern clubs like **Bolton** and **Huddersfield** but seemed to find his niche as the star attraction in **Jimmy Bloomfield**'s enterprising **Leicester City** side of the early 1970s. He wouldn't have been quite as effective without Len "Solly" Glover thundering down the wing – with a lot more pace than any of Glover's horses ever showed. But Frank was a showman in a team which, on its day, could beat anybody – even if that day didn't come often enough to save Bloomfield's neck.

Worthington was too much of an individualist to fit Don Revie's utilitarian vision of the perfect England side (although he got a look-in under Joe Mercer's caretaker regime), but he consoled himself with the kind of off-the-pitch lifestyle which would fill today's *Sunday Sport* for a year. It's all chronicled in the nudge-nudge wink-wink autobiography *One Hump Or Two*, the very title a sign that Frank could be as coarse off the pitch as he could be sublimely subtle on it.

The autobiography is, though, notable for its superb flickerama and a fine tale about a Caribbean pre-season tour which climaxed with Frank and Alan Birchenall meeting Omar Sharif at a party. The international playboy, upon meeting two of Leicester City's finest, pronounced himself "deeply moved".

Frankie's career eventually fell into the kind of nomadic pattern which marked Bestie's declining years, with spells at Bolton, Leeds, Birmingham, Tranmere, Brighton, Sunderland, Southampton, Preston, Stockport, Hinckley Town, even the Philadelphia Atoms and Mjilby AIF in Sweden. But he was of great service to Leicester, not just because of the goals he scored, or the skill he showed, but because his antics inspired a young Filbert called Gary Lineker.

82 THE MICKY THOMASES

Only the name is the same

There's only two Michael Thomases. One will always be best remembered for putting the finishing touch to the most thrilling climax to an English league season of all time; the other for a group of angry men attempting to cut off his penis after he'd slept with one of their wives.

To the relatively sensible Michael (rather than Mickey) first. Lambeth-born Michael Thomas captained the England schoolboy, youth and under-21 teams, went on to play for his country and had a distinguished career at **Arsenal** and **Liverpool**. But it is for the split second during a match between those two sides at Anfield that he'll always be remembered.

In the final game of the season, Arsenal travelled to the home of the English champions needing to win by two clear goals in order to lift the title. After nearly two minutes of injury time, and with the Liverpool players and Scouse crowd already celebrating, Alan Smith slipped the ball through to the midfielder, 30 yards from goal. Thomas thundered down towards keeper Bruce Grobbelaar, and in a moment of extraordinary coolness slipped the ball into the net. The result is still burnt into the memories of both club's supporters, and even formed the climax of a book and feature film, *Fever Pitch*.

Arsenal's Thomas was the model pro. The same could hardly be said for

Manchester United's Mickey, who isn't remembered with any great love by United fans. Thomas personified the Dave Sexton years of dull football, and was generally considered to be a lower-league star got lucky. The pressure got to him, and Thomas admitted he had played several games still drunk from the night before. He also enraged the nation by implicating himself in shameless gamesmanship in a match against Ipswich Town. After what looked like a possible dive for a penalty against the Suffolk side, Thomas smirked and – unforgivably – winked at the *Match Of The Day* cameras, earning Jimmy Hill's eternal disapproval.

> *"The game's about glory… going out and beating the other lot, not waiting for them to die of boredom"*
>
> *Danny Blanchflower*

Off the pitch, his life was equally lamentable. His former glamour model wife took exception to his boozy, womanising behaviour and smashed up their home, even demolishing a glass door with her feet. She wasn't the only one to be upset: Mickey was later caught *in flagrante* with an old sweetheart, now married to someone else. Her husband's associates stabbed him a dozen times in the buttocks with a screwdriver, later leading to gags about Thomas being lucky to escape without brain damage. Slipping out of consciousness, Thomas could recall his assailants debating whether to "cut his dick off". "If we can find it," joked one. He didn't fare much better elsewhere. At **Chelsea** he commented to new chairman Ken Bates that he'd like to "give one" to an attractive young girl who walked by. It was Bates' daughter-in-law.

Possibly Thomas's lowest ebb, though, was when he was convicted of passing counterfeit £10 notes and sentenced to 18 months in prison. As he was taken down, Thomas at least had the wit to enquire: "Can anyone change a tenner for the phone?" But in terms of great memories, this Michael Thomas would surely gladly swap places with his namesake from Arsenal.

DANNY BLANCHFLOWER

This isn't your life

What has Spurs legend Danny Blanchflower got in common with Noel Gallagher and Bill Oddie? For the answer we need to rewind to the 1970s and a certain TV show. When the amiable presenter Eamonn Andrews approached his unsuspecting victim with his famous big red book and the magic words, "Danny Blanchflower… this is your life", the response was unexpected. "No it bloody isn't," retorted the Ulsterman, walking away. His response (Oddie and Gallagher

Eric Cantona in one of his crazy walk-on parts

declined more politely) briefly made Blanchflower the most talked-about man in Britain, but it summed him up: individual, outspoken and uncompromising.

The name Danny Blanchflower has become synonymous with skilful, buccaneering football. As an adventurous player and captain, he led **Tottenham** to the Double in 1961 and Northern Ireland to a World Cup quarter-final in 1958. But it was his attitude to the game that won him most fans. "The game's about glory," he famously said. "It's about doing things in style, with a flourish. It's about going out and beating the other lot, not waiting for them to die of boredom." His quote became the unofficial definition of "the Spurs way" of playing – and has been an albatross around the club's neck ever since, as a succession of managers failed to produce a team like Bill Nicholson's. One of the main reasons was that they didn't have players like Blanchflower.

The attacking wing-half played for **Glentoran**, **Barnsley** and **Aston Villa**, and served in the RAF during World War Two, before turning up at White Hart Lane. Intelligence and skill were his strongest points, and, true to his maxim, Blanchflower was constantly on the attack. Some managers considered him something of a luxury player, although Blanchflower countered: "It's bad players who are the luxury, not the skilful ones."

Footballer of the Year awards in 1958 and 1961 soon put paid to his critics, and his extraordinary performances in the Double year helped Spurs cruise to the title. They retained the FA Cup and reached the European Cup semi-finals next season, too, as Blanchflower amassed 56 caps for Northern Ireland.

Blanchflower was as articulate off the pitch as he was on it, working as a respected newspaper columnist, and eventually managing **Chelsea** and his country. "He would wax lyrical about football and its relation to life," remembers **George Best**, who played for his Northern Ireland team. "Football and its relation to endeavour. Football and its relation to a canteen cup. To ask him anything about football was to invite a reply as epic as one of Milton's poems."

His most famous line, however, was perhaps "pass the hot milk, please" – coined in a Shredded Wheat advert. So Blanchflower did eventually show up on the small screen – and the big one, playing himself in the Spurs-themed *Those Glory Glory Days*. Just as long as you didn't try to tell him that this was his life…

ERIC CANTONA

No seagulls or trawlers please

"I am happy to be crazy," **Eric Cantona** once said. "The world in which we live is boring. If you're different, you are considered crazy." Anyone with the vaguest interest in English football over the past 10 years cannot have escaped Eric Cantona's craziness: he was one of the finest players in the Premiership and probably its maddest. His antics at **Manchester United** are well documented – the kung-fu attack on a Crystal Palace fan, the seagulls following the trawler "explanation" and the inspirational play that led the Red Devils to the Double.

Less well known is what came before, and has followed since. Before his move to **Leeds United**, Cantona played for six French clubs, and the way he is admired in England (recently being voted Manchester United's player of the century) is greeted with a Gallic shrug on the other side of the channel. His reputation in his homeland is that of a maniac and agitator. Looking at his behaviour during his French domestic football years, it's easy to see why: controversy followed Cantona at every stop along the way to Auxerre, Martigues, Marseille, Bordeaux, Montpellier and Nimes.

> ***"I am happy to be crazy. The world in which we live is boring. If you're different, you are considered crazy"***
>
> *Eric Cantona*

At Auxerre he punched team-mate **Bruno Martini**, and when challenged by seven angry opponents after an ill-tempered reserve match, he put four of them in hospital. Montpellier colleague **Jean-Claude Lemoult** had Cantona's boots thrown in his face after a perceived indiscretion, while France manager **Henri Michel** was once dismissed as "a shitbag", earning the fiery forward a year's ban from the international side.

At **Marseille** he threw the shirt on the ground in disgust, and while at **Nimes** he chucked a ball at a referee. After being suspended for two months, Cantona dramatically announced his retirement. He was back within weeks.

Cantona eventually decided that France did not suit his skills, came to England, and the rest is history. Since returning home, he has entered a profession the French take as seriously as the British take football: the cinema. It was a typically awkward choice for Cantona, but he has since won great acclaim for his performances. British cinemagoers will have seen him sporting dubious period facial hair in the movie *Elizabeth* with **Cate Blanchett**.

In France he has had some excellent roles: his debut *Le Bonheur Est Dans Le Pré* won him rave reviews for the relatively sedate role of a duck farmer named Lionel, although the film suffered somewhat from the shameless and unlikely product placement of his sponsor, Nike.

However, a degree of typecasting since has shown what his people really think of him: in three films he's played a violent maniac. In *Les Enfants Du Marais*, he had a major role as a moody boxer; in *Question D'Honneur* as a moody boxing promoter; and in the comedy *Mookie*, as a moody boxer who befriends a chimp. His latest outing, in *L'Outremangeur* (*The Overeater*), sees Cantona play a greedy cop, wearing a 160-pound fat-suit.

It's ironic that the French couldn't understand this most Gallic of men's singular football gifts. It may be that his role on the screen could finally persuade them to take the crazy genius of Cantona seriously. Then again, maybe not.

KYLE ROTE JR

Yanks for the memories

Having attributed his presidential victory to America's soccer moms, Bill Clinton should perhaps have offered up a vote of thanks to **Kyle Rote Jr** too. In the 1970s the Texan emerged as the NASL's first all-American hero, proving to a nation of Bud-slurping armchair quarterbacks that heck, maybe those soccer guys really were real athletes after all.

Rote's father had played professional "football" as wide receiver with the **New York Giants**. The teenage Rote Jr was expected to follow in his uniform – until he and his gridiron team-mates spent an afternoon kicking a "soccer" ball around. They were spotted by a passing Englishman from Blackpool, **Ron Griffith**, who insisted on showing them how to do it properly. Rote's interest deepened and he eventually concentrated on the sport at college, becoming the number one pick in the NASL draft of 1973 and signing for the **Dallas Tornado**.

Rote instantly became Rookie Of The Year with 11 goals and 10 assists, but ironically it was only when he took the US version of *Superstars* by storm that he really made the American public take notice of soccer. In the 1974 edition of this made-for-TV trash decathlon, he beat NFL icon OJ Simpson, pole vaulter Bob Seagren and tennis player Stan Smith to take the *Superstars* crown. A year later he could only finish third, but in 1976 he regained his title, beating a rather eclectic field that included English athlete David Hemery, actor Robert Duvall and Lou "Hulk" Ferrigno, and in 1977 he made it a hat-trick of wins. (And he didn't fall off his bike or shoot the table once.)

Rote, who once spoke at the White House on behalf of Gerald Ford, scored 47 goals for the Tornado over six seasons, before playing a farewell season with the **Houston Hurricane** in 1979. Instead of putting his feet up, however, he then took a year off to work with Mother Theresa. He holds a degree in psychology, and these days spends his time running his own sports agency, representing Major League Baseball and basketball stars.

ALLAN SIMONSEN

Valley of dreams

In 1977, **Allan Simonsen** was voted European Footballer of the Year. Five years later, he was playing for **Charlton Athletic**. But it wasn't drink, drugs or gambling which led to the Danish superstar's reduced circumstances: it was his own free will. To get an idea of how unlikely Simonsen's move from north-east Spain to south-east London was, imagine **Rivaldo** signing for **Grimsby Town**. The tricky attacking midfielder was a popular figure at **Barcelona**, with whom he spent three years and won the Cup Winners' Cup, but when Diego Maradona pushed the quota of foreign players above the permitted maximum, Simonsen was deemed surplus to requirements.

He was put on the market for £300,000 and was expected to move to Italy, but Addicks chairman Mark Hulyer was nothing if not ambitious and stumped up the cash to take the star to the old Second Division. Hulyer reasoned that the mid-table strugglers would recoup the outrageous outlay through sponsorship and additional gate receipts – more than 2,000 saw Simonsen's reserve-team debut – but the big figures never rolled in, and his wages of £1,500 a week (then an enormous sum) were another stumbling block.

On the pitch, Simonsen inspired Charlton with nine goals in 16 matches and some performances which fans still talk about, but when it became clear his salary couldn't be paid he packed his bags, making his swansong in a dismal 7-1 defeat at **Burnley**. It was a decidedly unglamorous end to what might have been

Simonsen: expect the Scottish national team to be his next managerial "challenge"

a fairytale season, and the outlay played a considerable part in Charlton's financial woes of years to come. Simonsen, though, had evidently acquired a taste for being the underdog: he rejected offers from Spurs and Serie A to rejoin Danish minnows **Velje**, his first club, and later resurfaced as manager of first the Faroe Islands and later Luxembourg. "I like a challenge," he later explained.

LAURIE CUNNINGHAM

The Black Pearl

Genius is an easy word to bandy about where favourite footballers are concerned, but **Laurie Cunningham** really was one man worthy of such an accolade – albeit in a flawed kind of way.

Ron Atkinson once said that Cunningham could run through snow and leave no footprints, such was his balletic grace, and he was certainly one of the most under-rated players ever to grace the English – and later Spanish – game. Cunningham, a winger, was the first black player to wear the Three Lions in a competitive international match (for England's under-21s) and he was arguably the most skilful footballer of his generation. Quite simply, few players in England could match Cunningham's gracefulness, attacking instinct or inventiveness.

The shy, slim (he weighed less than 11 stone) Londoner began his career as an apprentice at **Leyton Orient** during the mid-1970s. Within months of his debut, his displays had prompted Johnny Giles to sign him for **West Bromwich Albion** (for £110,000 in 1977) and he quickly became one of the hottest properties in football. Giles was soon on his way but the gung-ho, all-attack style of his successor – Ron Atkinson – suited him perfectly, and he narrowly missed out on League Championship success in 1979. But against **Valencia** in the Uefa Cup that year he put in a performance that marked him out as a world-class talent, running ragged a side including such luminaries as **Rainer Bonhof** and **Mario Kempes**. **Real Madrid** were quickly alerted, and a bid of £995,000 secured his move to Spain. (Folklore has it that he travelled to Madrid during the summer of 1979 to demand a move to the Bernabéu.)

> ***"He took the hardest option of all – I was delighted to see him make the Cup final "***
>
> *Ron Atkinson on Laurie Cunningham, who missed the 1983 Cup final of his own accord*

The "Black Pearl" scored on his debut, but his dream move soon turned into a nightmare as he was subjected to cynical tackling. Injuries inevitably set in and, before too long, Cunningham had been reduced to a journeyman. He tried his luck briefly at a number of clubs – Manchester United, Marseille, Sporting Gijon and Leicester City among them – before joining **Wimbledon** in March 1988. He promptly picked up an FA Cup winners' medal as the Crazy Gang registered their famous Wembley win over Liverpool, and it earned him another crack at the Spanish League, this time with Rayo Vallecano. But just as his career looked to be getting back on track he was killed in a car crash near Madrid, aged just 33.

Cunningham's contemporaries described him as one of the most athletic figures in the game, a world-class talent who could ghost past players with his sublime skill and pace. But there was a darker side to his story. One of the first black players in England, Cunningham was subjected to racist abuse from opponents and the terraces, but while Albion team-mates **Cyrille Regis** and **Brendon Batson** simply rammed the ignorance back down their throats, Cunningham felt the injustice more keenly.

In May 1979, an all-black team was put together to play the Baggies in a testimonial match for Len Cantello. Cunningham featured alongside the likes of Regis, **Garth Crooks** and big **Bob Hazell**, but felt that an important point could be made by keeping the side together to tour England. "We have the basis of a very good squad and it would be ideal to be kept together," he said. "I am sure more people would want to see our side."

Just how big a person Cunningham could be is revealed by the fact that during a loan spell at at **Manchester United**, he found himself in the frame for a place in the 1983 Cup final but was unhappy with his lack of fitness. He knew that the Cup final could be his big chance to revive his career but confessed to United boss **Ron Atkinson** that he felt he would "let the lads down" if he played. It was a display of professionalism that made a big impression on Big Ron. "There was so much at stake for an individual who was desperate to prove so much, but he took the hardest option of all," remembers Atkinson. "That was why five years later I was delighted to see him make the Cup final with Wimbledon."

Few would argue with that.

MALCOLM ALLISON

A touch of glamour

The enduring image of **Malcolm Allison** will be that of the fedora-hatted, cigar-smoking playboy, a model on each arm, posing for the cameras. That he was also one of the finest coaches England has ever produced is often completely overlooked. Allison's personality, high-profile managerial failings and even his headgear all overshadowed everything he achieved on the training ground. Had he stuck to what he knew, his life and career might have been very different, but then Allison was a man spurred on to ever-greater acts of showmanship by the twin demons of drink and a deep-seated need for the limelight.

> *"We will win the European Cup. European football is full of cowards and we'll terrorise them"*
> *Malcolm Allison on Man City*

The latter stemmed from his time as a player at **West Ham**; in 1958, Allison was the finest defender on the Upton Park books, but he contracted tuberculosis and was confined to a sanatorium. On his return, he lost his place to a young **Bobby Moore** and never really recovered from the blow. On the surface, at least, it spurred him on: after a managerial apprenticeship at **Plymouth**, he pitched up at **Manchester City** as Joe Mercer's assistant in 1965 and set about turning an average Second Division side into league champions playing with flair and style.

While Mercer's nous in the transfer market was responsible for much of City's success, it was Allison's work in making the Blues the fittest, most adept passing side in the country which really sealed the deal. His techniques were years ahead of their time and reflected his own, unlikely, hard-working habits as a player. When he stepped out of Mercer's shadow to take over the hot seat in 1972, however, the cracks began to show.

Within a year, he was off to **Crystal Palace**, where he changed the strip, widened the pitch, and posed in the team bath with porn star Fiona Richmond. Razzmatazz was introduced to Selhurst Park, to the extent that players were even given nicknames in the club programme: **Don Rogers** was dubbed The Troublemaker, **Tony Taylor** The Road Runner and **Charlie Cooke** The Card Shuffler. The club shop began selling mini-fedoras and the fans were enthused, but Palace never achieved anything more than an FA Cup semi-final appearance and plenty of media coverage. Cue a return to City, via Plymouth once more.

This time Allison went mad with chairman Peter Swales' chequebook and blew millions on **Steve Daley** and **Kevin Reeves** to spark hyper-inflation in the game. It became clear Allison was out of his depth, so off he shuffled for a world tour taking in Kuwait, Portugal and Bristol, a journey that ended in alcoholism, huge debts and life in a nursing home.

BEST OF TIMES

Best opened his first nightclub in Manchester in October 1973 with two entrepreneurial friends. They paid £10,000 for the Club del Sol on Bootle Street. The venue was renamed Slack Alice after the Larry Grayson comedy character. Among regular visitors were Jimmy Tarbuck, Bruce Forsyth, Bernie Winters, Mick Jagger, Leo Sayer, Bryan Ferry, David Essex and Phil Lynott. It was here that Best met US Miss World Marjorie Wallace – who was already dating racing driver Peter Reveson, Jimmy Connors and Tom Jones.

RAYMOND KOPA

In the red corner

In May 1968 France came to a standstill for two weeks. Ten million workers downed tools, while in Paris 800,000 students and workers marched through the capital demanding the fall of de Gaulle's "police state", better salaries and more favourable working conditions. Alongside the protesters – and rioters – were a small group of French international footballers. They too had their grievances, and their leader was **Raymond Kopa**.

Kopa was a natural choice as rabble-rouser – a Polish immigrant, he was always something of an outsider to the French. Born Raymond Kopszewski, his name was shortened to Kopa to help his host nation pronounce it. Like most immigrants in his adopted hometown of **Noeux**, Kopa was destined for a life down the mines, not one of public prominence. As a child, he worked alongside his father quarrying coal for a living. A hand injury put an end to that career, but Kopa was about to start earning with his feet.

The creative inside forward was spotted playing for Noeux by **Angers**, who signed him up. Even his skills on the football pitch seemed somehow alien to France – he played more like a Brazilian, and was often scorned in his early days for dribbling the ball too much. He impressed for Angers, however, and eventually transferred to France's premier side **Reims** in 1950, helping them to dominate French football for the next six years. They even reached a European Cup final, where they faced the mighty **Real Madrid**. Kopa's sublime skills had already caught the attentions of the Spanish giants, and he took to the field knowing that his transfer to the Bernabeu was assured. Reims lost that game, but the man now known as "the Napoleon of Football" was not to lose many more.

From 1956 to 1959 Kopa played with Puskas and di Stefano in one of the best teams the world had ever seen, winning the European Cup three times on the bounce. The last, strangely, was against Reims – to whom he transferred back the following season, his greatest. Kopa was the undisputed star player at the World Cup in Sweden in 1958, laying on most of **Just Fontaine**'s record 13 goals, and he wound up European Footballer of the Year.

He played 45 times for his country, and *France Football* placed only Platini and Zidane ahead of him in a recent list of great French players. But his career was to end amid controversy, as Kopa began to campaign for player power. French clubs held property rights over players until they were 34 – meaning they could only break free of contracts with their side's blessing or once they were washed up. Kopa became a thorn in the authorities' side, and played a huge part in getting players improved rights. He was a revolutionary on and off the pitch.

Vic Buckingham calls Don Howe to ask him to perfect his Cruyff turn

THE HARD MEN *From pin-prickers to leg-biters*

In January 1971, **George Best** was fined £250 for accruing three yellow cards in 12 months, a disciplinary record the tabloids described as "appalling". Today, such misdemeanours would be the work of three weeks to the average defender. To look back on yesteryear as a golden age of flair would, however, be inaccurate.

Put simply, as long as there have been 11 men and a ball, there have been players willing to bend the rules to get their own way. For some, be it through bad luck, repeatedly bad timing or simply an absence of any other creative talent of their own, the ability to foul and cheat has become a defining characteristic.

This can be traced back to 1930s' legend **Wilf Copping** who, though a fine player, is most fondly remembered for his chiselled jaw (he never shaved before a match, to intimidate the opposition) and crunching two-footed tackles. George Allison rebuilt Herbert Chapman's great Arsenal side around Copping, a former miner from Barnsley who learned his trade at **Leeds**, where he was known as "The Iron Man."

It worked. The Gunners took the league twice during Copping's five-year tenure, and he also starred in the "Battle of Highbury" between England and Italy in 1934, in which it is generally agreed his behaviour was the most antagonistic of any of the sinners on show. Bill Shankly, who blamed a Copping tackle for his different-sized ankles, recalled: "He didn't need to be playing at home to kick you – he would have kicked you in your own back yard or in your own chair… He had no fear at all."

The legend of the hard man was born, but it was in the 1960s and 1970s that such players became venerated by a media hungry for headlines and controversy. **Ron "Chopper" Harris** of Chelsea, Liverpool's **Tommy Smith**, **Norman Hunter** of Leeds and the omnipresent **Nobby Stiles** were full-blooded but generally fair. It was their clashes with each other that were the most unpleasant. **Billy Bremner** – and the entire Leeds team he played in – was less palatable but retained a scampish charm.

However, it was the players who didn't necessarily seek trouble but didn't run from it who were the hardest. **Dave Mackay** bossed the Spurs midfield so ruthlessly he inspired them to the Double; later, the likes of **Mark Hughes** and **Alan Shearer** would marry skill to brute force and get away with it. **Graeme Souness, George Graham** and **Alex Ferguson** would become Championship-winning managers by building their teams around hard men and defending them to the hilt.

Man-marking, meanwhile, was largely a Continental invention; **Claudio Gentile**'s shocking handling of Diego Maradona during the 1982 World Cup was its most brutal example, but Argentina's **Carlos Bilardo** was reputedly even more unjust, pricking opponents with a drawing pin before running away.

Then there are the hotheads; **Roy McDonough** holds the record for red cards (15 in all, not counting "friendlies") in a career of thuggery that took in Southend, Colchester and Cambridge. **Mark Dennis** wasted his talent with woeful challenges and a hatred of referees while at Southampton. **Vinnie Jones**, for all the cartoon posturing, was genuinely fearsome (ask Liverpool). And as for **Roy Keane**…

VIC BUCKINGHAM

He Got Rhythm

If any single incident best encapsulates the eccentricity of this much-travelled coach, it is the affair of the emergency team meeting. Vic Buckingham's reign as **Fulham** manager (from 1965 to 1968) is not remembered by fans with much affection – he is usually blamed for dismantling the team and presiding over the sale of such talents as Rodney Marsh at bargain prices – but the players will never forget him. Or the emergency team meeting.

> ***"I'd like you to introduce the overhead bicycle kick into your game "***
>
> *Fulham manager Vic Buckingham coaches Don Howe*

The Cottagers' form had dipped and Buckingham felt that an emergency meeting was needed to clear the air. The players turned up at the Fulham ground, anxiously wondering if they were to be subjected to one of Buck's two-hour team talks. Instead, Vic strolled into the dressing room, sat down, read the paper and, when he'd finished it, just got up without saying goodbye and left.

He may have done it just to wind the players up, but it could also have been to accentuate his carefully acquired reputation as the game's eccentric English aristocrat. Born in Greenwich, the wing-half-cum-left-back signed for **Spurs** in 1935. His playing career was interrupted by World War II but he was the kind of player who looked more stylish on a cigarette card than on the pitch.

He began his coaching career winning the FA Amateur Cup with **Oxbridge** side **Pegasus** in 1951, joining Bradford Park Avenue that same year, going on to manage **West Brom** (with whom he won the FA Cup in 1954), **Ajax** (where he helped discover Johan Cruyff), **Sheffield Wednesday**, **Fulham**, **Ethnikos** and **Barcelona** (where, as at Ajax, he was succeeded by Rinus Michels).

Although he was a disciple of Arthur Rowe's push and run school of football, he brought his own ideas to training, once ordering his players to run up and down the terraces at Fulham because: "We need more danger in the team." After Rodney Marsh had cracked his ankle and another player had needed 25 stitches, Buck decided the level of danger was sufficient to move on to more conventional training. He would later sing George Gershwin's *I Got Rhythm* to Marsh in a vain attempt to convince the player his dribbling was interrupting the flow of the team.

At Barcelona, who he helped turn around in the early 1970s after one of the club's most traumatic eras, he is best remembered for wearing tweed jackets and silk ties, drinking cocktails, playing golf and gossiping about horse-racing. To his

THE MEN IN BLACK *Eight officials of note*

KEN ASTON

One of the few referees who can claim to have changed the game as we know it. Ken Aston devised the system of yellow and red cards in the wake of the fiery England-Argentina match during the 1966 World Cup, when Bobby and Jack Charlton only learned the next day that they'd been cautioned. Aston was struck by the solution as he drove home in his MG. "...the traffic light turned red," he later recalled. "I thought, 'Yellow, take it easy; red, stop, you're off.'"

Aston always retained a philosophical approach. "The game should be a two-act play with 22 players on stage and the referee as the director," he once said. "There is no script, no plot, you don't know the ending, but the idea is to provide enjoyment."

TOFIK BAKHRAMOV

Better known as "the Russian linesman" (even though he was from Azerbaijan) who decreed that **Geoff Hurst**'s shot did cross the line to put England 3-2 up against West Germany in the 1966 World Cup final. Swiss referee Gottfried Dienst didn't see the incident and turned to Bakhramov, who as Kenneth Wolstenholme informed us, could only speak Russian and Turkish. "I still don't know if the shot was in or not," admitted Dienst not long before he died. "I have to say that I was standing in a poor position for that shot, exactly head-on instead of diagonal to the goal. I wouldn't have allowed the goal if Bakhramov hadn't pointed to the middle with his flag."

Asked once to explain his infamous decision, Bakhramov simply replied, "Stalingrad".

PIERLUIGI COLLINA

A football icon not for his resemblance to Uncle Fester, but for his ability to officiate with firmness and fairness while missing very little – a combination that has won him the respect of fans and players alike. (For the record, he lost his hair in the space of a fortnight after an attack of alopecia.) The Italian (a financial consultant by day), took up refereeing in his teens, following a brief playing career in which he failed to live up to the standards he sets as an official. "For a defender, I don't think two red cards in five or six years is out of the ordinary. It can happen to anyone, can't it?"

JACK TAYLOR

A butcher from Wolverhampton who achieved World Cup immortality when he became the first referee to award a penalty in the final. The Germans hadn't even touched the ball in 1974 when Johan Cruyff broke straight up the field from kick-off and was tripped in the box by Uli Hoeness. "You are an Englishman," a perceptive Franz Beckenbauer hissed angrily at Taylor.

Impressively, he also once halted a pre-match pitch invasion at Stamford Bridge in the 1970s by marching into the centre circle and relaying a warning over the PA that he'd wait until midnight to start the game if he had to.

CLIVE THOMAS

Known as the Terror of Treorchy and the source of deep-seated grudges from the Maracana to the Mersey. In 1977, Everton were locked 2-2 with Liverpool in an FA Cup semi-final when a **Duncan McKenzie** header clipped **Bryan Hamilton**'s hip on its way into the Liverpool net. Thomas ruled it out, despite there being no offside flag or handball. To this day, all he will say of the incident is: "there was an infringement"; it's still bitterly contested by Everton supporters.

One year later in the World Cup, as Brazil and Sweden were drawing 1-1 in Buenos Aires, **Zico** headed into the net in the dying seconds. Thomas ostentatiously disallowed it, claiming he'd blown for time while the ball was in mid-air. Brazil's appeal was unsuccessful but it was the end of Thomas's international career.

TOM "TINY" WHARTON

"The last time I saw you, you were in evening dress, and I must say you're better at the dancing than the football." It was this kind of remark (to Stranraer's flamboyant **Freddie Laing**) that helped to turn Tom "Tiny" Wharton into a landmark in Scottish football. Instantly recognisable because of his 6ft 4in height, the Brylcreemed behemoth seemed to tower over even the likes of **Billy McNeill**. Football journalist **Doug Baillie**, a colourful centre-half with Falkirk and Dunfermline in the 1960s and 1970s, noted on Wharton's retirement that it was almost a pleasure to be booked by the man. "I've warned you before about your tackling, Mr Baillie. I'm going to have to caution you this time, Mr Baillie. What is your name please, Mr Baillie?"

ARTHUR ELLIS

Perhaps the first referee to achieve star status in Britain. Ellis's most celebrated 90 minutes came during the 1954 World Cup when he officiated at the "Battle Of Berne" between Brazil and Hungary. He awarded two penalties, and sent off three players for fist-fighting – one of them a Hungarian MP. A Brazilian defender was hit by a bottle thrown from Hungary's bench, and the defeated Brazilians brawled with the Hungarians in their dressing-room afterwards. Ellis sat drinking tea at the time. It was perfect training for his later role as umpire of *It's A Knockout*.

JIMMY HILL

The saviour of an early televised game when he replaced an injured linesman. During an Arsenal-Liverpool match in the early 1970s, a linesman pulled a muscle and play was held up while an appeal was made for a qualified referee. "After five minutes, nothing had happened and I could see The Big Match becoming The Abandoned Match," recalled Hill. "So I rushed down to see if I could help – I'd taken a referee's course as a player. It turned out I was the only qualified "applicant" under about 60 and when referee Pat Partridge saw me, he said, 'You'll do, Jim. Get changed – and make it quick.'"

If you were to be beaten by a bow-legged winger, you'd want it to be Garrincha players and to officials, it seemed as if the club had somehow hired Professor Henry Higgins from *My Fair Lady*. But his innate self-confidence rubbed off on the team, who loved it when he would airily dismiss Real Madrid as "just a bunch of show-offs". And he could, for all his reserve, show passion. In training the week before a game against **Real Betis**, someone had scrawled the word "Betis" on a blackboard. "Betis?" he growled. "Who are they? F*** Betis" and with that he kicked the blackboard to the ground.

"We need more danger in the team"

Vic Buckingham orders his Fulham players to run up and down the terracing

His revived Barça were enough of a threat to Real for Franco's regime to allegedly fix the referee for a vital Spanish Cup quarter-final between the two rivals. The promise of Buck's reign petered out as his health (and his back) worsened and he was forced to leave, but he passed on the club to Michels knowing he had restored its sense of pride and the players' belief. He had done something very similar at Ajax in 1959, never really winning the big prizes but spotting the gawky promise of Cruyff and encouraging the team to play fluent, passing football.

Bobby Robson, who played under Buckingham at West Brom, described him as "an astute tactician who was not afraid to take on board the hard lessons learned from the Hungarians and experiment." Indeed, such was his enthusiasm that, at the Hawthorns, he called in his defender **Don Howe** for a chat about how the player needed to improve his game. Howe waited nervously as his coach noted: "There's just one area of your game I'd like you to improve upon…" "What's that?" asked Howe anxiously. Buck paused and said: "I'd like you to introduce the overhead bicycle kick into your game". To this day, Howe isn't sure if Buckingham was joking.

GARRINCHA

Bird on the wire

Popular opinion has determined that Pelé is the greatest footballer of all time. Ask a Brazilian, however, and they'll tell you **Garrincha** was the daddy of them all (often literally, as well as figuratively). Yet while Pelé hid his indiscretions well enough to end up an ambassador for Brazil, sport and Viagra (something Garrincha never needed), his older, more entertaining team-mate is best-known for dying in poverty aged just 49, having squandered his money and spurned advice from former team-mates and the fans who worshipped him. Given the nature of the man it couldn't have happened any other way.

Pelé grabbed the glory because he scored the goals and came out with the snappy one-liners; Garrincha was educationally sub-normal, but put a ball at his feet and he could beat any defender in the world. Most of Pelé's greatest goals were supplied from Garrincha crosses and he has acknowledged that he could not have won three World Cups without him; the pair lost only one of 60 matches (in the 1966 World Cup) while on the same side. Garrincha had first graced the world stage when a player revolt led to his inclusion in the 1958 squad. In 1962, with Pelé injured, he stepped from the shadow of his friend to win the ultimate prize in Chile almost single-handed. Sadly, the 1966 World Cup proved to be his international swansong.

As a man, Garrincha (or "Little Bird" as his name translated) was a mess. He walked out on his wife and eight children to live with a jazz singer and fathered innumerable offspring through brief dalliances, including one while sneaking out of training camp at the 1958 World Cup in Sweden. He also drank to distraction, a problem exacerbated by an early retirement from the game. In truth, however, he had always known the end would be premature – he'd been unable to walk as a child and only an operation as six-year-old had given him mobility, though his legs were left permanently curved.

Brazilians' continuing obsession with Garrincha – thousands lobbied the authorities and threatened boycotts when his statue was moved from a public area of the Maracana Stadium to a VIP enclosure – can be explained by his status as the ultimate Malandro, the mystical slave figure to which his countrymen all aspire. The Malandro breaks free from his masters and lives a life full of joy and style yet lacking in any discipline. Some would say Garrincha took the concept too far; to Brazilians, who still well up at the mere mention of his name, he got it just right.

THE CLUBS

From the playing fields of the great public schools to a railway sidings just off the A3

Celtic's Joe McBride takes training to a new level in 1965

Princess Margaret ***"Mr Labone, where is Everton?"***
Brian Labone ***"In Liverpool, ma'am"***
Princess Margaret ***"We had your first team here last year"***
Exchange at the 1966 FA Cup final

CORINTHIAN CASUALS

The next time a high-profile footballer is required to perform community service for misdemeanours of a criminal nature, he should be made to carry it out at the King George V Playing Fields just north of Kingston, south-west London. For it is on this under-developed patch of grass, where any noise from the few dozen spectators is drowned out by passing trains, that the true spirit of football lives on – in an odd sort of way.

Corinthian Casuals are indeed alive and well, and still linked in essence to the club which epitomised sporting virtue in the 19th and early 20th centuries. It was in the 1880s and 1890s that the Corinthians – formed in 1882 as a side to challenge Scotland in a friendly – became one of the finest sides in the game, although this claim was never tested as their strict public-school ethos meant that they didn't enter a competition until 1900. The club was about playing well and, above all, fairly, rather than winning matches, though they did this pretty effectively too, seeing off **Manchester United** 11-3 in a 1904 friendly, the Reds' record defeat. Sportsmanship was paramount, and if Corinthians were awarded a penalty, their player would deliberately miss it as to score from the spot was the act of a cad; similarly, if Corinthians conceded a penalty, the goalkeeper would stand aside to leave an empty net (these rules survived until the 1980s).

The team quickly became ambassadors for football, visiting Asia, Africa, Europe and the US to play prestigious friendly matches; their global legacy can be seen most obviously in the famous Brazilian side who share their name and in **Real Madrid**'s aping of their all-white kit. Corinthians merged with Casuals, a leading London amateur side, in the 1930s, and the club still exists in the lower echelons of the Ryman League, still fiercely amateur and still endearingly quaint. To this day, a red card is often punished by being sacked from the club, while swearing or answering a referee back brings a hefty fine. Handlebar moustaches are, however, no longer compulsory.

ST PAULI

During the first eight decades of their history, Hamburg's **FC St Pauli** had given no indication that they might become one of football's most unusual professional clubs. True, they were formed in the sleazy area that includes Hamburg's famous red-light Reeperbahn district, but that didn't mean they were had to be different. The 3,000 or so die-hards who followed St Pauli in their comfortable Second Division life even regarded the posh **SV Hamburg** as a bigger brother, not a rival.

Then, in the 1986-87 season, things suddenly changed. The St Pauli players heard a chant from the stands that made them look up in surprise. "Never again fascism, never again war!" some fans shouted, adding: "And never again Third Division!" These people weren't old men with dogs – they were kids in leather jackets with spiked hair, and they were back in greater numbers for the next home match. And the one after that.

By the end of the season, St Pauli had almost doubled their average attendance, thanks to this peculiar section of the football-loving public who felt alienated by the corporate identity of big clubs such as Hamburg or **Bayern Munich**: the young, the politically aware, the socially disaffected.

It may defy belief, but it took these enthusiastic members of the sub-culture

Whether it's team photographs or fans' attire, St Pauli like to do it a bit differently

only a couple of years to effectively take over the club. In 1989, they created the first German football fanzine, then successfully fought St Pauli's move to a shiny domed stadium. That same year, the cover of the official matchday magazine for the game against Bayern featured a heavily-tattooed wild-man with a raised fist and a headline reading: "Class War!"

Today, St Pauli's revamped magazine covers art, politics and music – but hardly any football. This is entirely in keeping with their credo of offering the unexpected. Walk into their decrepit but charming Millerntor ground and you won't hear Europop over the tannoy but AC/DC's *Hell's Bells.* Scan the 20,000 regular home fans and you'll see punk rockers, anarchist squatters, prostitutes and bikers rather than insurance salesmen and bank clerks. The makeshift visitors' loo is a donation from a German rock band. The official club store looks just like an alternative record shop, complete with pierced kids in hooded sweaters behind the counter. Buy a scarf and you'll find it carries a skull-and-crossbones – a semi-official logo that also features on the back of the players' shirts.

Ah yes, the players. Well, they knew what kind of club they were joining. When St Pauli enjoyed their second stay in the Bundesliga (1988-1991), their regular goalkeeper was a man who had lived in a crash pad, looked after disabled children and done social work in Nicaragua. In 2001, the club bought an expensive team coach then airbrushed it until the thing looked ready for the scrap heap and stencilled the words "Get out of the way!" across the front. A year later, the official squad photo was taken in a prison yard – with the players handcuffed to each other (see "Colour Section").

In late 2002, a 50-year-old Motorhead fan was elected club president. He's a gay activist who sometimes performs in drag in one of the theatres he owns. When he faced the press for the first time, he wore blue jeans and a skull-and-crossbones cap. His name is Cornelius Littmann, but the journalists all called him "Corny". Just another normal day at FC St Pauli.

BRISTOL ROVERS

Any club which claims Jeffrey Archer among its celebrity fans and revels in the nickname "Gasheads" deserves a break. They've changed nicknames, grounds and managers with disturbing frequency, but **Bristol Rovers** are just that kind of club. The players run out to the soporific strains of *Goodnight Irene* – is it any wonder the team have underperformed in recent years, clinging to the lower reaches of Division Three for dear life?

Founded in 1883, Bristol Rovers win a trophy, on average, every 60 years: they were champions of Third Division South in 1952 and 1973 and of the Third

Division in 1989-90. So the bad news for middle-aged Rovers fans is that they aren't due to win anything again until they're dead and buried in their Number 12 shirts with "Gashead" on the back. Their nickname has changed several times – from the Purdown Poachers to the Black Arabs (after the colour of the founders' shirts and a local rugby club called Arabs) to the Blues to the Gasheads (after the proximity of their old ground to a gasworks).

> ***"When it's 11 against 12, soccer becomes sad. I feel like crying"***
> *Ronaldo sticks the knife into Juventus*

The club's golden age was in the 1950s when they dominated the Third Division South. They twice beat sides 7-0 (Brighton and Swansea) and reached the last eight of the FA Cup in 1951. In 1954, Rovers made the most astonishing signing in their history, buying **Youra Esha Pera**, aka the Assyrian Wizard, the first Iraqi to play League football in England. The forward almost didn't play, getting lost at Victoria Station and then being refused a permit by the Home Office. Questions were asked in the House of Commons and Youra was allowed to stay and given a job at a local colliery. He played for the club's third team but, on the brink of earning professional forms, returned to Iraq.

Youra's departure meant that he missed out on the club's finest moment: a 4-0 victory over Matt Busby's babes in the third round of the 1955-56 FA Cup. Of late, Rovers have been bedevilled by financial problems. They were forced to sell their old Eastville ground to a greyhound racing company to pay their debts, moving to Bath City's Twerton Park before sharing the Memorial Ground with a rugby club. A happy knack of discovering strikers (**Bobby Zamora**, **Marcus Stewart**, **Jason Roberts**, **Barry Hayles**, **Jamie Cureton**) has also been undermined by the practice of selling them at knockdown prices.

DUKLA PRAGUE

There's only one real reason anyone in the UK really remembers the name **Dukla Prague**. In 1986, Birkenhead punk satirists Half Man Half Biscuit released their debut single, *The Trumpton Riot*. On the B-side was the now-legendary track, *All I Want For Christmas Is A Dukla Prague Away Kit*, a celebration of the madness of Subbuteo (reproduced elsewhere in this book). Dukla remain a cult for men of a certain age to this day. You can purchase that very maroon and claret kit on the internet, and the club itself still does a fair trade selling away strips to baffling English visitors. They'll set you back about 120kc (£3.50), including a badge which you have to sew on yourself. Unfortunately, this supplemental income hasn't helped Dukla's fortunes, and in 1997 the side reached the ultimate low, leaving their home ground to merge with **Marila Pribram** and assume their name. Dukla's decline has been a spectacular one.

In the 1960s they were one of the strongest sides in the whole of Europe, reaching three European Cup quarter-finals and one semi-final (losing to **Celtic** in 1967), beating the great **Ajax** side that had hammered Bill Shankly's **Liverpool** 5-1, and drawing 2-2 draw with the mighty Real Madrid.

But Dukla's strength was based on communism rather than popular support. Formed in the 1950s from the Czech army (named after Dukla, the village where the Czechs had fought off the Nazis in WWII), the club could call up any player on their general's orders. The generals were good managers: they soon picked Josef Masopust, European Footballer of the Year in 1962, who led Dukla to five national titles. The fall of communism meant iron curtains for Dukla. They clung on through the 1980s, even winning the national cup in 1990, but the army's support of the club collapsed in 1994, and there were "financial irregularities".

JUVENTUS

Italians have never made good losers. A football defeat can't simply be explained by the fact that the opposition were better than you – there's always an underlying, sinister reason behind defeat: the ref is bent, the opposition are cheats or on drugs. Perhaps in a land of the mafia and widespread political corruption, this attitude is understandable, but one thing's for sure: as the team at the top of the Italian tree, **Juventus** are always going to be the side everyone else is accusing. Italy's favourite – and also most hated – team, Turin's Old Lady are controversial for numerous reasons. Bankrolled by Fiat's Agnelli family – and in part by Libyan leader Colonel Gadaffi's family – the Zebras have long been regarded in Italy as fat cats using their huge spending power to buy the Serie A title. Their support in Turin is largely based around southern economic migrants (often treated with derision in the north), and they have an unhealthy contingent of glory-hunting fans to annoy those of other teams. And that's all before you get to the drugs and the allegations of bribery.

"We all know Juventus benefits from favouritism," said then-Inter star Ronaldo in 1998, after a controversial penalty incident had sent the title to Turin. "They can punish me but I won't stay silent. When it's 11 against 12, soccer becomes sad. I feel like crying." The allegations were treated seriously, and were even raised in the Italian parliament, leading to a scuffle among politicians. The drug scandals are just as explosive. Roma manager Zdenek Zeman caused a huge stir in 1998 by accusing Juve of using "the chemist" to transform the physiques of players like **Gianluca Vialli** and **Alessandro Del Piero**. "I was surprised by their sudden bulking up," he said. "I thought such changes only occurred after years of work."

Juve are far from alone in Italy for these scandals, however, and the problems shouldn't detract from the club's greatness. In the 1930s the likes of Orsi, Monti and Ferarri thrilled Turin as Juve won five straight titles. In the late 1950s, Welsh giant **John Charles** became a folk hero alongside brilliant, temperamental Argentine **Omar Sivori**. And 1972-86 saw their awesome dominance. Vialli, **Zidane** and the **Baggios** would all come later, as Juventus amassed 27 titles. They've sacrificed flair for efficiency in recent years, but the Old Lady remains Italy's greatest footballing success story. Just don't expect other Italian teams' fans to admit it.

JUVENTUS BUCURESTI

Communist eastern Europe was a law unto itself when it came to changing the names of football teams: all over the place Dynamos were becoming Metalurgs and Racings changing to Spartaks, but surely none can match the record of Romanian side **Juventus Bucaresti**. Over the course of five consecutive seasons, the side's name changed five times. As if that wasn't confusing enough for the fans, the next year the club was moved to a completely different city.

Starting out as Juventus Bucuresti, they were founder members of the national league and Romanian champions in 1930. They survived the war and competed under their old name in the 1946-47 championship. It was when the communists got involved that things really went crazy: in the 1948 season, the name was changed to Distributia Bucuresti; in 1949 Petrolul Bucuresti, in 1950 Competrol Bucuresti and (the same year) Partizanul Bucuresti, and in 1951 Flacara Bucuresti. This still wasn't enough. In the 1952 season, the team moved to the oil town of Ploiesti. They kept the name Flacara (Ploiesti), but were relegated at the end of the season. Promoted immediately, they played as Flacara until 1956 when they became Energia Ploiesti, and, finally, Petrolul Ploiesti. This proved a lucky name as they won the league in 1958, 1959 and 1966, and haven't felt the need to change the title since – despite five further relegations and promotions.

RENTON

Which team were the first football "Champions Of The World"? You'd be forgiven for thinking Uruguay, but that ignores the claims of a small village side from Dunbartonshire called **Renton**. Back in 1888, they were Scottish Cup winners, and a match was arranged with their English counterparts, **West Bromwich Albion**, for the grandiose title of World Champions. Renton proudly took the title, beating the Baggies 4-1 at Hampden Park in front of 6,000 spectators.

Their worldwide glory wasn't to last long, though. Renton did go on to become founder members of the Scottish League in 1890 but they were expelled after a mere five games. Their crime was playing a game against **Edinburgh Saints** – a team the Scottish FA ruled were professional. Renton would never recover: without league football their top players were lured to bigger clubs, and by 1895 they were a struggling team on the way to oblivion.

On their way down, they gained a reputation as bad losers. One newspaper was disgusted at Renton after they lost to **Vale of Leven**: "Renton are not taking their defeat like men. They feel sore about the reception they got from the Dumbarton crowd. But who is to blame? No-one but themselves. They have long thought that there was only one team in Scotland – the Renton. They think differently now."

NEW YORK COSMOS

For a few years in the 1970s, the **New York Cosmos** were the coolest team on the planet. **Pelé** and **Franz Beckenbauer** strutted their stuff in front of 80,000 in

Franz Beckenbauer confuses the Yanks with one of those new-fangled soccerballs

UNITED BY ANY OTHER NAME

Liverpool won the League last season while unlucky Chelsea were denied promotion to the top flight after an FA committee gave Benfica extra points because some of their opponents hadn't turned up. In other words, last season was a pretty typical affair in the south-west African state of Namibia.

In Britain, naming football clubs is a simple, none-too-creative, business in which the three key factors are: location, location, location. But as the gospel of football spread across the globe in the early 20th century (the unlikely missionaries often being British sailors, dockers and railwaymen), foreign clubs aped the Brits.

So forget all that nonsense about "there's only one..." There are at least two other Manchester Uniteds on the planet (curiously, neither has been sued yet) and three Liverpools, while the number of Arsenals reaches double figures, if you include the odd amateur side in an over-30s league in Tennessee.

ARSENAL LESOTHO

Roots This South African kingdom won independence in 1966 and the national side, gloriously nicknamed **The Crocodiles**, played their first international five years later. In 1983, a bunch of Arsenal fans in the capital Maseru thought it would be fun to found a club which, touchingly, and unimaginatively, they decided to call Arsenal. They are not alone in paying such homage: there are Arsenals in Argentina (where they have just won promotion to the First Division), Guadeloupe, Mexico and Guyana, where the Gunners play in the evocatively-named Milk Stout League.

Uncanny coincidences The boys from Maseru are called Arsenal (okay, **Arsenal Lesotho** to be precise), their nickname is the Gunners, they play in red and white and they won the League and Cup double in 1989 and 1991. Yep – the very same years George Graham's Arsenal won the League. They have won the title once more since (in 1993) and clinched the Lesotho Cup (which, intriguingly, is run as a mini-league) in 1998, the year Arsenal beat Newcastle 2-0 to claim the FA Cup.

EVERTON (CHILE)

Roots Legend in Valparaiso has it that when a bunch of Anglo-Chileans decided in the summer of 1909 to start their own football club, they called it **Everton** because one of the founders had an Everton mint in his pocket. As the original Everton had toured South America that year, and ships from Liverpool often docked at the port of Valparaiso, the truth may be more obvious and much duller. The club was forced to move to the seaside resort Viña del Mar in 1942. Free-scoring **René Meléndez**, somewhat inevitably dubbed the club's Dixie Dean, helped win the first two championships (1950 and 1952). The club have won the Chilean

League on only one occasion since, in 1976, and now play in the country's Second Division, where they are perennial promotion contenders.

Uncanny coincidences **Corporacíon Deportiva Everton** did win the Chilean Cup in 1984, the same year Everton beat Watford 2-0 to lift the FA Cup. And the Chilean club's ground Sausalito has staged three World Cup qualifiers involving Brazil and a semi-final (back in 1962) won by the tournament runners-up. Goodison Park did exactly the same in 1966. A deeply trivial footnote, but proof of what Sting famously referred to as "the devastating principle of synchronicity".

LIVERPOOL (URUGUAY)

Roots At the turn of the century, Montevideo played host to many English football teams trying to jazz up their pre-season training. Most of these teams sailed from Liverpool, which may explain why in 1915 a bunch of Franciscan students from the Colegio de los Capuchinos de Nuevo Paris in the Uruguayan capital, decided to call their new club Liverpool.

Uncanny coincidences Teams called Liverpool, Dublin and Bristol were all based in Montevideo and competed in the Uruguayan league between 1915 and 1923. And the Uruguayan Liverpool's first game of league football was a 1-0 victory against Newcastle. Montevideo's Liverpool have never finished higher than fourth in the Uruguayan Premiership and their best performance against a foreign club was a 1971 4-3 victory in a friendly with Werder Bremen.

MANCHESTER UNITED (GIBRALTAR)

Roots With a population of 31,000, this slice of limestone rock can only support amateur football. Manchester United were founded in 1962 by local football fans. "We wrote to Manchester United to ask permission to use their name and got a letter back from Sir Matt Busby telling us to go ahead," says United's current manager (and former player) Brian Askuez.

Uncanny coincidences Manchester United FC have won Gibraltar's league seven times (1975, 1979, 1980, 1984, 1995, and 1999) and its cup three times (1974, 1977 and 1980), a fitting display of domestic dominance. They also play other teams with such familiar names as Lincoln and Wolves (although they are officially known as the Rock Wolves). Gibraltar is not affiliated to Fifa and its application to join Uefa is described as "pending." Askuez says: "We do manage to play friendlies, mainly in the UK, Spain and Morocco, but otherwise we play against other clubs in Gibraltar".

the Giants Stadium, while the celebs hanging out in the dressing room read like a who's-who of 1970s' cool: the Rolling Stones, the Monty Python team, Robert Redford, Alice Cooper. It all happened in a mad whirlwind that owed everything to American entrepreneurship and a get-go attitude, but ultimately the foundations for this New York soccer dream were built on sand.

The Cosmos were set up in 1971 to join the recently-established North American Soccer League. Initially playing in the decrepit Randall's Island Stadium and drawing crowds of around 5,000, it took a series of ambitious moves to propel them suddenly into the big time. Former Welsh international **Phil Woosnam**, NASL commissioner, asked Englishman Clive Toye to help build the club. English coach Gordon Bradley was installed, but Toye knew they needed a big signing to promote soccer in the Big Apple. The pair wooed major executives from Warner and Atlantic Records to help buy players, and Toye persuaded the now-retired Pelé to turn his back on offers from European clubs because "if you got there you can win a championship. Come here and you can win a country." The Brazilian legend went for it – and won. His arrival in 1975 put around 50,000 on the gate straight away.

For a while, the glamour was irresistible. Teams including Pelé, Franz Beckenbauer, **Carlos Alberto**, **Giorgio Chinaglia** and **Johan Neeskens** (as well as former **Aldershot** and **Hartlepool** defender **Malcolm Dawes**, **Keith Eddy** of **Barrow**, **Watford** and **Sheffield United** and **Barry Mahy**, who made 21 appearances for **Scunthorpe**) won eight out of every 10 games they played. They scooped the title in 1972, '77, '78, '80 and '82, and during the evening they partied with the best of them at Studio 54. Alice Cooper charmed Pelé sufficiently to be given a shirt, which he later wore on stage in the city. It seemed things could hardly get better, but the bubble was to burst.

There was interference from executives, as Toye remembers: "We had one asshole telling us that we had to change the way the game starts, and have Pelé and Beckenbauer juggling the ball in the centre circle like a circus act." In addition, the quality of opposition was often appalling, leading to a lack of competition for the Cosmos, and when Pelé retired, the glamour disappeared. Sponsorship never came in, and the league gained a reputation as a retirement home for ageing talent. Like every other attempt to wean Americans off native sport, the style was never backed by substance.

WEST HAM UNITED

In the official history of **West Ham United**, **Trevor Brooking** notes that "Football at Upton Park has always been about more than just results, it's about playing the game the right way, playing with style and flair". The obvious rebuttal to this claim consists of just two words: **Julian Dicks**.

Still, one East End hard man qualifies, rather than negates, Brooking's point. West Ham is, famously, the club that founded its own unofficial football academy decades before the shiny official academies sprang up like mushrooms across Britain. In Cassattari's Café in the 1950s, players like Malcolm Allison, Dave Sexton, Frank O' Farrell, John Bond and Noel Cantwell would discuss football tactics, trying out ruses with salt and pepper pots. Although the name of **Ron Greenwood** is usually associated with the Academy, he didn't become the club manager until 1961, although, like Allison, he thought English football should learn from the havoc the Hungarians had wreaked on England in 1953. Allison's views would have a massive influence on **Bobby Moore** and John Lyall. But, from the style of play adopted by **Coventry City** under Cantwell in the 1970s, one can only assume the Irish defender wasn't listening. The terms "progressive football" and "Ernie Hunt" don't often appear in the same sentence.

But that's West Ham for you, a club whose reputation for playing good football was cemented by the holy trinity of England's 1966 World Cup triumph: Moore, **Martin Peters** and **Geoff Hurst**. The club conveyor belt continues to deliver such talents on an astonishingly regular basis (**Alan Devonshire**, **Ray Houghton**, **Rio Ferdinand**, **Joe Cole**, **Michael Carrick**, **Frank Lampard**, **Jermain Defoe**). The tradition that such talent is cherished by the club's discerning fans lasts as long as it takes you to go to the Boleyn Ground on a frustrating Saturday afternoon and hear the Hammers faithful baying "F***ing kick it!" at the wonderboys.

West Ham's relegation was widely mourned because the club is perceived, with some truth, to have stuck to its guns – this is one London club which probably won't hand the keys for the manager's office to George Graham. Sometimes you wonder if the fans themselves might not have preferred a different tradition: that of winning trophies. Still, being renowned for playing fluent attractive football is a happier fate than being famous for being infamous (**Millwall**) or for being the team of the 1980s (**Crystal Palace**).

SKONTO RIGA

If you think the Old Firm's dominance of Scottish football is boring, just be grateful you don't live in Latvia. Since independence, the club's primary professional club, **Skonto Riga**, have won the league 12 times on the bounce. With only eight teams in the top flight, and only four of them properly professional, it's been a walkover for Skonto, who have attracted the best players and coaches over recent years. The dominance is getting embarrassing.

"I'm bored," admitted the club's most popular player, Georgian international midfielder Alexander Rekhviashvili, in a recent interview. "Our goal for every season is to win the **Latvian Championship**, but there are no more than four financially stable teams and the results are predictable." Rekhviashvili went on to say that he wanted to play in Italy or England, as well as adding (and something may be lost in the translation here) that "Ireland is not a bar of chocolates".

Even when they're not playing well, things go right for Skonto. Last season they were almost pipped to the title by rival club **Ventspils**, as the two sides finished equal on points, with Skonto holding a better goal difference. Excited at the prospect of somebody else winning the league, the Latvian FA decided to waive the rules and ignore the goal factor; instead there would be a league playoff. Skonto won 4-0.

RAPID VIENNA

Rapid Vienna have clapped their way into football history. Fifteen minutes from the end of every game at the Gerhard Hanappi Stadion, the home fans start clapping frantically, even (with a fine sense for English puns) rapidly, to encourage the boys in green and white. The tradition dates back to the pre-war years and a game, lost to memory but enshrined in myth, when Rapid were on the wrong end of a humiliating scoreline (4-1 or 5-1, opinions differ) and the fans started clapping after 75 minutes, their applause inspiring the team to snatch a draw.

Why the fans behave like this is probably, ultimately, less important than the fact that they do still do it – at every game. And although, through repetition, the inspirational effect has worn off, you can still detect a glimmer of extra urgency in the team. This hasn't stopped Rapid's decline – they were big in the 1930s, bigger still in the 1950s (when, inspired by midfielders Ernst Happel and Gerhard Hanappi, they beat **Real Madrid** and **Milan** in the **European Cup**), and still quite good in the 1980s, when Hans Krankl was the genius in residence. Rapid still pride themselves on a passionate never-say-die kind of play which comes straight out of the English football school – but then the club was founded by hat factory employees who changed the name from Wiener Arbeiter-Fussballklub to Rapid to give their club a more English-sounding name.

Rapid still proudly call themselves a people's club and the people have been known to take matters into their own hands, staging a peaceful sit-in on the pitch after one barren spell of form in 2001-02. Rapid's drift has been more painful because **Austria Wien** now have a players' budget as big as the other nine clubs in the Austrian top flight combined. But Austria are the posh club, said to "have been founded in coffee house smog" by the working class fans of Rapid.

Unlike a lot of clubs, for whom the past is a burden to be borne or something to be redefined according to the needs of this season's marketing campaign, Rapid are proud of their past and give seats for life to legends. On matchdays, the club erect a massive marquee where beer and sausages are dispensed at decent prices, and even the players have been known to drop in for a chat. It's all a long way from the world of the high-pressure English club – and all the better for it.

BERWICK RANGERS

England and Scotland are the oldest football rivals in the world. The two sets of supporters love to hate each other, and any idea to bring them together in a positive manner is generally doomed. Most fans would laugh off the idea of a football shirt with the Scottish Lion alongside the English Lion as a pipedream. But that would be reckoning without the big bag of contradictions that is Berwick-Upon-Tweed, where the two lions adorn the town's football strip. Berwick is an English town (several miles south of the border) where the residents have Scottish accents. The town's football club, **Berwick Rangers** (who are actually based in Tweedmouth, south of the river), play in the Scottish Football League. Needless to say, things can get confusing during an international between the countries.

Berwick Rangers' faithful show there's no identity crisis on the Scottish border

"Aye, it can get a bit crazy around here for internationals," says Ian Oliver, a lowland Scot who has worked as groundsman for Rangers for 27 years. "Our support comes from both north and south of the border – it's probably half and half. The staff at the club are generally English, but the players tend to be Scots and all of them live in Edinburgh."

The club have used their location to good effect over the years. Formed in 1881, "the wee Rangers" initially competed in the Northumberland League, playing tough teams like **Newcastle**. They discovered the easier option of switching to the Scottish Border League in 1898, walloping the likes of **Peebles Rovers** to win the title. They returned to the rigours of the English game a year later, before rejoining the Scottish League in 1905, where they've remained ever since. The high point in the club's history came in 1967, when they beat the big (Glasgow) Rangers 1-0 in the Scottish Cup first round.

PENAROL

> *"The sight of a Penarol shirt makes me sick. I want them to lose, even against foreigners "*
> *Nacional supporter*

"Almost all South Americans are football mad," observed American writer John Gunther in his 1940 book *Inside Latin America*, "but none are madder than the stout citizens of Uruguay." It's fair to say that the passion for the game remains as strong as ever on the continent that gave us **Garrincha** and **Diego Maradona**. But while Brazil and Argentina may have best represented this obsession in recent years, Uruguay led the way in the first half of the 20th century.

It all started in Montevideo in 1891, when British gentlemen working on the railways formed the Central Uruguayan Railway Cricket Club. Football rapidly became the preferred game, and 20 years later the team changed their name to **Penarol** and became the country's dominant force, forming an intensely passionate rivalry with city-mates **Nacional**.

Like a Latin version of **Celtic** and **Rangers**, the sides share virtually every league title, battling against familiar-sounding teams – Liverpool, Wanderers – whose names betray their English roots. Penarol (club motto "you'll be eternal like time and you'll flower each spring") have the upper hand, and in the 1960s were a truly great side – defeating European champions Real Madrid on several occasions with fabulous players like **Pedro Rocha** and **Pepe Sasia**.

"We Uruguayans belong to Nacional or to Penarol from the day we are born," says writer Eduardo Galeano. "That's the way it's been since the beginning of the century." Prostitutes in the Montevideo bordellos used to compete for fans' trade by sitting in doorways wearing club strips, and Galeano recalls a fellow Nacional fan's sentiments that "the sight of a Penarol shirt makes me sick. I want them to lose every time, even against foreigners." Even other South American nations recognise the fervour of Uruguayan support: "Other countries have their history, Uruguay has its football," runs the popular phrase.

But passion has its ugly side. Uruguayans have developed a reputation for professional fouls and mindless thuggery (profiled effectively at numerous World Cups) and this win-at-all-costs mentality is at its height during the Montevideo derby. Recent highlights include a huge, ugly brawl in the centre circle during a 2000 fixture and the multiple arrests for fighting of bad-boy Nacional striker Richard Morales.

With things as close as ever in the championship, little looks set to change on the domestic scene, while on the world stage it remains incredible that a nation of just 3.3 million has made such an impact (including two World Cup wins, in 1930 and 1950). With the likes of Alvaro Recoba currently impressing, who knows when Uruguayan football could rise again?

PARTICK THISTLE

Alan Hansen recalls a pre-game Saturday morning training session at **Partick Thistle**, with the team in the middle of a bad losing streak. "The manager Bertie Auld said 'I'm going to announce today's team now, then we're going to have a practice game without any opposition. We'll knock the ball about a bit, score a few goals, and that will get our confidence back.' After 15 minutes the score was 0-0 and Bertie was going mental. After 30 minutes it was still 0-0 and he had changed the team for the afternoon. It's actually quite difficult playing against nobody."

The story sums up the fortunes of Glasgow's third club, who are destined to always be the bridesmaid to the giant Old Firm sides. But while they may never have won the league, Partick offer something entirely different to the Glaswegian football scene. Where between **Rangers** and **Celtic** there is loathing, at Partick there's just humour. They even see fit to mock their auspicious rivals' petty bigotry in their chants:

"Hello, hello, how do you do?
We hate the boys in royal blue
We hate the boys in emerald green
So f*** the pope and f*** the queen."

At 127 years old, the club are certainly well established, and there have been glory years: between 1954 and 1959, the Jags contested three Scottish League Cup finals – unfortunately failing to win any. Their time finally came in 1971, when Thistle defeated a mighty Celtic side containing nine internationals using a young and largely untried team. Rae, Lawrie, McQuade and Bone were the goalscorers in a miraculous 4-1 triumph – it's kept the Thistle fans going ever since. The Jags have also enjoyed two outings in Europe – the 1962-63 **Fairs Cup**, where they beat **Glentoran** only to lose to **Spartak Brno** of Czechoslovakia, and 1971-72, when they were thrashed by **Honved**.

Firhill has even become a favourite haunt for celebrity Glaswegian football fans. Billy Connolly is among the most notable, and was recently joined by actor Robert Carlyle and *Pop Idol* flop Darius Danesh. A suspicion is often aired in Glasgow that any celeb proclaiming their love for the Jags is merely avoiding the abuse that will be heaped upon them from 50 per cent of Glasgow if they nail their colours to the mast of either Old Firm side, but it all adds a touch of glamour to following the city's underachievers.

AC MILAN

If there's one club that sums up everything good, bad and ugly about Italian football, it's **AC Milan**. Their history covers glory and shame, brilliance and bluster, technical genius and boardroom chicanery. They are Italy's flashest club (no mean feat), its most successful European campaigners, and there's even a nutty president to boot. Scarily, he's also Italy's prime minister and top media mogul. Imagine a hyper-egotistical Tony Blair cross-bred with Rupert Murdoch and Martin Edwards (a worrying thought, granted) and you're getting close to understanding Silvio Berlusconi.

"I'm condemned to win and in fact I've always won," said the former cruise ship singer recently, when asked how he could govern his country and support his Milan team while a political corruption storm raged all around him. In other words, he's not bothered. Why should he be? A self-made billionaire, Berlusconi has already been prime minister with his party Forza Italia (the name is based on a terrace chant), lost the role and then bounced back with a series of ambitious construction plans. But his achievements with AC Milan remain his proudest.

Berlusconi has presided over six league and four European Cup wins for the *rossoneri* since he bought the bankrupt side in 1986, meanwhile drawing viewers to his three TV channels. He was also crucial in the creation of the Champions League, where Milan have thrived. His brilliant coaches even helped rid Italy of a reputation for boring football. Berlusconi is determined to keep things

Milan, a club condemned to win; must be hard for the fans

FUNNY BUSINESS

The strange synergy between the worlds of football and comedy isn't restricted to matchdays at White Hart Lane: for a halcyon period during the 1960s and 1970s, every club worth its salt had a funnyman on the terraces, and preferably in the boardroom too. The trend began with music-hall favourite Tommy Trinder (catchphrase: "You lucky, lucky people"), who became chairman of his beloved Fulham in 1957 and stayed for 20 years. Norman Wisdom began life as an Arsenal fan but switched allegiances to Brighton when he moved to the area after the war, later becoming a director of the club. Eric Morecambe performed a similar role for Luton Town in the 1970s, slipping mentions of the club into routines and becoming such a popular figure that the Kenilworth Road hospitality suite is still named after him. Jimmy Tarbuck became a regular face in the Liverpool dressing room during the 1970s and often travelled with the team on official functions. He's now president of the Reds' Celebrity Supporters Club, which can also count Stan Boardman among its numbers. Bernard Manning has been a Manchester City hanger-on for decades, while Des O'Connor was once a "nippy winger" on Northampton Town's books.

interesting: earlier this year he suggested the game should be livened up with more substitutions and penalties. Milan's fortunes have reflected his political career: they thrashed **Barcelona** 4-0 in the 1994 European Cup final as Berlusconi swept into government; when he was forced to resign over corruption investigations, his team lost the European Cup to **Ajax**; as he won a 2001 landslide, Milan hammered Inter 6-0.

"With all its faults football is beautiful, because it is a metaphor for life," he reckons. There's no doubt that Milan's life has been an interesting one. There were the glory years of the 1950s and 1960s, when the likes of **Gianni Rivera** and **Cesare Maldini** helped win six scudetti. Then there was the low period of the 1970s, when president Felice Colombo was caught match-rigging, Milan were twice relegated and new president Giuseppe Farina fled Italy with a fortune of players' money. After those two, even Berlusconi was a breath of fresh air.

Appointing Arrigo Sacchi from then little-known Parma was a masterstroke. He signed the Dutch trio of **Marco van Basten**, **Ruud Gullit** and **Frank Rijkaard** and his sides won with style, playing some of the finest football Europe has seen. In the 1989 European Cup, **Franco Baresi** and **Paolo Maldini** were rampant as Milan swept aside Real Madrid 5-0 and **Steaua Bucharest** 4-0 in the final. Fabio Capello's Milan were just as cool: in 1992 they won Serie A without losing a game; the next autumn they won a string of matches 5-4, 7-3, 5-3 and 5-1. With Maldini leading Milan to another European Cup (his fourth) last year, there's no guessing where Berlusconi's adventure will end. Perhaps in prison and shame; maybe with further glory. Either way, Milan's fortunes will probably follow those of the man.

ROCHDALE

"If we stay there much longer, they might as well rename the league Rochdale Division Three." So moans one downtrodden fan on a website dedicated to the Lancastrian football club that must rank as England's least successful league side. It was never going to be easy for **The 'Dale**. Situated bang in the heart of northern rugby country, the old mill town has over recent years become absorbed into Greater Manchester, with the huge, glittering temptation of Manchester United just on the doorstep. No wonder Rochdale's 9,125 capacity stadium, Spotland, is barely a quarter full for most matches.

Rochdale's history is a litany of terminal averageness, punctuated with the odd near-miss. Even way back in 1919, when the club applied for Football League status, there was disappointment. Seven clubs applied for six places and Rochdale missed out. Things haven't got much better since. They finally made it into Division Four in 1921, and have spent the rest of their history trying – and mainly failing – to get out of it. Only six seasons have been spent in the heady realms of England's second-worst league, with a ninth-place finish in the old Division Three the all-time highlight. Rochdale did outdo themselves to reach the final of the **1962 League Cup**, only to be crushed 4-0 by **Norwich City**.

Rochdale fans dream of a pie, a pint and Premiership football

No-one paid much attention. The 'Dale have even failed to whip up a rivalry with neighbouring **Bury**, who respond by ignoring them.

Buried in the basement league since 1972, last year Rochdale finished 18th. "Last season was one of the worst in recent memory," moans one gloomy supporter, predicting: "I expect us to struggle this year."

SAINT ETIENNE

The French like their sport with plenty of pathos. Cyclist Raymond Poulidor won the hearts of the nation by never winning the Tour de France, and in the late 1970s, a football team from a bleak town in the middle of nowhere won lasting popularity by repeatedly failing to win the European Cup. Even the revelation that the team was funded by the proceeds of tax evasion has done little to damage the treasured image of **Saint Etienne**.

For most of the 1960s and 1970s, Saint Etienne *were* French football. Known as *Les Verts* for their distinctive green strip, they won 10 League titles, six French Cups and, more importantly for a country that venerates flair, played with a beguiling mix of passion and artistry. Saint Etienne were loved as a national institution, but club president Roger Rocher had eyes for a bigger prize.

In 1976, they became the first French team in nearly 20 years to reach the final of the European Cup. Unfortunately, their opponents were a grimly efficient **Bayern Munich** team. *Les Verts* played elegantly, hit the post twice and lost 1-0. Intent on winning the Cup, Rocher brought in expensive stars like **Michel Platini** and Dutch international **Johnny Rep**. Saint Etienne MkII responded by qualifying for Europe again and then self-destructing.

The cup run ended with a disastrous 7-2 aggregate defeat to **Ipswich**. Suitably chastened, the team then went on to blow their chances of a domestic League and Cup double. To make things worse, Platini left for Italy amid rumours that his wife Chrystele and team-mate **Jean-François Larios** were becoming unusually friendly. Rocher, meanwhile, spent his time writing letters to the Pope.

Nobody knows whether the Pontiff ever replied, but Rocher certainly needed help, either divine or otherwise. A police investigation found that money from gate receipts and the club shop was being used to help players pay their taxes. Over 900,000 francs had been paid to Platini in cash. Rocher went to prison and Platini reached for his chequebook.

Without a benefactor, Saint Etienne struggled on but relegation was inevitable. The club spent most of the next 10 years inhabiting the strange world between the First and Second Divisions, waking up to a succession of false dawns before a consortium of businesses took over and put finances on a surer footing.

AFC WIMBLEDON

Football supporters often get a poor deal – yet even the most long-suffering fans would be hard-pushed to feel quite as aggrieved as the former followers of **Wimbledon FC**. On May 28, 2002, to almost universal disbelief, a three-man FA Commission gave official sanction to Wimbledon chairman Charles Koppel's plans to move the club almost 70 miles from their temporary base at **Crystal Palace**'s Selhurst Park to the promised land of Milton Keynes, home of the concrete cow. Within two months, a new club born from the ashes of the FA's decision were playing their first game in front of a capacity crowd and signing a six-figure sponsorship deal. It was the start of one of British football's most remarkable and uplifting tales – and it isn't finished yet.

The roots of AFC Wimbledon (it stands for "A Fans' Club") can be traced back to 1991. That was when Wimbledon – the unfashionable, philistine underdogs who rose from humble non-league roots to unleash **Vinnie Jones** and land the FA Cup – abandoned their historic Plough Lane home on safety grounds and began sharing Selhurst Park, while ostensibly searching for a new HQ in the London borough of Merton. For a variety of reasons (mostly dubious, say former fans), such a ground never came and Koppel came up with a radical solution.

The weeks following the FA's ratification of this solution were a whirlwind. Within two days, the Dons Trust (a supporters' organisation set up to spearhead a move back to Merton) had voted to walk out en masse, set up a new club and enter it in the Combined Counties League, seven rungs below the Premiership.

AFC Wimbledon played their first match on Wednesday 10 July, 2002, in front of 4,657 at **Sutton United**'s Gander Green Lane. When their league campaign got underway, 4,215 squeezed in to the ground they now share with Kingstonian in south-west London, and many more were locked out. Meanwhile, Wimbledon – now known to ex-fans as Franchise FC – opened to a crowd of 2,476 and hit a record low in November when just 664 paying spectators turned up for **Rotherham**'s visit in the Worthington Cup.

At the end of their first season, AFC Wimbledon finished third (out of 24 teams), losing only five games and scoring 125 goals in their 46 matches, as well as mystifying opposing teams whose average gates were somewhere around the one-man-and-a-dog mark. AFC fans' eventual aim is to return their club to the Premiership with their own ground, preferably passing their ex-club on the way down. Given the fairytale nature of their short history to date, it isn't quite as far-fetched a dream as it might sound.

SHEFFIELD WEDNESDAY

Should I survive for four years after my final parent dies and if **Sheffield Wednesday** manage to keep trading, my relationship with this most desperate of clubs will be the longest of my life. Its defining characteristic is pain.

I can still see the last seconds of the 1993 FA Cup Final replay. In fact, if I'm truthful, I see them most days. **Andy Linighan**'s header in the last seconds of extra time; **Chris Woods** flapping like the jessie we all knew he was; poor, heroic, exhausted **Roland Nilsson** (international commitments had forced him to play twice in 24 hours) collapsing on the line as the ball bobbled past him. That miserable night, shuffling silently down Wembley Way, I decided Wednesday could hurt me no more.

We had, I reasoned, had a few – not to be confused with many – great times along the way. There was that fabulous night at **Blackburn** when **Jack Charlton**'s warriors recovered from a goal down to almost ensure promotion from the old Third Division. Typically, Wednesday almost cocked it up the following Saturday at **Exeter**, but that has long been forgiven. There was dear old **Brian Joicey** scoring a scrambled late equaliser against **Oxford** on April 19, 1975, but only because it was Wednesday's first home goal since the previous 14 December.

There were the swashbuckling promotion teams so masterfully marshalled by Howard Wilkinson and Ron Atkinson, when the Steve Burtenshaw years and home defeats to **Mansfield Town** were almost forgotten. There was Mel Sterland and David Hirst and glorious victories over **Sheffield United** when it really mattered. Oh and there was the mad season of 1981-82 where I saw every game, home and away, but that's just me. Really, it's just me. Of course I was wrong about Wednesday's capacity to hurt me after 1993. It just goes on. Atkinson's second spell; **Danny Wilson**'s inability to handle **Paolo Di Canio** (who needed support rather than suspension); **Paul Jewell**'s tactical ineptitude; the imports who didn't care (a big, angry hello to **Gilles De Bilde**, **Petter Rudi** and **Wim Jonk**), and those who cared as much as I do but weren't good enough (a big, sad nod to **Darren Wood**, who memorably listed "doing Wednesday quizzes" as his hobby in the programme).

Over nine successive 1990s top-flight seasons, money was raised from a share issue, from a European tour (Wednesday were England's third-best team in 1992) and what seemed to be sensible husbandry, albeit the sort where **Larry May** rather than **Mark Wright** was the big-money centre-half. Then one morning in 1999, we woke up to find we were paupers, with a team to match. Where did the money go? We'll never be told. That's the Wednesday way.

Now Wednesday are back where they were a few weeks after Joicey's goal in 1975: Division Two, or "Division Three" as it was then. Sheffield United's exploits hardly helped, nor did their successful signing of Wednesday's under-achieving winger **Owen Morrison**. Did relegation hurt? Like septicemia.

Still, at this level there's no more hurt to be caused (yeah, right), but I bet Andy Linighan caresses his FA Cup winner's medal every day.

John Aizlewood

THE GAMES

It's only 22 men and a ball, but every so often it's pure poetry

Bobby Smith is sandwiched during an exhibition game for England at Wembley

"Here's Hurst. Can he make it four? He has! He has!"

Hugh Johns' less well-remembered commentary of the 1966 World Cup final, on ITV

HUNGARY 7 ENGLAND 1 (1954)

Six-three could have been a fluke. True, never had the English been so outpaced and outwitted. "I came off the pitch wondering what we had been doing for all those years," said a shell-shocked **Tom Finney** after the game. "The Hungarians were so much better in technique it was untrue. The first thing they did was to come out 20 minutes before the game to warm up. We had never done anything like that – you'd have thought England would have cottoned on. And we'd never seen a deep-lying forward before." Yet it was the return match the following May which confirmed that some kind of seismic shift had taken place in the game of football and that England were definitely no longer the masters.

In Budapest, tram drivers who hadn't been able to get time off to watch the game signalled the score to each other with gestures, flashing lights and horns. In the mines, each new goal was chalked on the side of the cages that took miners down to the coalface. **Ferenc Puskas** says "a million people tried to buy tickets for the game but only 100,000 could officially get in. Some friends took pigeons in so they could fly their tickets to their friends." Fans and pigeons looked on as England were duly annihilated 7-1 – their worst defeat of all time.

> **"Malcolm, it was like playing people from outer space"**
>
> *England defender Syd Owen tells Malcolm Allison about Hungary*

Tactically and technically the Hungarians were a world apart, carving the naïve English to pieces. Puskas' explosive left foot netted twice, inside-right **Sandor Kocsis**' powerful aerial dominance showed why he had the nickname "Golden Head", and **Nandor Hidegkuti** was once again rampant. Then there were the raids of right-half **Josef Bozsik** (a member of the rubber stamp Hungarian Parliament) and the

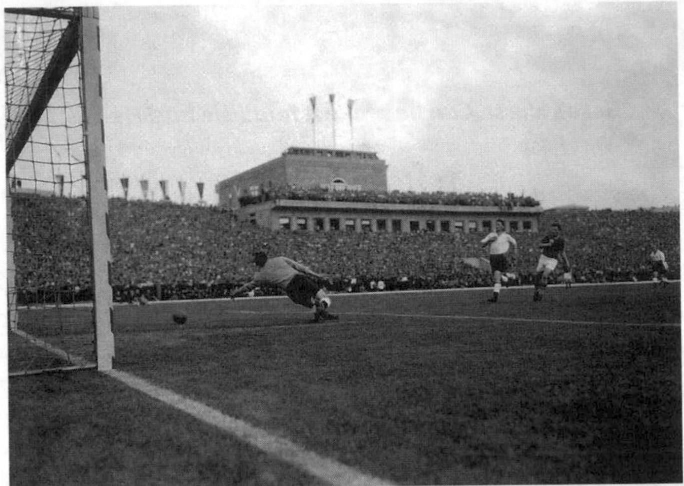
Puskas slots past England with consummate ease during England's record 7-1 defeat

masterful wing play of Lazslo Budai and Zoltan Czibor. The English left Budapest aware that a new era of football had arrived and that they must adapt – it wasn't enough for Walter Winterbottom to simply ask his centre-half Harry Johnston whether he wanted to man-mark Hidegkuti, get the reply that he'd rather not, and leave it at that. "This was the nearest thing to telepathy on a football pitch that I have ever seen", Finney recalled later. The humiliation probably did England some good: a 14-4 drubbing on aggregate couldn't be ignored, and tactics would have to change. Although Brazil's 1970 team are usually described as the greatest team of all-time, the Hungarian side were probably even more impossibly gifted and revolutionary. From 14 June, 1950 to 17 November, 1955, their record would be: Played 50, Won 42, Drawn 7, Lost 1, For 215, Against 58. It's just a pity the "Lost 1" statistic refers to a World Cup final.

WALSALL 2 ARSENAL 0 (1933)

The cover of the programme for Walsall's January 1933 fixture against Arsenal in the FA Cup third round says it all. "Big guns come to Walsall" reads the caption, alongside a drawing of a gigantic military man aiming 10 cannons at an angry-looking teddy bear armed with a stick. "Is this the way to Wembley?" asks the Field Marshall, representing the London team who were on their way to winning three championships and becoming one of the greatest sides in Arsenal's history. "Yes, for one of us!" replies the irate ursine.

In the end, neither side would reach Wembley that year, but Walsall would pull off the greatest shock in FA Cup history (sorry Hereford fans). While Arsenal's side contained several England internationals, Walsall were stranded in the lowly Third Division (north). Walsall fans thought defeat so inevitable that the ground was only half full, with 11,149 turning up to Fellows Park.

Walsall tackled hard and limited Arsenal to one chance in the first half, a **Cliff Bastin** shot blocked by Saddlers keeper **Joe Cunningham**. With **Harry Salt** and **Jack Bennett** grafting in midfield, and skipper **Sid Bird** leading by example, the miraculous happened in the second half. Striker **Gilbert Alsop** won a corner, then headed home from **Freddy Lee**'s kick. Newly confident, Alsop raced into the box minutes later and received a frustrated kick from Arsenal defender **Tommy Black**. The penalty was coolly converted by **Bill Sheppard**. Alsop and Bird were carried shoulder-high around the pitch at the end of an afternoon that half the OAPs in Walsall still claim they witnessed. Arsenal manager **Herbert Chapman**, blaming Black for the Walsall goals, sent the player home and promptly sold him to Plymouth.

ENGLAND 0 BRAZIL 1 (1970)

This group match was the unofficial World Cup final of Mexico 1970. A crowd of 70,950 packed into the Guarlajara Stadium to see world champions England take on a rampant Brazil side. Much was made of the clash between the planet's finest forward, **Pelé**, and its most immaculate defender, English captain **Bobby Moore**. Images from the match are still carved on the psyches of both nations: **Gordon Banks** flipping across his goal to scoop Pelé's downward header over the crossbar (Pelé inwardly cursing, then applauding) **Jairzinho**'s stunning raids down the flank; Moore outwitting Pelé on numerous occasions with his flawless timing.

There's the agonising memories of **Alan Ball** rattling the crossbar, and **Jeff Astle's** miss with the goal at his mercy. Then there's the goal, simplicity itself. **Tostao** drifting in a cross, Pelé squaring the ball in the coolest manner imaginable, and Jairzinho thundering forward to hammer the ball home.

This was the most competitive game Brazil faced en route to winning the Jules Rimet trophy to keep. Which made England's 3-2 defeat in León against West Germany all the more painful. One Scottish international, who watched that notorious quarter-final, had to admit: "I had a lump in my throat. I had to get out of the stadium before anyone noticed the tears in my eyes."

ESTONIA P-P SCOTLAND (1997)

Games are often called one-sided, but Scotland's 1998 World Cup qualifier against Estonia took the description to ridiculous extremes. After a series of disagreements, the Scots found themselves kicking off at Tallinn's Kadriorg stadium with no opponents at all, while the Estonians sat round at their training ground in a huff. How it all happened was farcical.

Originally scheduled to kick off at 6.45pm, the match was brought forward to 3pm by Fifa after Scotland expressed reservations about the quality of the stadium's floodlights. Estonia objected strenuously, even claiming that some of their players would be "at work" during the afternoon, but Fifa stood firm. Neither side would budge, so Scotland found themselves taking to the pitch at three with only the referee and two linesmen as company. **Billy Dodds** kicked off to **John Collins**, the ref blew up, and the Scots were proclaimed 3-0 winners by default. Collins punched the air in mock celebration.

But that was just the start of hostilities. "We believe Scotland were afraid of us," raged Estonian FA vice-president, Iaver Pohlak. "They had injuries and we think that they wanted to avoid this match. Our players were 100km away in a training camp and it was impossible to get them here." Scotland denied it ("we

Craig Brown examines the controversial floodlights at the Kadriorg Stadium

are deeply disappointed," said coach Craig Brown) and got on the first charter back to Glasgow. Ludicrously, as the Scots sped home, the Estonians turned up for the match at the original time of 6.45pm – even beaming out the floodlights across the empty stadium to prove that they worked.

The fingers of blame were pointed firmly at Fifa. The baffling affair left several questions to be resolved: would players get their caps for the second-long "game"? Was **Gary McAllister** (banned for one game) still suspended? In the end, Fifa buckled and ordered the game to be replayed in Monaco (it finished 0-0). All in all, it was one of the more unusual days out for the Tartan Army, and gave a new meaning to the phrase "there was only one team out there today".

REAL MADRID 7 EINTRACHT FRANKFURT 3 (1960)

Simply the best game of football ever to have been played. Commentator Kenneth Wolstenholme called it "Swan Lake on turf". But what is it that keeps the mythical appeal of the 1960 European Cup final at Hampden Park so fresh?

For one, there was the score. **Real Madrid** beat **Eintracht Frankfurt** 7-3, a margin that shouldn't be allowed in a respectable cup final. And the 137,000 amazed souls present would tell you it could have been more – Madrid hit the woodwork three times, and Frankfurt rattled the crossbar, too.

More important still was the sheer quality of football on show, especially from Madrid. Real may have won the European Cup for the four previous years, but even those legendary sides couldn't compete with the holy trinity of Ferenc Puskas, **Alfredo di Stefano** and **Paco Gento** – not to mention **José Santamaria** and **Luis Del Sol**.

Yet it was the Germans who started best, taking an early lead through **Richard Kress**. The Glaswegian crowd knew Frankfurt were no mugs – they had demolished **Rangers** 6-1 and 6-3 in the semi-finals. Di Stefano levelled on 26 minutes, and from then on in, it was all Madrid.

> ***"We believe Scotland were afraid of us "***
>
> *The Estonian FA's laver Pohlak after the no-show game in Tallinn, which later ended in a draw*

Puskas, by now aged 33, was playing his first ever European final, and he played as though it might be his last, with an invincible display. (He almost didn't play: a late apology for accusations he'd made that Germany's 1954 World Cup winning squad had taken performance enhancers averted a possible German boycott of the final). The man known as *Canoncito pum* – "little cannon bang" – for his extraordinary shots put Madrid in the lead with a goal from nothing, bringing the ball down on the goal-line and blasting it home from the narrowest of angles. In the second half, Puskas – who liked to juggle soap in the showers with his left peg to entertain his team-mates – was unstoppable. He put away a penalty, then a rare header, to make it 5-1, at which point Real began to showboat, doing outrageous tricks to massive applause from the Hampden crowd. Puskas made it six, and while Eintracht added a couple of consolation goals as Madrid poured forward relentlessly, di Stefano added Real's seventh.

Eintracht sportingly formed a guard of honour to clap their conquerors off the pitch, but they must have been traumatised: they never appeared in the final of Europe's top competition again. Real, meanwhile, were the new heroes of Glasgow. Huge crowds cheered their bus around the city and away at the airport.

SCOTLAND 1 PERU 3 (1978)

Scotland's World Cup campaign of 1978 was a fine lesson in not counting your chickens. The nation's qualification for Argentina was met with xenophobic optimism bordering on the hysterical – not even a warm-up defeat to England (who hadn't qualified) could dampen the feeling that the Scots had a chance. Manager Ally McLeod – alias "Mohammed Ally" – whipped up the fervour by predicting, optimistically, that the cup would be coming back home with the Tartan Army.

> ***"I would like to thank Scotland and Mr McLeod for the team they presented us with "***
> *Peru manager Marcos Calderon*

Their first game against Peru was considered a pushover. Scotland didn't even bother having a warm-up match against South American opposition beforehand – after all, Peru had three players (**Hector Chumpitaz**, **Hugo Sotil**, **Teofilo Cubillas**) who had played at their peak at the time of the 1970 tournament. Staying in Alta Gracia, worrying reports emerged from the Scots camp about boozing, gambling and womanising, while the hotel and training facilities were poor.

McLeod's team selection was also widely criticised. He picked almost the same side that had just lost to England: **Derek Johnstone** was overlooked despite his 41 goals for Rangers that season and **Bruce Rioch** and **Don Masson** got the nod despite being badly out of form with Aston Villa and Notts County respectively.

Things initially seemed to be going well for the Scots. They took the lead on 15 minutes, with **Joe Jordan** pouncing on a parried Rioch shot. After this, Peru

ON THE SPOT

"It is loading a bullet into the chamber of a gun and asking everyone to pull the trigger. Someone will get the bullet – you know that – and it will reduce them to nothing. Fairness is not even an issue." Thus spoke **Christian Karembeu**, erstwhile **Middlesbrough** and **Real Madrid** star, after seeing Holland dismissed from Euro 96 at the hands of a penalty shoot-out.

When it comes to a shoot-out, your perspective is shaped entirely by the outcome – it is decisive, inarguable, and still the only way to separate teams after 120 minutes of fruitless football. Karembeu may have been bitter, but **George Best** wasn't – the Manchester United legend was the first man ever to score in a shoot-out, as the Reds overcame **Hull City** 4-3 in the semi-final of the short-lived Watney Cup in 1970. The shoot-out got a mixed reception – newspapers were enthusiastic, fans less so – but soon took off as the only way of avoiding marathon replays (in the late 1940s, with the FA decreeing that cup ties be settled on the day, several lasted over three hours with extra time). The NASL introduced a widely ridiculed rival system, with players running from 35 yards out to try and slot home.

The 1976 European Championships were decided from the spot, with Czechoslovakia inflicting the only ever shoot-out defeat on a German side. The German FA told them not to worry because everybody knew that the Germans were no good at taking penalties, and paid the players their win bonuses.

The title of longest shoot-out is contested by several games, but the 2001 West Riding Amateur League Cup clash between **Storthes Hall** and **Littletown** probably has the best claim. It was abandoned after 34 consecutive kicks went in –a lack of floodlights meant car headlights were the only illumination. A 1987 FA Cup tie between **Aldershot** and **Fulham** was settled in the Shots' favour after 28 kicks, though a Costa Rican game in 1997 saw a reputed 38.

And the oddest shoot-out? In the late 1890s, a circus challenged **Leicester Fosse** players to take penalties against a football-playing elephant. Three successive players failed to find a way past the beast, but Fosse star **William Keech** used sleight of eye to deceive the keeper, winning 3-2 after three kicks apiece (the elephant, it seems, could score as well as block).

turned on the style. The "old man," 29-year-old Cubillas, orchestrated the game from midfield, while pacy wingers **José Munante** and **Juan Carlos Oblitas** tore into a slow Scottish backline. Ally's army looked like a disorganised rabble. Forty-two minutes in – it was a wonder it took that long – the Peruvians equalised, as a sleek move saw **Teofilo Cueto** blast home. After the break, it was pure Inca magic. The Scots missed a penalty, Masson's shot being saved easily, and McLeod admitted the mistake of playing him and Rioch, as both were subbed.

It was too late. A blistering 20-yard shot from Cubillas gave Peru the lead, and he capped a wonderful performance with the third, bending a free-kick round the Scotland wall with the outside of his boot. "I would like to thank Scotland and Mr

A Celtic pensioner celebrates victory over Inter Milan's "Ambre Solaire men"

McLeod for the team they presented us with," said Peru manager Marcos Calderon afterwards. It was "the end of the world," admitted McLeod. For Ally's management reign it certainly was: a draw with Iran ("In the name of Allah go" the tabloids should have said) and the thrilling defeat of Holland didn't save him his job or, oddly, take the World Cup back to Edinburgh.

CELTIC 2 INTER MILAN 1 (1967)

"They were sleek and tanned like film stars. Ambre Solaire men. On our side there were quite a few with no teeth and we had blobs of Vaseline on our eyebrows to block the sweat. It must have been funny." **Celtic**'s **Bobby Murdoch** was quick to notice the physical differences between the mighty **Inter Milan** and the Glaswegian side as they lined up to face each other for the 1967 European Cup final. But the contrasts did not stop there. Inter, the overwhelming favourites, had won the top European prize in 1964 and 1965, and had been unlucky not to triumph in 1966, too; Celtic were new to European finals and many of the players had never even set foot in a foreign land before their continental campaign started.

Inter were footballing millionaires capable of buying any player they fancied; Celtic were all local lads born within 20 miles of the East End of Glasgow – the side had cost just £42,000 to assemble. But while the Celts may have been the unsophisticated underdogs facing the continental aristocrats, their strength was very much in their humble backgrounds.

> ***"We must play as if there are no more games, no more tomorrows"***
> *Jock Stein fires up Celtic*

A uniquely talented group of players, they had performed together for many years and understood each other's games inside out. "Together they are a team – a real team," said their manager, Jock Stein. He was the side's other great asset, like fellow scot Sir Alex Ferguson decades later a master of tactics and the psychological game, telling his team "we must play as if there are no more games, no more tomorrows" as they stepped out onto the pitch at Lisbon's Estadio Nacional.

The match was a contrast of styles too. Inter were the great exponents of *catenaccio*, fielding a virtual eight-man defence. Stein, meanwhile, wanted to be remembered "for the football we played. We want to make neutrals everywhere glad we qualified." Celtic did just that. Despite going 1-0 down within eight minutes to a penalty, Stein's plan to overwork the Italian defence worked a treat. Winger **Jimmy Johnstone** and **Bertie Auld** were rampant, and on 62 minutes, Celtic equalised with an exhilarating volley from the edge of the box by **Tommy Gemmell**.

The Scots piled on the pressure, and with five minutes remaining, Inter buckled. Stevie Chalmers scored the winner, turning in a Murdoch effort on goal. The ensuing pandemonium after the final whistle included Gemmell enraging an ice cream vendor on the side of the pitch by asking for a cooling ice but – understandably – not having any money to pay. And the Celtic lads may not have looked like movie stars, but they didn't entirely neglect their images. Bobby Lennox had made sure his false teeth were stashed in the back of the net in case they did win: "I didn't want them getting pictures of me flashing a pair of gums."

HAMPTON 3 AYLESBURY 1 (2003)

Chances are you've never been to the Beveree Stadium, tucked into an anonymous corner of south-west London called Hampton. The ground, with an official capacity of 3,000, is surrounded by houses, some quite posh. That might be a problem if Hampton & Richmond Borough FC a) ever attracted more than a few hundred souls; b) attracted fans who like to shout and stamp their feet and c) gave those fans cause to shout or stamp their feet.

The Beavers, as they're known (to the potential discomfort of the club's promising women's team), were in the Ryman Premier League when, in February 2003, they met Aylesbury United. The home fans were silent as usual, and Aylesbury went ahead after five minutes. So far, so predictable.

Then the wonderfully named Ashley Sestanovich tried to run through the entire Aylesbury defence. Weaving into the box, he lost the ball to United's Mark Burgess and fell over. He lay there, prone, not looking as if he was appealing for anything, but shamed by his own ineptitude. The game seemed about to resume when the assistant referee flagged for a penalty. After furious Aylesbury protests, Richard O' Connor levelled from the spot for Hampton.

Sestanovich, possibly inspired by the away fans' incessant chant of "dirty cheating bastard", then dribbled through most of the Aylesbury defence to hit a 20-yard screamer into the roof of the net. Even the Aylesbury fan website felt obliged to note later that it was "a goal worthy of winning any match… but he's still a diving cheat". In other words, Sestanovich had done to Aylesbury what Diego Maradona had done to England in 1986.

To add insult to, well, insult, he then skipped past three defenders to play a low ball across the area for Andy Cyrus to run on to and score. The crowd didn't spill onto the pitch and Kenneth Wolstenholme didn't declare on the tannoy that it was all over, but for the home fans among the crowd of 302, the elation was almost as intense – but much more short-lived: the Beavers only picked up one more home point that season and were relegated.

THE WILLIE CARR FLICK

You can always tell when an event has reached cult status by the number of people who claim to have witnessed it first hand. On that basis October 3, 1970 was an event like no other in the history of **Coventry City** Football Club because they somehow managed to cram more than 200,000 people into a ground with a capacity of little more than 40,000. Today, almost 33 years on, you still bump into 25-year-olds in the city who swear blind that they saw the "Willie Carr flick" in the flesh.

I didn't. Like the rest of the country I had to rely on *Match of the Day* to see, if not the greatest goal scored by a player in a sky blue shirt, certainly the most audacious. There were 10 minutes to go in the match against the champions **Everton**. City were leading 2-1 and were awarded a free kick in a central position on the edge of the penalty area. While the four-man wall steadied itself, the carrot-haired Carr stood over the ball, pincered it between his heels, and flicked it up. As it fell, the stocky figure of Ernie Hunt struck a perfect right-foot dipping volley over the wall and into the top corner of **Andy Rankin**'s goal.

The Everton manager Harry Catterick described it as something you would find in a circus, but that is why it is so special to City fans. The club produced better players than Hunt and Carr, they won more important matches than this one but rarely had an event at Coventry sparked such national interest.

Ernie Hunt, complete with sideburns

It was a piece of audacious skill that allowed many fans to ignore the years of struggle against relegation, those periods under Gordon Milne in the late 1970s when the team played such sterile football and even perhaps the criminal squandering of early 1980s talent that saw the likes of **Mark Hateley**, **Gary Thompson**, **Danny Thomas** and **Gary Gillespie** depart. Fans at other clubs may have witnessed wonder goals much more regularly. But few will ever have seen a goal that within 24 hours was being copied by children up and down the country. People compared the skill to that displayed by the all-conquering Brazilians who just four months earlier had won the World Cup playing beautiful football. Ironically, although it was Carr's flick, by signing for **Wolves** he disallowed himself from achieving cult status so it is Ernie Hunt's volley that is warmly remembered by Coventry fans. The FA had the last word, banning all such free-kicks. Spoilsports.

Tom O'Sullivan

ENGLAND 3 ITALY 2 (1934)

There was certainly enough at stake when England met Italy at Highbury in November 1934. For starters, the game was considered a battle to decide who were the best team on the planet. Coached by Vittorio Pozzo, who had taught at a language school in Derby prior to World War One, Italy were the World Cup winners, having beaten Czechoslovakia 2-1 in Rome to become the first European team to lift the trophy. But England were considered the old masters of the game, and hadn't entered the World Cup to give the rest of the world a chance. England had never lost at home to a European side, but a confident Italy felt they could end that proud record. To add to the heady mix, Mussolini expected sporting excellence from his nation's teams, and there were huge win bonuses on offer, further adding to the players' desperation to beat England.

The home side, meanwhile, were a tight unit, and virtually a club side – **Frank Moss**, **George Male**, **Eddie Hapgood**, **Wilf Copping**, **Ray Bowden**, **Ted Drake** and **Cliff Bastin** were all **Arsenal** regulars and well-used to playing at Highbury. Straight from kick-off, England piled forward, winning a penalty after just 30 seconds. Italian keeper **Carlo Ceresoli** saved **Eric Brook**'s effort, but the

Manchester City forward got his own back quickly, smashing home two great goals within 10 minutes – a powerful header and free kick. In the 15th minute, Drake's excellent solo goal made it 3-0 to England, and all hell broke lose. Shell-shocked and staggered by the hard English tackling, the Italians started kicking out. The game would become known as the "The Battle of Highbury".

Hapgood had his nose broken, and after the game Brook's arm needed an x-ray, Drake had two black eyes and Bowden was limping. Italy's wonderful forward **Giuseppe Meazza** scored two fine goals to make it 3-2 in the end, but England stood firm. Returning home in shame, and with England now adjudged the best team in the world, Italy had to wait until 1938 – when they would retain the World Cup – to be restored in Mussolini's eyes.

KIEV 3 NAZIS 2 (1942)

The scene is the Ukraine in 1942. German tanks had rolled into Kiev, leaving a trail of blood and destruction, and local Major General Eberhardt decided that good relations between locals and the occupiers should be promoted. His idea was to boost morale by staging a football match between the Germans and Ukrainian champions **Dynamo Kiev**. The Kiev team had been captured by a football-supporting Wehrmacht officer who decided to spare their lives.

Things did not go the way Eberhardt had planned. Despite being physically weary, the Ukranians' skills shone through, and they took an early lead. Eberhardt threatened the side with the firing squad at half time if they did not lose, but buoyed by the crowd, the Kiev players romped to a 4-1 win. The players were not shot, but Eberhardt was in trouble. A rematch was organised, with the Kiev players banned from training, and on lower rations. They won 6-0. Humiliated, Eberhardt brought in a crack Hungarian side, **MSG Wal**, to do the job: the visitors were duly hammered 5-1 and then 3-2 in a rematch.

The Kiev players thought as long as they won, they'd stay alive: the Nazis would want revenge on the pitch. But Eberhardt was under massive pressure to avoid a further PR disaster. An unbeaten German Army side, **Flakelf**, were lined up to finally topple the malnourished Ukranians. With a crowd comprised entirely of Wehrmacht, Kiev's players were informed this was their last chance: win and they would die. They won 3-2. As their winner flew in, members of the SS began taking potshots at them: after the game all but three were executed. A team statue now stands in Kiev, but many in the city will tell you that the games never took place, and were the invention of the (equally hated) Communists.

USA 1 ENGLAND 0 (1950)

England's first venture into the World Cup, at Brazil 1950, was not a happy one. Not only did one of the pre-tournament favourites not win the trophy, they were humiliated by the USA in what remains one of the biggest upsets in football history. The match – later dubbed "The Game That Shook the World" – was played in Belo Horizonte ("beautiful horizon"), in front of a crowd of Brazilians rooting for the underdogs against the mighty English.

> ***"England have been beaten by the Mickey Mouse and Donald Duck team "***
>
> *The US press rubs it in*

The disparity between the teams could not have been greater. England had the likes of Tom Finney and **Billy Wright** (**Stanley Matthews** was rested for this "easy game"). The US had sent a hastily-assembled band of amateur players. Ironically, many of the players were in fact expat Scots, with more reason than most to want to beat the English. Greenock-born star **Eddie McIlvenny** led the Yanks out, chosen as captain precisely because he was Scottish and could inspire the team against the Auld Enemy, and manager Bill Jeffrey was born in Edinburgh. Among their line-up were a hearse driver, a student and a teacher. Rated 500-1 to

The despair of defeat: Steve McMahon and Liverpool crash to Wimbledon

win the game by one London bookmaker, the US were expected to lose by seven or eight goals (they had, after all, recently lost 9-0 to Italy and 4-0 to Scotland). Even the Americans didn't feel they stood a chance, partying until the early hours the night before the game. But 39 minutes into the match, after wave after wave of frustrating English attacks, Haitian-born forward **Joe Gaetjens** – who worked as a dishwasher – scored a wonderful diving header to give America the lead.

The hungover "Americans" held on to their slim lead against the run of play, and the shock victory was confirmed. Gaetjens was carried shoulder-high around the stadium. The press in England thought that the wires were mistaken when the 0-1 score came through – thinking it more likely 10-1 to England, who were wearing blue shirts for the only time in history. A New York paper's headline read: "England have been beaten by the Mickey Mouse and Donald Duck team." Fast forward 43 years and *The Sun* would greet a similar shock with "Yanks 2 Planks 0."

"It was a big upset," admitted Gaetjens. "They should have won, and nine times out of 10 they would have. But that game was ours." It was a happy story, but Gaetjens met a tragic end. Returning home to Haiti, he was arrested by dictator Francois "Papa Doc" Duvalier's gangster militia in 1964, because his family had worked for the opposition. It is thought he died in captivity. We'll be getting reminded about it all over again soon – because the story of the match is currently being made into a Hollywood movie.

ITALY 4 WEST GERMANY 3 (1970)

While it might have been a World Cup semi-final, for 90 minutes there was little out of the ordinary about Italy's 1970 match against West Germany in Mexico City. Italy had taken an early lead inside the gigantic Azteca Stadium and then, as expected, closed up shop defensively. It was a tribute to the Germans' determination that they'd kept going and managed to squeeze a late equaliser out of the game. Inspirational sweeper **Franz Beckenbauer** powered his side forward and, in the 90th minute, **Karlheinz Schnellinger** found the response to **Roberto Boninsegna**'s early goal for the Italians.

But as the match went to extra time, few present could have expected a goal-fest. What followed, though, was extraordinary: the only match in World Cup history to produce five goals in extra time. Fortunes fluctuated at a startling rate. **Gerd Müller**, that year's Golden Boot, gave the Germans the advantage straight away with his ninth goal of the tournament, but **Tarcisio Burgnich** brought things all-square again three minutes later. Just before the break, **Luigi Riva**, Italy's star forward, thumped in a left-footed effort from outside the box to make it 3-2 to Italy. It seemed, for once, that Italian coach Ferruccio Valcareggi was prepared to gamble on his side's formidable creative instincts. Italy kept pushing, but the Germans, with characteristic ruthlessness, would not lie down.

Amazingly, Müller headed home his 10th goal of the finals to bring it back to 3-3. But the Italians were to have the final word against their industrious opponents. After good approach play from Boninsegna, European Footballer of the Year **Gianni Rivera** fired home what was to finally prove the winner. It was a breathtaking end to what had started out as a relatively tedious game. The Germans fell to the ground shattered, but it also took the wind out of Italy: the massively talented side looked desperately tired in the final – never a good time to face the best team in history. Pelé's Brazil beat them 4-1.

WIMBLEDON 1 LIVERPOOL 0 (1988)

Really, it couldn't have happened any other way. In the weeks prior to the 1988 FA Cup final, media build-up had focused on the "greatest mismatch in Cup final history", with wild predictions of record scores as League champions **Liverpool** sought to become Double winners against clogging paupers **Wimbledon**. The year before, **Coventry** had overcome the odds against **Tottenham**, but that was only a minor upset, we were told, and wouldn't be repeated 12 months on.

In reality, the Dons' victory doesn't really register on the footballing Richter scale (they did, after all, finish seventh in the league, albeit 30 points shy of the Reds), but the manner of the win makes it a classic. Having spent the evening before the game in the pub on coach Don Howe's advice – their hotel was "very nice, but not very Wimbledon" – Bobby Gould's side exhibited the disdain for reputations that had seen them terrorise the top half of the First Division, with **Vinnie Jones** and **John Fashanu** staring out their opponents in the tunnel and screaming obscenities as the sides walked out.

Many claim Jones' early lunge at **Steve McMahon** took the bite out of Liverpool's midfield, but the game really turned on **Peter Beardsley**'s first-half disallowed goal; wiped out, comically, because the referee had already blown to award a Liverpool free-kick for an earlier foul on the same player. The rest is history: **Lawrie Sanchez**, that most ordinary of midfielders, rose to head **Dennis Wise**'s free-kick home, and **Dave Beasant** became the first goalkeeper ever to save a Cup Final penalty when he stopped **John Aldridge**'s spot-kick. June Whitfield, the underdogs' sole celebrity fan, was later spotted dancing with delight in the streets of Wimbledon Village.

> ***"They say Wimbledon was a fairytale, a miracle – it was hard work and correct planning "***
> *Owner Sam Hammam on 1988*

NORTH KOREA 3 PORTUGAL 5 (1966)

South Korea may have caused a stir at the 2002 World Cup, but they were 36 years behind their bitter enemies from the north when it came to creating a buzz about football from the Korean peninsula. To say North Korea were the surprise package of the World Cup in England in 1966 would be an understatement – it was miraculous they even got to these shores. Britain didn't have any formal diplomatic relations with either part of Korea at the time, and getting visas was problematic. The side were eventually allowed to participate – provided that the North Korean national anthem wasn't played. Not much was expected, even by the team themselves, or their "Great Leader", Kim Il-sung.

"Before we left for England, the Great Leader told us we could not expect to win the World Cup, but we could win one or two games," remembers **Pak Doo-ik**. The side were based in Middlesbrough, playing their "home" games at Ayresome Park. They lost their opening game 3-0 to the Soviet Union, but won Teesside hearts by drawing with Chile 1-1 in the next match, and then incredibly beating Italy 1-0 thanks to Pak Doo-ik's goal in the last group game. They were

RECORD VICTORIES

Thrashings, tonkings, hammerings – call them what you like, there's nothing like a really massive football victory. In the club game (at a professional level, at least), they happen pretty rarely these days. Anything over seven goals merits the spelling-out of the number for the disbelieving public on the *Grandstand* vidi-printer, and a startled inflection in the voice of the normally-calm reader of the classified results. Even the Premiership can only offer a feeble 9-0 battering of Ipswich by Manchester United back in 1995 as its highlight. For the daddy of them all, we have to rewind 118 years, to the home of the "smokie" and the first round of the Scottish Cup, just a few years after Association Football had been codified.

Back in September 1885, Aberdeen amateurs **Bon Accord** had been drawn away to **Arbroath**. Nobody expected the minnows to triumph as they strode out at Gayfield Park, but the margin of their loss still required a staggering football incompetence: the Red Lichties ran out 36-0 winners. According to press reports, Arbroath keeper Jim Milne did not touch the ball for the entire match, and spent much of it sheltering from the rain under a spectator's brolly, puffing on a pipe. Rampant right winger **Willie "Jocky" Petrie** racked up four hat-tricks and one for good measure, and his 13 goals still stand as a British record.

Things could have been worse, mind you. The referee admitted after the match that he had spared Bon Accord's blushes by wrongly disallowing seven Arbroath goals for offside. Two years later **Hyde United** recorded a humiliating 26-0 loss to the mighty Invincibles of **Preston North End** in the English FA Cup, but for the only other senior match making it past the magic 30-goal mark, we have to turn to international football and, strangely enough, Australia.

Although never a footballing force themselves, the Aussies' qualification route for the World Cup has offered up some plumb fixtures against island people who are barely familiar with the game. Rugby-loving Tonga (who provide Australia and New Zealand with some of their finest oval-ball players) saw their hapless side demolished 22-0 back in April 2001, but that was just a taster for what would happen against American Samoa (an unincorporated territory of the US with a population of 63,000) later the same month.

Ranked 203 in the world – ie last – the American Samoans arrived in Australia on the back of a 13-0 loss to Fiji and an 18-0 battering by Tahiti and had lost several players due to passport problems. Only sanctioned for international competition in 1998, the inexperienced Samoan side must have been fearing the worst.

It duly happened, as Australia netted so frequently that the referee lost count of the score (it finished 31-0). After the match, Australian striker **Archie Thompson** – who bagged 13 strikes despite previously having netted only one international goal – said, cruelly, that "their one attack consisted of getting just over the halfway line." Thompson became the first 13-goal striker in history to be dropped for the next match. Serves him right for being so cocky.

Gerry Armstrong rises from obscurity to immortality with one swing of the boot

through to the quarter-finals, facing **Eusebio** and the might of Portugal. "The players couldn't believe how much the local community supported them," says Dan Gordon, producer of a British documentary film about the side. "At every game the chant of 'Korea' went up in the stands."

Korea kicked off playing very attacking football, stunning the Portuguese with a first-minute goal from **Park Seung-jin. Lee Dong-woon** made it 2-0 on 20 minutes, and **Yang Sung-kook** immediately added a third. Korea seemed on course for a semi with England (when the score was flashed up at Wembley, fans assumed it was the wrong way round). A penalty awarded against the Asians turned the tide. Eusebio scored it to make it 3-1, and from then on, Portugal dominated. Eusebio scored again before half-time, and 15 minutes into the second half, got his hat-trick. He added a fourth, and **Augusto** finished off the miracle comeback. "They came from the other side of the world as 1000-1 no-hopers," read a *Daily Mirror* report. "They leave world football wondering how far they will advance in the future." The answer, unfortunately, was nowhere: North Korea would never play in the World Cup finals again.

NORTHERN IRELAND 1 SPAIN 0 (1982)

The top scorers list at the 1982 World Cup had a slightly disjointed look to it. It was no surprise to see **Rossi, Rummenigge** and **Zico** occupying the top three slots, but nestled behind them, with four goals, was the unlikely figure of Watford fringe striker **Gerry Armstrong**. Northern Ireland had arrived on the world footballing map, and had made quite an impression. Perennial underdogs even when George Best made it into the squad, the Irish side of 1982 was the finest in the country's history, with **Pat Jennings**, **Norman Whiteside** and **Sammy McIlroy** three world-class performers gelling just at the right time and propping up a ragged assortment of under-achievers and bit-part players.

> ***"Billy Bingham told us to feed on the crumbs and that's just what we did. It made us feel 10 feet tall"***
> *Billy Hamilton*

Even so, nobody expected much when the boys in green were drawn in a group with hosts and joint-favourites Spain and a resurgent Yugoslavia, especially as Best – in the twilight of his career with Hibernian in Edinburgh – had missed out on his chance of a finals appearance after having a drink-induced nightmare when being watched by manager Billy Bingham.

Northern Ireland did themselves the power of good by holding the Yugoslavs to a goalless draw in their opening match but then blew it all by being kept to 1-1 by minnows Honduras in Zaragoza and were left needing victory against the almost-qualified hosts to ensure a passage to the second round. Sheer determination – and some fierce tackling – kept the Spaniards in check in the first half, and immediately after the restart, **Billy Hamilton** bundled Spanish hardman **Miguel Tendillo** off the ball ("If anyone deserved a slap, he did," Hamilton later commented) and delivered a cross which goalkeeper Arconada flapped at and pushed into the path of a grateful Armstrong.

Even the dismissal of **Mal Donaghy** on the hour didn't help the hosts, with Jennings in inspired form, and Northern Ireland were through, moving into the Madrid hotel the cocky Yugoslavs had already booked for the second week. Sadly, the second round of group matches saw them meet Austria and a rampant France, and they were soon on the plane home, but the victory lifted the nation and is still remembered by misty-eyed fans. And Armstrong? He went back to Vicarage Road and continued to struggle for a regular first-team spot, scoring half his World Cup tally during the entire ensuing season in the Second Division.

TEN CHEEKIEST GOALS OF ALL TIME

1. Dion Dublin, Coventry v Newcastle, 1997

Shay Given catches a cross and, as the players drift upfield, Dublin hides behind him. The keeper rolls the ball out, Dublin skips round him and passes into the net.

2. Johan Cruyff, Ajax v Helmond Sport, 1982

Ajax captain Johan Cruyff runs up to take a penalty. But instead of shooting, he passes the ball forward and to his left. Team-mate Jesper Olsen, running into the area, passes it back to Cruyff, who places the ball past the gob-smacked keeper.

3. Gary Crosby, Nottingham Forest v Manchester City, 1990

City keeper Andy Dibble casually rests the ball in the palm of his hand like a waiter. It's inviting enough for Gary Crosby, who nods it out of his hand and scores.

4. Dean Saunders, Sheffield United v Port Vale, 1998

Saunders reaches the ball a second after the Vale keeper has slid it out. The striker bounces the throw-in off the retreating player's back and curls it around him.

5. George Best, Northern Ireland v England, 1971

Gordon Banks throws the ball into the air to punt it upfield. Best nips in, dinks the ball over Banksie's head and taps it in – but it's wrongly disallowed.

6. Tomas Brolin, Leeds v Sheffield Wednesday, 1996

Brolin miscontrols a cross and tumbles, but a defender's clearance bounces off the roly-poly one. The keeper's follow-up hits Brolin on the head and goes in.

7. Roger Milla, Colombia v Cameroon, 1990

Colombian keeper Rene Higuita thinks he'll dribble round some Cameroon players. Milla nips the ball off his toes, runs half the pitch unchallenged and scores.

8. Steve McManaman, Tottenham v Liverpool, 1996

McManaman's scuffed shot looks to be heading straight to Ian Walker. But as the keeper kneels to collect, it hits a large divot and bounces over his shoulder.

9. Masashi Motoyama, Kashima Antlers v Shimizu S-Pulse, 2002

During a cup match between these J-League sides, a Kashima player commits a foul in the Shimizu penalty box. Players from both sides stop as the keeper positions the ball for a free kick. But the referee hasn't blown and Motoyama pops the ball in.

10. Pat Jennings, Tottenham v Manchester United, 1967

Keepers are meant to stop goals, not score them. Kenneth Wolstenholme is shocked into silence in the Charity Shield when Jennings' punt bounces over Alex Stepney.

THE SHRINES

From the Maracanã to Hackney Marshes, the grounds where dreams are (sometimes) played out

Football by night, Milanese-style

"Where's the dog track?"

Luther Blissett, on swapping Vicarage Road for the San Siro

THE MARACANA

Aptly, the biggest football stadium in the world is the spiritual home of the finest team in history – Brazil. The gigantic, spaceship-like Maracanã was purpose-built for the 1950 World Cup, and to cope with the soccer-mania gripping the country, they had to make it big – very big. The home nation hosted Uruguay in the final that year, and an incredible 199,854 spectators crammed inside. There was so little room that some even stood on the roof. The home side lost 2-1, but a new world record for attendance at a football match was set – and is unlikely ever to be beaten.

A workman puts the finishing touches to a revamped Maracanã in 2000

History has been made at Rio's Maracanã again and again: the stadium saw Pelé's 1,000th goal fly into the net; Sinatra, The Beatles and the Stones all played gigs there. Located in the EstAdio Mario Filho quarter (named after the great player), the ground also hosts the home games of Rio's favourite team, **Flamengo**. When the visitors are city rivals **Fluminense**, the atmosphere is appropriately carnival-like. Unfortunately, the Maracanã is beginning to show its age. It has been badly maintained and was threatened with demolition in the 1990s. With crowds under 10,000 not unusual, the financial situation was dire.

It took an appeal from Pelé – who described Maracanã as a "sentimental and indispensable feature of Brazilian life" – before the Brazilian government agreed to fund modernisation. But the Maracanã still has problems. Parts of it are still unsafe, limiting capacity to around 80,000, and the latest threat comes from an unusual source: urine. Fans determined not to miss games by visiting the toilet are renowned for using the terraces as their own personal lavatory – as the Rio sport authority's president says: "From a very young age, Brazilians learn they can relieve themselves anywhere." Ammonia from the urine has penetrated the concrete and acted like acid on the steel girders, causing serious damage. The Maracanã's long-term future is still in doubt; let's hope the Brazilian fans haven't quite literally pissed their history up the wall.

> ***"English – you created soccer but we teach you how to play it"***
>
> *Fans' banner at the Maracana*

STAIR PARK

Stranraer's ground has been given the second part of its name with very good reason: it's slap bang in the middle of a picturesque public park (no word on the stairs, though). When the ball bounces out of the ground there are always a couple of pesky kids on hand to run away with it, and at one end of the stadium a team of boys are employed to fetch wayward shots out of trees and bushes.

Other park activities can interfere too: there's often orchestral music being piped through the air, as the ground is right next-door to the bandstand. Equally pleasant is the view of the sea from the back of the club's marvellous new main stand. Located a mere 90 minutes away from Northern Ireland, opposition fans often give Stranraer's support abuse for being Irish rather than Scots, but Blues fans have got the last laugh: supporters of the club get a discount on the Stena Line ferries to Belfast. And there aren't many clubs where you can arrive by boat.

ESTADIO NACIONAL

The magnificent Estadio Nacional in Lisbon is fast becoming Portugal's forgotten stadium. Perhaps it's the location – nestled deep in the peaceful pinewood forests 10km outside the capital. Or maybe it's the spate of arena-building sweeping across the nation in anticipation of Euro 2004 – the biggest sporting event Portugal has ever hosted. There's no doubt the Estadio Nacional has fallen behind the magnificent Da Luz ground in the pecking order, and the new José Alvalade stadium looks impressive, too. But it would be a shame if the old national stadium was to be overlooked entirely.

For starters, its history is rich: it was here that Bill Shankly told Jock Stein: "John, you're immortal" after his **Celtic** side (later nicknamed the Lisbon Lions) had won the UK's first European Cup in 1967, and there have been many great games since. There's also a serene woodland atmosphere that no other major stadium in the world can rival. Cut into the heart of the forest, the changing rooms and toilets are covered with weeds, while on the east side of the stadium, seats have been replaced with stone benches rising up to a vast, impressive marble rostrum. Throw in a huge mural of **Eusebio** in his pomp, and it's a one-off. Unfortunately, it doesn't see much action now: only the Portuguese Cup Final and athletic meetings come here these days.

MOLINEUX

There's something about a floodlit match – the cold, the way noise carries through the night air, the Bovril still on sale at some League grounds and the luminous green carpet of a pitch – that makes the game extra exciting. We're spoilt in the present age of twice-a-week Champions League matches, but back in the 1950s floodlit football was a real rarity. Leading the way were **Wolverhampton Wanderers**. Molineux became the first major British ground to be fitted with floodlights in the summer of 1953. The team celebrated in style by lining up a series of high-profile friendlies against the cream of European opposition – another first for the Black Country club, and a blueprint for exciting European nights to come at places like Anfield and Old Trafford.

Using a system of just 60 lamps, which cost just 7s6d (38p) to run for the night, Wolves' first opponents were a South African XI in September. The home side donned luminous satin shirts to take advantage of the lighting. Next came the likes of **Spartak Moscow** (who were beaten 4-0), **Racing Club** of Buenos Aires (defeated 3-1) and **Moscow Dynamo** (beaten 2-1). But it was the visit of

The legendary Billy Wright still presides over Molineux

Honved, "the best team in the world", that really won the flashy new set-up fame. Wolves beat the **Puskas**-inspired Hungarian champions, who had among their number several players who had recently beaten England 6-3 at Wembley.

Millions watched Wolves win 3-2 on TV that night (as well as the 54,998 fans in Molineux), and clubs soon began to follow suit and install floodlights themselves. The only people complaining were the local cinemas, who said night matches robbed them of business. Unfortunately, Wolves' fortunes on the pitch were on the wane within a decade. Molineux remained one of the finest stadiums in the country – even when one of its banks was little more than grass – and now finally has a decent team to grace it again. The massive orange arena recently saw itself promoted to the Premiership.

DRILL FIELD

The 3rd of May 2002 saw a piece of football history, as **Northwich Victoria** took on **Congleton Town**. It may not sound like a particularly enticing fixture, but the final whistle brought down the curtain on an incredible 128 uninterrupted years of football at one of the game's original homes – the Drill Field. Despite the efforts of local supporters' groups, Northwich had finally bowed to financial pressure and sold their stadium to be developed into a housing estate. "It's madness," said Clive Penny, treasurer of the Drill Field Trust, about the mooted move to a new stadium. "The Drill Field is our lifeline, in the centre of town and it's adequate for the crowds we're ever going to need." But the ground has now gone the same way as Wembley's twin towers. It brought to an end the stadium's proud record as "the oldest surviving football ground in the UK, therefore the world," according to the FA. Northwich had played there since 1874.

Other grounds have put in claims to rival the Drill's record, however. Bramall Lane is certainly very old, but the current front-runner as the UK's first pitch is London's Vincent Square, which has been the Westminster School's playing field since the 1850s. Also in with a claim is **Hallam FC** in Sheffield. Their field was used for cricket matches as early as 1804, and supporters claim football was played there in the 1850s, too. Northwich, meanwhile, are now ground-sharing with **Witton Albion** and looking to move into their new stadium soon.

> ***"It'll never replace plastic"***
>
> *Ray Harford – whose QPR team played on a synthetic pitch – inspects Coventry's grass effort*

GRIFFIN PARK

Brentford may not be the most glamourous club in the capital, but at least their 5,000 or so loyal punters are never short of a drink – the Bees' Griffin Park is the only ground in the country with a pub on every corner. It's perhaps unsurprising, considering that the land used to be owned by the Griffin Brewery (hence the name). The pubs – The Griffin, The Royal Oak, The Princess Royal and The New Inn – are all pretty friendly, even being described as "quaint" on one fans' website. That's certainly a rarity inside Greater London's football territory, so many away fans arrive early in a bid to drink a pint in all four alehouses before the game (**Stan Bowles** can normally be found in one of the quartet, holding court).

It may not last though: Brentford announced in November 2002 that they were hoping to sell Griffin Park and move to a new stadium a mile away. With the old place looking pretty run-down – one stand still doesn't have a roof, though the others are a lucrative form of aerial advertising as they are visible from planes landing at nearby Heathrow – many are keen for the new stadium plans to go ahead, though progress to date has been slow. Their only gripe will be about the lack of boozers. As one website editorial runs sternly: "If the move goes ahead, expect pressure from fans to move our pubs brick by brick."

VICTORIA ROAD

It's certainly seen some strange happenings over the years, Victoria Road. **Hartlepool United** were the unluckiest club in the country during the First World War: the ground managed to take a direct hit from German bombing before aerial bombardment was even fashionable. In 1916, a German zeppelin on a bombing mission to the Teesside industrial area found itself under attack from a Royal Flying Corps pilot, and was forced to jettison its load over Victoria Road. The main wooden grandstand was destroyed. A "temporary" replacement was erected instead – which lasted until the 1980s.

As if that wasn't enough, the ground's mascot, H'Angus the Monkey, was recently elected the Mayor of Hartlepool on a "free bananas for schoolchildren" platform. The simian talisman is well-known for his antics at Victoria Road. Few, however, expected him to win the £53,000-a-year job – much to the embarrassment of Downing Street, and the delight of the Hartlepool faithful, who haven't had much to cheer since Brian Clough kicked off his managerial career at the club. Perhaps we shouldn't be surprised at these bizarre antics – the side are known as the Monkey Hangers, after locals apocryphally lynched a chimp they mistook for a French spy during the Napoleonic wars.

NOU CAMP

The Nou Camp is more than just a football stadium. For 118,000 regular visitors, it is their (unrecognised) country's headquarters, a cathedral of all things Catalan. Far more than **Barcelona**'s footballing pedigree (which in continental terms is fairly average – they've won the European Cup just once), the stadium and its fanatical support are what make Barça one of the biggest clubs in the world.

The side's popular appeal has always been massive. Moving to a larger ground became necessary way back in 1950, when Slovakian superstar **Ladislao Kubala**'s lure meant the old Les Corts stadium – which held an impressive 60,000 – was simply not big enough. Club president Galobart purchased the land from which the new stadium would rise, but it took seven years, 288 million pesetas and a new president (Francesc Miró-Sans) before the Nou Camp was ready for action. It was worth the wait. An amazing 93,000 could pack inside, and the site has subsequently seen visits from some of the best-known people on earth – from Bruce Springsteen to the Pope. Indeed, God's emissary on earth preached to a full house before being presented with Barcelona membership card number 108,000 – presumably laminated as "His Holiness". There have been several other candidates for

A policeman and horse double the average gate at Hartlepool's Victoria Road

WARTIME GROUNDS

"Uwe Rosler's granddad bombed Old Trafford," read a popular Manchester City T-shirt in the mid-1990s, as the fans attempted to annoy their Mancunian rivals. While Rosler senior probably wasn't implicated directly, it's certainly true that United's famous ground was heavily damaged by German bombing during World War Two. All around the country, bitter football foes pulled together to help each other in the face of a common enemy. City even let United play their home games at Maine Road after a 1941 raid destroyed United's main stand and terracing. Arsenal and Spurs may baulk at the thought of a North London groundshare nowadays, but as the blitz pounded the capital, the Gunners played home games at White Hart Lane. A 1,000-pound bomb had destroyed the roof of the North Bank, and the rest of Highbury was being used as an Air Raid Patrol Centre. Meanwhile, Birmingham's St Andrews was shut down by the chief constable, who was worried about air raids. Quite rightly, it transpired: the ground was hit 18 times, and the Blues shared Villa Park. Even Southampton ended up playing a few games at Portsmouth's Fratton Park after The Dell sustained bomb damage. Swindon Town's County Ground became a POW camp, with huts built on it, while Tranmere Rovers' Prenton Park was used to send out smoke signals to confuse German aircraft looking to bomb Liverpool docks. Even the national stadium did not escape. Wembley's pitch was oil-bombed – there wasn't much damage, but it was messy.

CULT FANS *Supporters-turned-stars*

KEN BAILEY

Now sadly passed to the great Wembley in the sky, Bailey was a ubiquitous and instantly recognisable England fan clad from head to toe in red, white and blue. A diminutive, balding civil servant from Bournemouth, his top hat and tails were always picked out by the 1960s TV cameras at England games.

DR FUN

The Scouse Ken Bailey. Liverpool FC's most famous Kopite, Dr Fun has been unmissable since the 1960s at Anfield in his red top hat and tails (with "Hiya Kids" sewn on the back). Accompanied at all times by his personal mini-me – dummy Liverpool Charlie – and a loud horn. Fun is really named Lenny Campbell and is a former seaman, lifeguard, club compere and Butlins redcoat from Huyton.

HELEN "THE BELL" TURNER

A legend on Moss Side, Mrs Turner is an 83-year old who has been following City longer than anyone can remember, urging on the team by ringing her bell. She was given a standing ovation by the faithful during the last game at Maine Road.

MANOLO THE DRUMMER

Always seen in the heart of the Spanish crowd, home or away, beating out a chant of "ES-PA-NA" on a drum, with forearms like ham shanks. Owns a bar opposite the Mestalla Stadium in Valencia, adorned with pictures of himself and his drum.

JOHN MR PORTSMOUTH FOOTBALL CLUB WESTWOOD

Love him or loathe him – and his incessant bugle and bell playing will assist you in the decision-making process – Westwood, who changed his name by deed poll, is the public face of Pompey's travelling charm offensive. This heavily tattooed antiquarian bookseller (honest) is strangely reminiscent of the childcatcher in *Chitty Chitty Bang Bang* in a garish top hat.

THE BIRDMAN

Colombia's travelling mascot and possibly the most famous fan in the world, the spectacular birdman is clad from head to toe in yellow and blue feathers and performs death-defying stunts to prove his extreme devotion to the cause. His greatest moment came during USA '94 when he was lowered from an upper tier on a wire so that he could flap his support from a great height above his countrymen.

TANGO MAN

Well-proportioned Sheffield Wednesday supporter Paul Gregory decided to paint his entire upper half orange (including bald head) before going to the match, soon evolving into the legendary "Tango Man". First came to national attention during a Rumbelows Cup fixture in 1991 when he stripped off in sub-zero temperatures. Often accessorises with a giant orange hand.

beatification on the famous pitch over the years too: it's said in Barça that if Kubala built the Nou Camp, **Johan Cruyff** filled it, and **Diego Maradona** meant the ground was too small. The little Argentine's genius helped to pack out an arena expanded to over 100,000 for the 1982 World Cup (where the Nou Camp had the honour of hosting the opening game). It's only improved since, with a full refurbishment taking place to celebrate the club's centenary in 1999.

Plans are afoot for more improvements to the surrounding area. What's more, the Nou Camp recently welcomed its 10 millionth visitor: a dinnerlady from **Stockport**. Stella Hughes, 64, was given the prize of a signed shirt and trip to see Barça play, despite the fact she doesn't like football and only went along because her husband wanted to visit the ground.

GLEBE PARK

Some clubs go out of their way to provide visitors with an intimidating welcome: towering stands, grand gateposts, "Welcome to Hell" banners – that sort of thing. Not **Brechin City**. At their charming Glebe Park ground, away fans are greeted by a lovely hedge. It runs around the entire perimeter of the stadium, carefully trimmed, and is, all in all, rather nice.

The topiary doesn't end there, though. Once inside Glebe Park, visitors won't be able to help but notice that one side of the ground – known officially as "Far Side and Hedge" – is indeed another well-tended hedgerow. As if that wasn't pleasant enough, the Main Stand, which accommodates just 300 punters, is charmingly overlooked by a church spire. The largest stand is the Trinity Road End, which seats 1,000. As Brechin's average attendance is around 450, booking tickets in advance isn't necessary. The arena may strike you as somewhere more suitable for a game of bowls than football, but at least there's a real personality to Brechin. Make your way round to the rear of the Centenary Terrace and you'll find the names and hand-prints of many of the supporters have been set into the concrete, Hollywood Boulevard-style.

OLYMPIC STADIUM

There can't be many venues more beautiful or historic than the Olympic Stadium, Stockholm – home of the Swedish capital's current top side, **Djurgårdens FC**. Built for the 1912 Olympics, the ground retains original features of castle towers, ivy-clad walls and decorated columns. Fans can admire walrus heads carved into the magnet-shaped dome's walls, completed by two tall towers and a beautiful arcade inspired by the Colosseum. There are sculptures of

Ask and Embla (the first human beings in Nordic mythology) and around 80 other carvings on the outside facades. It's more than you can say for Wembley.

The site was designed by ambitious young architect Torben Grut, who was personally selected by Victor Balck – the father of Swedish sports – to help bring the Olympics to Stockholm in 1912. The games and stadium were a roaring success. Among the highlights was Jim Thorpe, a 24-year-old American Indian who won both the pentathlon and decathlon. "You, Sir, are the greatest athlete in the world," Sweden's King Gustav V told him at the medal ceremony. Thorpe replied: "Thanks, King."

OLD TRAFFORD

Despite **Roy Keane** recently taking a swipe at Old Trafford's limp atmosphere and dismissing some fans as being more interested in eating prawn sandwiches in their corporate boxes than watching the football, it is still one of the finest stadiums in the world. Old Trafford has played host to 93 years of **Manchester United** history (Sir Bobby Charlton famously once called it "The Theatre of Dreams" for all the glory he had witnessed there), World Cup and European Championship games, two FA Cup finals, and in May 2003 became the first British club stadium to stage the Champions League final.

It was hailed as "the most remarkable arena" by the Sporting Chronicle when it opened for business in February 1910. Built at a cost of £60,000, and with a capacity of 80,000, Liverpool were the first visitors and played the role of party poopers by winning 4-3.

Old Trafford's famous Stretford End, home of United's most vocal fans, was bulldozed at the start of the nineties, and coupled with United's dominance on the home front, it means that Premiership games can sometimes lack atmosphere. However, the stadium can still crackle with an awesome energy and excitement, especially on European nights under the floodlights. "When you go out on to the pitch, it's like switching on a radio and turning the volume up," says **George Best**. "One moment there is silence, the next you are swamped in an amphitheatre of noise. I can still recall the way the hairs on my neck when I first went out. It was truly exhilarating."

THE BERNABEU

The story of **Real Madrid**'s stadium is the story of the one man – Don Santiago Bernabeu – who fired Real Madrid to greatness. A close friend and ally of General

Just a few of the eighty-odd pitches available at Hackney Marshes

Franco (for whom Real was a plaything), Bernabeu played for the club as a teenager alongside his brother Marcelo in the 1920s. The ground was far more humble back then: they played at Campo O'Donnell – a pitch next to a rubbish tip that these days is a Disney theme park.

By the 1930s Bernabeu was on the board at Real, and although the civil war interrupted matters, by the Second World War he had become club president. By 1953 Real had the finest stadium in the country, and **di Stefano** and co to fill it with magic. Located on one of the Spanish capital's main avenues, the Bernabeu feels right at the heart of Madrid, ringed with bars, elegant plazas and palaces. Holding 106,000, the Bernabeu has hosted every major game in world football – including a World Cup final, three European Cup finals and a European Championship final, as well as those of Europe's most successful club side.

HACKNEY MARSHES

They may call Old Trafford the Theatre of Dreams, but if you want to see thousands of football aspirations being acted out all at once, you'd be better off heading to Hackney Marshes. Every weekend players of all shapes, ages, sizes, races and abilities congregate on an expanse of green in north-east London to try to emulate their personal heroes. The Marshes represent what's happening all over the UK on a grand scale: with 87 full-size pitches, Hackney possesses the largest collection of playing fields in Europe, hosting over 100 matches on the sport's traditional grass roots day – Sunday.

There are dozens of teams contesting numerous leagues: for men, women, children and different ethnic communities. This can sometimes lead to tension: Turkish teams, for example, are kept on the northern half of the Marshes, as far away as possible from the Kurdish sides at the southern end. The Marshes were originally bogland, and were filled in by debris left over from air raids on London during the Second World War. By the end of the war, 350 acres had been reclaimed. Inevitably, the pitches have been graced by some of the finest Cockney players ever in their early careers, including the most famous sportsman on the planet, **David Beckham**. **Terry Venables**, **Ian Wright**, **Paul Ince** and **Ugo Ehiogu** are other notables to stride out onto the famous pitches. None of them can compete with **Fred Rosner**, mind. The Austrian came to the UK during the war, founded his own side, **Downham FC**, and has now played over 2,000 games on the fields. He was still playing at the age of 76.

THE NUMBERS

The figures that make the football world go round

Malcolm Allison indicates how many models were in his bath today

"Both sides have scored a couple of goals, and both sides have conceded a couple of goals"

Peter Withe

Figures are the stuff football is made of. Without the stats, we'd never be able to prove **Andy Cole** was a better **Manchester United** forward than **George Best** or that **Steve Guppy** is a more accurate crosser than **David Beckham**. Countless pub arguments have been settled since the advent of the Opta Index.

Certain numbers have taken on a special significance. To followers of Brazil and Argentina, the number 10 shirt will always represent, respectively, **Pelé** and **Diego Maradona** (the latter shirt was retired at one point so as not to burden promising young Argentines with the weight of history). At the other end of the scale, seven current Premiership clubs (**Birmingham**, **Bolton**, **Fulham**, **Leicester**, **Manchester City**, **Middlesbrough** and **Southampton**) do not have an "unlucky" number 13 on their books.

The seven shirt has traditionally been British sides' most treasured number, worn by artists like Best, Beckham and **Cantona** at Manchester United and **Dalglish** and **Keegan** at **Liverpool**. At **Sporting Lisbon**, however, the seven is avoided like the plague, having been a source of constant misfortune since **Luis Figo** vacated it in 1995. Five different players have worn it in that time; two missed whole seasons with injuries before leaving the club, two more never settled and left, and one – Bulgarian **Ivaylo Yordanov** – had just recovered from a major car accident when he was diagnosed with multiple sclerosis. The last wearer of the shirt, **Marius Niculae**, asked for the number nine instead.

Twenty-three is Beckham's number at **Real Madrid**, apparently modelled on basketball superstar **Michael Jordan**. It hasn't proved too lucky for Jordan, however, whose father was killed in a hold-up on 23rd July, 1993. Manchester City and **Cameroon** both retired the 23 shirt after **Marc Vivien Foe** died while wearing it in 2003. Several apocalyptic cults, including those who believe in the "Illuminati", have adopted 23 as a sign of evil – 2+3=5, which represents the Devil's pentangle, while two divided by three is 0.666. W is the 23rd letter of the alphabet, and the internet (or "WWW") is the root of all evil. Good luck, Becks...

Without his lucky cap, Lev Yashin was powerless to stop the shots flying past him

1

Lev Yashin may or may not be the greatest goalkeeper the game has ever seen but he was certainly the most persistent. Most boys might have surrendered all thoughts of the sporting life after they'd failed as an athlete, boxer, basketball player and, finally, as a centre-forward in the factory football team. But after finding a niche keeping goal in ice hockey for the Dynamo sports club in Moscow, he grew to hero-worship **Alexei Khomich**, who kept goal for the club's football team, and decided to switch sports. After two years on the bench, he came on as a sub in 1951 only to concede a goal within minutes. But he kept going, accruing caps (78 in all for the USSR), honours (he is the only keeper to have been voted European Footballer of the Year) and nicknames. Journalists couldn't decide which animal to compare him to (the options included octopus, spider and panther). But then Yashin had always been hard to categorise. As a lanky, ungainly schoolboy his classmates regarded him as a freak. As a lanky, graceful No 1 he kept 270 clean sheets, saved 150 penalties and wore two caps every time he ran onto the pitch – one was always stashed behind the goal.

Only **one** team have won the World Cup outside their own continent: Brazil. And they've managed it twice – in vastly different surroundings. Back in 1958 the team of **Pelé** and **Garrincha** travelled to Sweden, and topped a group that contained England and the Soviet Union en route to lifting the trophy after a 5-2 win over the hosts. Then in 2002, in the first finals hosted in the Far East, **Ronaldo**, **Rivaldo** and **Denilson** shone as the Brazilians breezed past World Cup perennials Germany in the final in Yokohama.

Also, "**one** team in Tallinn" was the now-legendary chant of the Scottish fans who made the trip to the Estonian capital for a game that kicked off with only Scotland on the pitch due to a dispute over the start time.

Miodrag Belodedici was the first eastern European to win the European Cup twice

Remember **two** points for a win? That was the way it used to work in the English Football League until 1981 when three points was instigated to spur teams on to attack.

"**Two**-horse race" has been the most overused phrase in English football over the last decade as **Manchester United** and **Arsenal** continue to keep their distance from the rest of the Premiership. Will Chelsea make it three?

Steaua Bucharest may have only scored **two** out of their four penalties in the 1986 European Cup final but that was **two** more than **Barcelona** in one of the lowest-scoring penalty shoot-outs in history. **Miodrag Belodedici** didn't take a spot-kick that night for Steaua but deserved his winner's medal. Five years later, when **Red Star Belgrade** became the second east European side to win the world's biggest club competition, Belodedici was in that Yugoslav side too.

Gunnar Gren: Albert Camus lookalike and one of a deadly trio of Milan strikers

3

Football has seen many great trios. Given the nationality of novelist Alexander Dumas and the title of his most famous book, any trio of gifted French players has been doomed to be dubbed "the **Three** Musketeers" since the combination of **Just Fontaine**, **Raymond Kopa** and **Roger Piantoni** in the 1950s. The great Swedish trio of **Gunnar Gren**, **Gunnar Nordahl** and **Nils Liedholm**, who helped make **AC Milan** one of the strongest teams in Europe in the 1950s, escaped the same fate only because they were born in Sweden and played their finest football in Italy's Serie A. The Gre-No-Li forward line, as it was dubbed, migrated south in 1949, just a year after winning their country the Olympic title. The **three** Swedes were almost as influential at AC in the 1950s, a decade in which the "Old Man" won four Scudetti, as three Dutchmen (**Ruud Gullit**, **Marco van Basten** and **Frank Rijkaard**) would be in the late 1980s and early 1990s.

For **three** successive seasons in the 1950s, **Leeds United** got drawn at home to **Cardiff City** in the FA Cup third round and, three times out of three, lost out 2-1 (or, to put it another way, the odd goal in **three**). Leeds did, however, manage to notch a win the next time the Bluebirds came to Elland Road (in the old Second Division in the 1962-63 season) – by **three** goals to nil.

Only **three** clubs have, to date, won the Premiership. **Blackburn** joined the exclusive club back in 1994-95, but since then Manchester United and Arsenal have made the title all theirs. Which presumably means that Messrs **Dalglish**, **Ferguson** and **Wenger** must be the **Three** Wise Monkeys.

Cypriots **Apoel Nicosia** have conceded double-figure scores in Europe **three** times (all in the Cup Winners' Cup), the only club with this unwanted record.

The Milan side of Ruud Gullit (left) and Mauro Tassotti didn't need to see the ball

The number of goals **AC Milan** scored against Steaua Bucharest in the 1989 European Cup final in Barcelona – and against Barcelona in the 1994 European Cup final in Athens. Often unfairly tagged a team of millionaires, the Milan of **Silvio Berlusconi**, **Arrigo Sacchi**, **Ruud Gullit** and **Marco van Basten** was the first Italian club side to be tactically innovative since **Helenio Herrera**'s **Inter Milan** updated *catenacccio* in the 1960s. Under Sacchi, Milan reinvented the classic 4-4-2 formation, introducing the pressing game. The back four would play up the field, constantly looking for the offside trap, and the midfield four would hunt in packs when they lost possession, retaining their shape when they had the ball to play quick, short passes. In black and white, it sounds almost prosaic, but as demonstrated by the likes of Gullit, van Basten and Dejan Savicevic, it seemed closer to poetry.

Four clubs have been managed by current Manchester United supremo **Sir Alex Ferguson**. He served his managerial apprenticeship at **East Stirlingshire** (where he would take to the streets with a megaphone to implore locals to come to the games), **St Mirren** and then **Aberdeen** – whom he steered to victory over Real Madrid in the 1983 European Cup Winners' Cup – before getting the nod from Martin Edwards to take the reins at Old Trafford.

And **four** was the number of times keeper **Gordon Banks** touched the ball when England played Malta in May 1971... from **four** backpasses.

Duncan Edwards, England's number five, who died in the Munich disaster

The number of the England shirt worn, all too briefly, by **Duncan Edwards**, the greatest of the Manchester United players to die in the Munich air disaster in 1958. His team-mate **Bobby Charlton**, himself one of the greatest players ever to wear an England and United shirt, said of him: "When I think of Duncan, I feel the rest of us were like pygmies". If he had not died from his injuries (typically, lying fatally injured in his Munich hospital bed, he asked the club coach: "What time's the kick-off against Wolves? I can't afford to miss that one") he might have led England to victory in 1966 instead of **Bobby Moore**.

Malcolm MacDonald struck all **five** England goals as **Don Revie**'s team battered Cyprus in a European Championship qualifier at Wembley on 16 April, 1975. Super Mac's' five-goal haul remains a record for an England player.

Five penalties were given by Bolivian referee **Ulysses Saucedo** in the 1930 World Cup finals game between Argentina and Mexico, a record for the tournament.

And **five** seconds was how long it took **Vinnie Jones** to get booked – a feat he managed twice, once playing for **Sheffield United** against Manchester City in 1991, and for **Chelsea** against the Blades a year later.

Liverpool boss Joe Fagan takes the European Cup (and a friend) on his travels

6

Liverpool, Liverpool, Nottingham Forest, Nottingham Forest, Liverpool and Aston Villa. That was the order in which, from 1977 to 1982, English clubs won the European Cup six times in a row. Apart from the 1977 final, in which Liverpool beat **Borussia Moenchengladbach** 3-1, the finals weren't great spectacles. Still, it's hard to begrudge **Nottingham Forest** winger John Robertson his moment of glory. His European Cup-winning goal against Hamburg in 1980 was recompense for his manager Brian Clough calling him "a fat dumpy lad who lives out of a frying pan, but give him a ball and some grass and he becomes Picasso". Liverpool won the European Cup again in 1984.

Previously, Spain had held the honour of the most consecutive European Cup wins. That was courtesy of the barnstorming **Real Madrid** side of the 1950s who reigned supreme for the first five years of the competition, but that run was ended by **Benfica** in 1961 despite Ferenc Puskas scoring a hat-trick in the final.

George Best, in his first game back after suspension, scored six goals – the highest by a Manchester United player in a single game – against **Northampton Town** in the fifth round of the 1970 FA Cup.

Stanley Matthews: always a competitor, even when playing on sand

The shirt number of right-wingers (footballers not politicians), from beefy, beer-loving Helmut Rahn to Stanley Matthews, David Beckham, "Jinky" Jimmy Johnstone, Grigorz Lato (a right-winger as a player and now a left-winger as a member of the Polish parliament) and the less-famous Neville Coleman, still the only British winger to score seven goals in one League game – for Stoke City against Lincoln City in 1957. Rahn is the maverick West German winger who, in the 1954 World Cup final, featured in his country's most famous line of football commentary: "Aus dem Hintergrund musste Rahn schiessen… Rahn schiesst! Tor! Tor! Tor!"

Seven is the highest number of goals ever conceded by England and came at the hands of the Magical Magyars – the Hungarian side of Ferenc Puskas and co of the 1950s. In a friendly played in Budapest on 23 May, 1954, Puskas and Sandor Kocsis both scored twice, with Mihaly Lantos, Nandor Hidegkuti and Jozsef Toth completing the scoring for the home team, to the visitors' embarassment. Manchester City's Ivor Broadis got England's consolation.

Wales lost by the same scoreline to the Netherlands in November 1996, as a Dutch side including the likes of Dennis Bergkamp, Clarence Seedorf and Frank de Boer ran riot in a World Cup qualifying game in Eindhoven.

Hristo Stoichkov, famous number eight and conqueror of the Germans in 1994

8

Since the war, **Juventus** have never gone more than **eight** seasons without winning the Scudetto. La Vecchia Signora ("The Old Lady") have won the Italian championship at least once in each of the last nine decades – a haul of 21 Scudetti, nine Copa Italias, three Uefa Cups, two World Club Cups, one European Cup and one European Cup Winner's Cup ensures the club is always having to fret about the size of its trophy cabinet. Although Juve are now synonymous with the Agnelli family, the owners of Fiat, they started out much more humbly. The club was founded by students in 1897 with kit loosely modelled on **Notts County**'s, thanks to the involvement of local British expats.

After France '98, when injury and illness prevented him from living up to the considerable pre-tournament hype, **Ronaldo** bounced back to form with **eight** goals for Brazil at the 2002 World Cup finals (including two in the final itself) to win the Golden Shoe award. It was the first time since the 1974 World Cup finals in Germany that any player had made it past the six-goal mark.

Eight was also the shirt number worn by Bulgarian legend Hristo Stoichkov as his country recorded a memorable quarter-final victory over the Germans in the 1994 World Cup. Bulgaria lost the semi-final to Italy. In his final appearance for CSKA in his homeland, Stoichkov wore the number four shirt – the number of goals he had scored against rivals Levski Sofia the week before.

Real's Alfredo di Stefano was the first player to truly let his football do the talking

9

While **Pelé** and **Maradona** will always vie for the honour of being the game's perfect 10, it is generally recognised that the art of centre-forward play was mastered to greatest effect by **Alfredo di Stefano**. George Best speaks of him in hushed tones as the finest footballer he ever saw ,while Best's mentor **Sir Matt Busby** said of The White Arrow: "He was one of the greatest, if not the greatest, footballers I have ever seen. At that time we had forwards and defenders doing separate jobs, but he did everything". As reticent off the field as he was eloquent on it, di Stefano won five European Cups in the all-white of Real, and, after becoming a naturalised Spaniard, was twice voted European Footballer of the Year. He was, as one journalist put it: "A man of supreme energy and science who hardly moved his boot at all when he shot, gliding the ball in as nonchalantly as if he was stamping on grapes".

Nine is also traditionally the number worn by the main striker, though in the era of squad numbers, the Golden Boot is now likely to go to someone wearing something else. (In the 1999 European Cup final, Inter's **Ivan Zamorano** wore the numbers 1 + 8 because Ronaldo was wearing the prized nine shirt.)

Nine England players have been given their marching orders – Alan Mullery (against Yugoslavia in Florence, 5 June, 1968), Alan Ball (Poland in Chorzow, 6 June, 1973), Trevor Cherry (Argentina in Buenos Aires, 12 June, 1977), Ray Wilkins (Morocco in Monterrey, 6 June, 1986), David Beckham (Argentina in St Etienne, 30 June, 1998), Paul Ince (Sweden in Stockholm, 5 September, 1998), Paul Scholes (Sweden in London, 5 June, 1999), David Batty (Poland in Warsaw, 8 September, 1999), and Alan Smith (Macedonia, 16 October 2002).

San Marino go nuts as they score from kick-off against England – and so do the fans

10

San Marino have never conceded more than 10 goals in an international. Norway racked up double figures against the men from this independent enclave of northern Italy in Oslo in September 1992. Since then, these part-time professionals have kept scorelines semi-respectable as they search for their first victory. So far, the closest they've come is two 0-0 draws: one against Lebanon and one against Turkey in a 1993 World Cup qualifier. While 48 games without a win is a record in international football, it's no disgrace given that you could fit the country's entire population into the San Siro and still have room for 8,000 Milan fans. San Marino were famed for being the only country whose lead goalscorer had bagged the grand total of one goal in international football. **Andy Selva** now has three to his credit, although he didn't score his country's most famous goal, after eight seconds against England in 1993.

Ten was the number favoured by the mercurial but flawed **Diego Maradona** for both club and country – and as such will be etched on the mind of every England fan, unable to shake the image of Maradona's outstretched arm knocking the ball past England goalkeeper **Peter Shilton**. (Or, for that matter, the image of Diego dancing through the massed ranks of the England defence for goal number two.)

Rosenborg players hear that Skonto Riga have gone a goal down

11

Rosenborg won their 11th League title in a row in Norway in 2002, a record bettered only by Latvia's **Skonta Riga**. **Dynamo Tbilisi** and **Dynamo Berlin** (now known as **FC Berlin**) won 10 in a row in Georgia and Germany respectively. As the official team of the East German secret police, the Stasi, Berlin's winning streak – from 1979 to 1988 – was marred by bizarre refereeing decisions and players being ordered to turn out for the side. Rosenborg's story is as unusual, if more uplifting. Coach **Nils Arne Eggen** could have been a ski-jumper, his first love, and admits that he switched to football as a teenager as much out of sheer cowardice as love of the beautiful game. It's also worth noting that all but two of Rosenborg's first team are Norwegian.

Eleven is not only the total number of players in a starting line-up but the total number allowed full-stop until 1965, when substitutes were introduced to the game (initially just for injuries but later for any reason) and those sides relying on a more "agricultural" tactical approach (ie kicking lumps out of the opposition to reduce the numbers) were forced to rethink.

Eleven goals is also a record for Scotland, Wales… and Ireland. For both Scotland and Wales, 11-0 is their most emphatic win and in both cases (the Welsh game in March 1888, the game involving Scotland in February 1901) the hapless victims were the Irish – who also had to endure a further 11-goal defeat in the same period, losing 13-2 to England in February 1899.

12

The highest number of goals scored in a single game at any World Cup finals. The two protagonists were Alpine neighbours Austria and Switzerland, with the former edging out the latter (and tournament hosts) 7-5 on 26 June, 1954.

Twelve is also the number of goals Pelé scored in World Cup finals tournaments – a total young pretender Ronaldo equalled in double-quick time. Pelé found the net six times in Sweden in 1958, once in each of the ill-fated (for him, anyway) 1962 and 1966 tournaments and four more times in 1970, including the final against Italy. His fellow Brazilian notched four in 1998 and an incredible eight in 2002.

THE CULTURE

Music, movies, books and comics – and Jossie's Giants

Superstars-era Kevin Keegan makes his bid for chart domination

> ***"Even readers of the* Boys' Own Paper *might have blanched – ludicrous beyond belief"***
>
> *Newspaper review of* Escape To Victory

FOOTBALL GOES TO HOLLYWOOD

You're 4-1 down at half-time. You're also down to 10 men as your star player has been carried off with a broken rib; the referee is bent in the opposition's favour; and your goalkeeper is a big-mouthed tosspot with two left feet and an understanding of the beautiful game that could be written on the back of a postage stamp with a thick black felt tip pen.

In a situation like this most people would pray for the ground to open up and swallow them. Incredibly, this is exactly what happens. A huge hole appears in the changing room bath, giving the players a heaven-sent opportunity to escape from the inevitable humiliation of the second half. Do they take it? Do they hell.

For reasons unfathomable to those watching, the players remain convinced they can win the game, and duly ignore the gaping hole. The only one who takes persuading (understandably in view of his first-half performance) is the keeper. But instead of hanging him upside down from a clothes hook and administering Deep Heat to his genitals, his team-mates beg him to continue. He justifies their touching faith with a blinding second-half display, saving a penalty in the last minute to secure a remarkable 4-4 draw.

John Huston made some great films, but *Escape To Victory* (the climax of which is outlined above) is not one of them. Its biggest flaw can be summed up in two words: Sylvester Stallone. Playing a character inspired by Steve McQueen's part in *The Great Escape* – minus the charm – Stallone is the solitary American internee in a German POW camp otherwise occupied by stereotyped British officers, instantly recognisable by the stiffness of their upper lips.

Unlike the Brits, Stallone – or Hatch as he is called in the film – is granted certain privileges by the Nazis. These include a personal supply of biological washing powder to keep his singlets and grandpa T-shirts sparkling white, and access to huge quantities of high-protein rations and a body-building gymnasium, to make sure he's fit enough to knock out Dolph Lundgren in his next feature film.

Unlike Hatch, John Colby (Michael Caine) has a scruffy uniform and a middle-aged paunch. Despite his appearance, he is in fact a former **West Ham United** and England footballer, whose working class origins are revealed in his London accent and his contempt for his fellow British officers. Colby accepts a challenge posed by Max von Sydow (playing the honourable German: the sort of role James Mason used to specialise in) to organise a football team from the prisoners to play a local German outfit.

Colby knows that British officers play rugger not soccer, so he insists on being able to choose his team from the enlisted men. This gives him access to several star players, all of whom seem to be called Terry, but are really **Bobby Moore**, **John Wark**, **Kevin Beattie** and **Mike Summerbee** in disguise. When the Germans move the goalposts by deciding to field a full international side, Colby strengthens his squad by demanding players from other Allied nations. A Trinidadian prisoner bearing an uncanny resemblance to **Pelé**, and a skinny fellow who looks like just like **Ossie Ardiles**, join the team. And from the labour camps of eastern Europe come **Kazimierz Deyna** and some skeletal actors with non-speaking parts.

> ***"He might be a great action man, but when it comes to football he hasn't got a bloody clue"***
> *Kevin Beattie on Sylvester Stallone*

Displaying a modicum of judgment, Colby decides there is no place in his all-star eleven for Hatch. But by listening to a radio made from paper clips and bits of string, the senior British officers realise the game – now due to be played in the centre of Paris – is really a fiendish Nazi propaganda exercise, the damage of which can only be averted by arranging a daring escape for the whole team. So Hatch has to slip out of the prison camp, make his way to Paris, contact the Resistance, have a brief fling with a gorgeous, pouting French minx, and then allow himself to be recaptured so that he can relay the escape plan to the rest of the team – a mission he accomplishes with such ease it's a wonder the other prisoners haven't bothered to try it.

But Hatch gets locked up in solitary confinement on return to the camp, and Colby can only get him released in time to learn of the escape plans by insisting the brooding, muscle-bound hero is his team's goalkeeper, now that his first-choice player has broken his arm. The Nazis find this sufficiently unlikely to insist on seeing the shattered limb, so Kevin O'Calloghan displays true British pluck by volunteering to have his arm subjected to heavy assault.

Before the game gets underway it's revealed that the referee has orders to ensure the Nazis win. Once the whistle has blown it also becomes clear that the ref is unaware of any Fifa directives outlawing the cynical tackle from behind,

CULT GERMAN FOOTBALL MOVIES

***Füssball Wie Noch Nie* (Football As Never Before)**

In the 1960s, there emerged in Germany a group of experimental film-makers who were obsessed with testing the limits of the medium rather than telling a story. One of them was Hellmuth Costard, who made a 1969 film called *The Oppression Of Women Is Mainly Discernible Through The Behaviour Of Women Themselves*, in which a woman – played by a man – does housework (and nothing else). A year later, Costard went one step further and filmed the 12th September match between Manchester United and Coventry City. All six cameras were on only one player – George Best. The resulting film runs for 105 minutes and has virtually no dialogue. Sometimes you can catch a glimpse of other players or even the ball, but for the most part you stare at Best standing on the pitch, and you listen to the crowd reacting to something you don't see.

***Das Grosse Spiel* (The Big Game)**

Das Grosse Spiel was made in July and August 1941 and released a year later, yet it is not a Nazi propaganda film. In fact it's a rather old-fashioned love story. The new player for the fictitious club Gloria 03 falls for an official's daughter but has to prove his worth before winning her heart. He does that by leading his team to the championship final and scoring the sudden-death winner. What sounds mundane is made remarkable by Sepp Herberger's contribution. The national manager (who would win the 1954 World Cup) brought many internationals to the set to make the match sequences more credible – and to get them away from the battlefront. He also came up with the idea of mounting movable cameras behind the goals, something which became commonplace only in the 1990s.

even when Dutch veteran **Co Prins** is scythed down like a tree uprooted by a Panzer tank. Typically, this is ignored by the German match commentator (**Anton Differing** performing a second-rate impression of David Coleman in jackboots) who raves as the ruthless Nazis rack up the goals.

With the help of a distinctly dubious penalty, clinically dispatched by the unsmiling German captain, the Allies approach half-time four goals behind and without Pelé, who has been forced to retire to the dugout after his efforts to play the beautiful game have been thwarted by defensive techniques learned from unarmed combat training manuals. But then the impossible happens: an unmarked Bobby Moore makes a late run into the German six-yard box to tap in a long cross from **Russell Osman** at the far post. Terry has scored and the Allies have discovered total football.

After refusing the chance to escape, Colby and the boys come out for the second half to give the complacent Master Race a good stuffing. Bewildered by the Allies' free-ranging movements and revolutionary tactics, the Third Reich's marking goes to pot. Ardiles is given the freedom of the park and, before you know it, the Allies have pulled two back and are looking for an equaliser. This is Pelé's cue, and he returns to the pitch, ignoring the pain of his broken rib. After his dazzling footwork leaves the whole German team falling dizzily into crumpled heaps, he crops up again to power an overhead kick into the gaping mouth of the Nazi net. In fact he does it several times, from different angles, twice in slow motion, and each time it goes in.

Ze Parisian crowd zey go wild, and just to prove again that he really is the decent, honourable sort of German who will go on to become a leading light in the post-war world, Max von Sydow leaps to his feet in spontaneous applause.

They thought it was all over. But it wasn't. An innocuous challenge by Ardiles in his own penalty area gives a German striker the chance to perform a manoeuvre later perfected by **Jurgen Klinsmann**. The referee has no hesitation in pointing to the spot. Can Hatch make the catch to save the match?

Natch. The penalty is feebly struck, and at just the height goalkeepers like, even this one. Before the ref can order it to be retaken and caution Hatch for wearing a jersey unbuttoned to the navel, the crowd follows the time-honoured **Millwall** practice of invading the pitch, encouraged by the Wehrmacht's unaccountable failure to provide any of their guards with ammunition for their guns. The barricades are swept aside and the players, disguised in suspiciously 1970s-looking clothing, are carried shoulder-high through the exits.

> ***"What kind of game is this anyway? For old ladies and fairies?"***
>
> *Sylvester Stallone struggles with the concept of* Escape To Victory

The film ends with Max von Sydow smiling enigmatically, doubtless dreaming of a European Super League, leaving unanswered the question of whether Michael Caine was recaptured on the outskirts of Paris wearing a hooded Adidas tracksuit top and platform shoes. Football, as they say, is a funny old game, but it's rarely funnier than when the film-makers get hold of it.

In fact, *Escape To Victory* is one of the better football films. The plot is no more ludicrous than, say, *Where Eagles Dare*, and there's even a shred (only a shred, mind you) of historical evidence for a propaganda-inspired football match between the Axis and Allies during World War II. The use of professional players also lends some semblance of authenticity to the training and match scenes. But the football itself rarely rises above the Stallone standard – clearly following the Method school of acting, Stallone trained so hard he broke a finger and damaged both knees; afterwards, he said that keeping goal made him "a walking blood clot" – and the film fails to escape the conventions of football coverage. It even

Gregory's Girl: John Gordon Sinclair's warm up to those Tesco ads

provides a commentator talking in clichés to describe what we can already see.

The plot of *Escape to Victory* is not a million miles removed from two earlier east European films. *Két Félidö a Pokolban* (also known as *Two Half Times In Hell, Eleven Men, and Last Goal*) is a Hungarian film made in 1961. This time it's Hungarian prisoners who play against the Nazis and they make their mass escape before the match, only to be recaptured. The Nazis sentence them all to death but insist on the match going ahead first. Like Michael Caine's team, they start badly, but get on top in the second half. Unlike *Escape To Victory*, however, the guards in this film do have live ammunition, and when the other Hungarian prisoners threaten a pitch invasion, they start shooting. The entire Hungarian team is mown down and the spectators, disperse leaving a solitary football on the pitch.

A similarly downbeat ending is preferred in the 1964 Russian film, *Tretiy Taym* (aka *The Last Game.*) This time the action is set in Kiev (see "The Games") and the Russian prisoners of war don't even get the chance to escape. They are given a simple ultimatum: lose or die. As you might expect, the Russians make a tardy start, but end up overwhelming the dark forces of the jackbooted oppression, only to be hauled in front of a firing squad when the final whistle blows. According to one source, the Russian actor **Gennardi Yukhtin**, who played the heroic Soviet keeper, was so impressive he was later invited to play professional

"Look Michael, if that Brazilian's gonna keep kicking the ball at me, I'm outta here"

football. It's hard to imagine Stallone having been granted a similar opportunity.

Neither *Two Halves In Hell* nor *The Last Game* is available in your local video shop, but if you're very unlucky, you just might come across *Hotshot*, a 1987 American film that is unmitigated crap. Rich kid wants to play professional football but God-fearing Republican-voting parents disapprove. Rich kid incurs wrath of local coach, so heads for Brazil to receive homespun wisdom and intensive coaching from retired, reclusive South American star (guess who?) and returns to Big Apple to score winning goal in crucial match, etc etc. *Variety* described it as "amateurishly made and acted," and damned the football scenes as "dull and uninvolving". Pelé is spared the hatchet – "Though he is not a professional actor and doesn't seem to speak much English, Pelé is a delight to watch for his smile and handling (sic) of a soccer ball" – but another review said simply that "there's not a single honest moment in the film."

> **"Pelé is a delight to watch for his smile and his handling [sic] of a soccer ball"**
> *US review of the risible* Hotshot

It's doubtful, though, whether *Hotshot* is the worst football film of all time. A much stronger contender is *Yesterday's Hero*, scripted by Jackie Collins. **Ian McShane** (whose father once played for **Manchester United**) stars as the heavy-drinking wreck of a great player (can't imagine who inspired that), given one last chance by an ambitious Third Division club, managed by **Adam Faith** and owned by an international rock star (**Paul Nicholas** plays Elton John with hair). The football bits aren't up to much, McShane's genius seemingly limited to extraordinarily little movement off the ball and side-footed square passes on it. But even these are works of cinematic genius compared to the rock star scenes, which consist of Paul Nicholas yelling, "Hello Amsterdam, New York, Paris, Tokyo, etc" in front of the same 20 extras who have been told to move about a bit and impersonate a crowd.

What do you mean, what happens? The Third Division club get to the FA Cup final, McShane leaves the bottle in the locker, and comes off the bench to score the winning penalty in extra time. There's a surprise then. John Motson supplies commentary and a cameo performance.

Ladybugs is another film about football that is rarely seen and deservedly so. It's a 1992 American feature about a girls' "soccer" team who are so utterly hopeless they can only be saved by the new coach persuading his nephew to dress up as a girl and wear a wig. *Empire* described this entirely believable scenario as "a five star no-no" and "a hopeless effort". *Variety* said it was "sexist, homophobic and woefully unfunny", singling out director **Sidney J Furie** for being "so bored with the material that he doesn't even bother to stage his soccer scenes correctly."

It isn't difficult to find dreadful films about football, but where do you find some good ones? Phil Crossley, a researcher at the British Film Institute (and a **Blackburn Rovers** fan), has tracked down more than 500 films, including documentaries, that have some connection with the game. These vary from the sublime – 30 seconds of a game between Blackburn Rovers and **West Bromwich Albion** in 1898, believed to be the oldest existing footage of a first class match – to the ridiculous (*Carry On Emmerdale* contained a saucy serial rogering scene in the dressing rooms during an FA Cup final).

> ***"Those patrons who think they will see a fine display of football will be disappointed"***
>
> *Nul points for* The Great Game

Crossley's research suggests the oldest surviving feature film about football is a 1911 silent melodrama called *Harry The Footballer*. The plot (dashing centre-forward kidnapped by opposition, but escapes just in time to lead his team into victory) probably wasn't new even in 1911. A rather more sophisticated storyline was employed for *The Great Game*, a 1930 British feature. One of the first films to intersperse genuine action scenes (**Arsenal** against **Huddersfield** in the FA Cup final) with the drama, it concerned a split between the manager and chairman of a club on the eve of a big match. The manager wants to pick a young player who just happens to be in love with his daughter. The chairman thinks there may be a degree of favouritism. The manager resigns in a huff and his players go to pieces in the first half, but he manages to get word to them to inspire them to victory.

A contemporary review of *The Great Game* described it as "an authentic and thoroughly interesting picture of Association Football," a sound recommendation if ever we heard one. The only known surviving print is now being restored by the British Film Institute, so there is a chance it will reappear one day. When it does, you will be able to see what is possibly **Rex Harrison**'s first appearance in a feature film.

One film that is accessible (it crops up on Channel 4 at times when nobody is watching) is *The Arsenal Stadium Mystery*, made in 1939. Taking a leaf from *The Great Game*'s book, it used action from a match between Arsenal and **Brentford** as the backdrop for a murder mystery melodrama played as a light comedy. In the film, Arsenal are playing an amateur team called Trojans, whose centre-forward suddenly drops dead on the pitch. The detective (**Leslie Banks**) suspects foul play, perhaps excessive use of the offside trap, but finally deduces that the striker was poisoned.

The plot twists and turns, but the real stars are the Arsenal team and manager **George Allison**, all of whom are heavily featured. During the newsreel sequence at the start (a device to introduce the Arsenal team), Allison is described as "born with a silver football in his mouth" – an image worth lingering over.

In 1952, *The Great Game* was remade with rather less success. This time it was played as a comedy starring Diana Dors, Thora Hird and John Laurie, with the football scenes cut to a minimum. "Those patrons who think they will see a fine display of football will be disappointed," snapped one critic. "There are only about three minutes' play in the whole film. While others expecting a sincere attempt to investigate the evils of the transfer procedure will be bored by the film's stupidity."

Stupidity and lack of decent action are the culprits in most football movies. Take, for example, *La Vida Sigue Igual* (*Life Goes On The Same*), a Spanish feature from 1969 starring Julio Iglesias. Strange as it may seem, Iglesias really was on **Real Madrid**'s books as a goalkeeper, but that's a poor excuse for this melodrama. With his career with Real out of the window due to a crippling car crash, he becomes a reclusive minstrel, composing execrable sings about love and pain and the futility of it all. Equally worth blowing up the telly to avoid is *L'Arbitro* (aka *Football Crazy*), a 1974 Italian comedy about a pompous referee and his love life. The presence of Joan Collins provides further incentive to steer well clear.

Collins might actually have enlivened the Yugoslavian epic, *Comrade President The Centre-Forward.* This 1962 masterpiece sounds like it ought to star Josip Tito as the striker-cum-revolutionary hero who scores a hat-trick in the World Cup final against the running dogs of imperialism, but it doesn't. Other obscure footy flicks include three Czech offerings: *Ivana In The Forward Line, Women Who Have Run Offside* and *The Goalkeeper Lives In Our Street.* Israel has also produced a film called *Fish, Football And Girls,* which features roughly equal amounts of each.

Arguably, the two best films about football aren't about football at all. The playing field scene in *Kes,* in which Brian Glover's bullying schoolteacher assumes the role of Bobby Charlton, is not only hysterically funny but tells you more about the British attitude to the game than a dozen lesser films. *Gregory's Girl* is another great picture, but Gregory's enthusiasm for the game is motivated by love for the girl who's taken his place in the team and in the end he transfers his affections to a girl who doesn't even play football.

Perhaps the only film-maker who looked at the spot-kick from the other direction was Wim Wenders in his 1971 existentialist feature *The Goalkeeper's Fear Of The Penalty.* In this, the central character fails to save an easy one for no apparent reason. He then goes on to commit a murder, ditto. Football as a metaphor for life, or life as a metaphor for football?

The history of football in films proves two things. First, not even a star cast, big budget and expert advice on the action scenes can make the drama created on the wide screen match that of a real game. And secondly, actors kick a ball with the same conviction as footballers time a punchline.

Stallone turns hero, Michael Caine calls for a taxi

BEAUTIFUL GAME, SHAME ABOUT THE FILMS

The good, the bad and the inexplicable – those football movies in detail

The Arsenal Stadium Mystery (1939)

Good football movies are almost as rare as good Elvis Presley movies. This British thriller has the unusual virtue of actually having a plot, which centres on the murder of a centre-forward of an amateur team playing Arsenal. Detective Leslie Banks sifts through the usual suspects (Tony Adams, the victim's agent) and ensures justice is done. The plot twists and turns admirably, but the real stars are the Arsenal team and manager George Allison, all heavily featured. ★★★★

The Great Game (1952)

This comedy drama (and remake of the 1930 movie) could teach Graham Taylor a thing or two about wasting talented players. Among the halfway-decent cast are Diana Dors, Thora Hird and John Laurie. Would have been far funnier with Thora Hird as the hard-tackling centre-half. ★★

Life Goes On The Same (1969)

Little-known Spanish drama with Julio Iglesias as a football-playing troubadour. Deserves to be even less known. ★

The Goalkeeper's Fear Of The Penalty (1971)
Popular in art houses, this exercise in cinematic existentialism takes the goalkeeper's predicament as a metaphor for contemporary angst (ie "We are all just waiting to pay the ultimate penalty"). This is actually a very respectable, if occasionally pretentious, movie which loses two stars only because there's not much footie in it. ★★

Football Crazy (1974)
Not a movie based on the famous song but the English name for an Italian comedy of manners about a self-important referee who finds it hard to focus on what's happening on the pitch as opposed to what's happening in his bedroom. This is understandable, as one of the things in his bedroom is Joan Collins. Under the new Fifa directive, this film deserves an automatic red card. ★

Yesterday's Hero (1979)
Ian McShane does his best impersonation of George Best. Jackie Collins takes responsibility for the script. Adam Faith is in charge of the team, Leicester Forest, who appear to have been named after a service station on the M1 and languish in the old Third Division. Suffice to say that if, as FA coaching director Charles Hughes maintained, running off the ball is 90 per cent of the game, McShane wouldn't even play for non-league Leicester United. ★★

Gregory's Girl (1980)
Bill Forsyth's charming tale of adolescence, football and sex has proved enduringly popular. Former *Crossroads* star Dee Hepburn pulls off a triumph of method acting as the fleet-of-foot female forward. John Gordon Sinclair looks so gawky he could be a natural for the movie of **Darren Anderton**'s life story. The Czech film *Ivana In The Forward Line* covers a similar theme but the would-be striker has to dress up in men's clothes and speak Czech. The other Czech film in the same genre is *Women Who Have Run Offside.* ★★★

My Life As A Dog (1985)
Not a football film as such, just a fine movie which happens to have football as the integral part of its plot – this critically acclaimed Swedish effort centres around our teenage hero's relationship with a girl who hides her emerging chest to keep playing for the local boys' side. ★★★★

Hotshot (1987)
Proof that Pelé can be dull. Tired old tale of poor little rich boy who flees to South America to learn about the beautiful game. Critics liked Pelé's smile. Unfortunately the script also gave him some dialogue. ★

When Saturday Comes (1996)

They opened wide the big book of northern clichés for *When Saturday Comes.* Sean Bean (who else?) plays Jimmy Muir, a gritty, **Sheffield United**-daft brewery worker with a talent for banging in the goals for his local pub team. With a gritty, unsupportive father and a gritty, simple brother grafting down t'pit, life's a struggle for the Muirs, and Jimmy's drunken ways suggest it's unlikely that he'll ever excel. Cue gritty local scout Pete Postlethwaite, who says "bugger" a lot and gets Jimmy a trial for the Blades. Our irresponsible hero responds by getting leathered the night before his trial and is unsurprisingly hopeless. A series of gritty events (accident down t'pit, unwanted pregnancy) leads Jimmy to a long dark night of the soul. The outcome is inevitable: after 10 minutes of *Rocky*-style jogging through the snow and fancy keepy-uppy, Jimmy lands a place at United. The climax stretches the boundaries of predictability, as Jimmy comes on as sub against **Manchester United**. Will he be able to hammer home a last-minute penalty, get the girl and reconcile himself with his dad? Have a guess. The football sequences are shoddy too, but overall, *When Saturday Comes* and its dreadful Def Leppard soundtrack just makes it into "so-bad-it's-good" territory. ★

There's Only One Jimmy Grimble (2000)

A blatant rip-off of two Billys: ballet-dancing film hit *Billy Elliott* and classic

Ricky Tomlinson comes over all Graham Taylor in *Mike Bassett: England Manager*

comic strip *Billy's Boots.* Young northern lad finds ancient boots belonging to pre-War goalscoring legend and is instantly transformed into a superstar, while dealing with a precarious home life and general deprivation. The football scenes are reasonably done, but it's hard to feel any sympathy for the key characters. ★★

Mike Bassett: England Manager (2001)

Ricky Tomlinson plays an inept **Norwich City** manager who becomes England boss by default when every other candidate is forced out of the running. The football scenes are mercifully brief, but the low-rent feel and generally lacklustre plot are not aided by cameos from Atomic Kitten and alleged comedian Phil Jupitus. There is but one genuinely amusing moment, when Bassett asks a posse of critical fans how they would turn things around; he is met by a detailed and intelligent analysis of the side's shortcomings, to which he responds "Oh, f*** off" before running onto the team coach. ★

Bend It Like Beckham (2002)

"Who'd want a girl who plays football all day but can't make chapattis?" So runs the central dilemma of likable Brit-flick *Bend It Like Beckham.* Asian teenager Jes (Parminder K Nagra) doesn't fancy being a solicitor; she wants to emulate her United and England idol. But her family "would have a collective fit" if they found out she was playing for the Hounslow Harriers women's team – they'd rather she was cooking with her mother. There's much clever comedy – and subtle social commentary – milked from the reverse prejudice of the insular Bhamra family, and the clash between traditional Asian values and modern, football-crazy Britain. And while the soccer scenes are occasionally unrealistic, it's also a fine love-letter to the sport. ★★★

WHEN TWO WORLDS COLLIDE: FOOTBALL AND POP

In 1970, pop music catered for the whole family: *Voodoo Chile* and *Woodstock* for the hip; *Tears Of A Clown* and *Band Of Gold* for the cool; *Wandrin' Star* for the prematurely aged – and *Back Home* for the football fan. *Back Home* entered the charts on 18th April, clawed its way to the top on 16th May and stayed there for three weeks, finally yielding to *Yellow River.* It hung around for another nine weeks and even made a brief reappearance in August, just as the plucky England vocalists who had mimed so unconvincingly on prime time British TV really were on their way back home from the World Cup. It wasn't as big a hit that year as Elvis' *The Wonder Of You*, or Mungo Jerry's *In The Summertime*; but it was bigger than Dana's *All Kinds Of Everything*, so at least there's that to be said for it.

Quite why **Back Home** was such a hit is a mystery. The formula was nothing new. Get the lads (and **Elton John** and physio **Les Cocker** on backing vocals) into a studio to sing some inanely patriotic lyrics to a supremely mediocre tune. Give it a hook in the chorus like a kick in the knee, chuck in some crowd sound-effects but, most of all, make it easy, make it cheap and make it quick.

Football records fall into three categories. There's the team anthem (with or without professional help) invariably timed for the FA or World Cup; then there's the footballer as "serious" solo artiste; and finally, there are songs about football by professional performers. The first (and by far the most numerous) category is, it must be said, largely composed of the most God-awful "music" that the human ear has ever been subjected to.

> ***"...A curious dream / I've never dreamed before / Stan Matthews on the wing for Stoke at the age of 84"***
>
> *Keele University students, 1964*

No one really knows when it all started. Jim Phelan, a record sleeve designer,

has done more than anyone in this country to bring together the crap and curiosities of footie records. His Exotica label has produced several compilation albums and CDs, on which you can find soccer songs performed by the Nolan Sisters, **Terry Venables**, **Jimmy Greaves**, **Jack Charlton**, the Victor Sylvester Orchestra, and **Franz Beckenbauer**. West Germany did a World Cup song in 1954, which appeared on an album of commentary on the final, but it's by no means certain this was the first World Cup promotional song.

To celebrate **Spurs**' 1960-61 Double, a bunch of session singers called The Totnamites sang a catchy little number in a chirpy, washing powder commercial sort of way called *Tip-Top Tottenham Hotspur*. It went something like this: "Tip-top Tottenham Hotspur, the greatest team of the year / Tip-top Tottenham Hotspur, raise your glasses and give them a cheer / Hooray for the Double and let's live it up / One drink for the league and one for the cup." It rose without trace.

Neither the ghastly Highland reel of *Men Of Scotland*, nor the Victor Sylvester *World Cup Cha-Cha-Cha* made it into the charts. Much better, but just as slow-selling, was *Stan Matthews* by Keele Row, one track of a flexi-disc EP produced by Keele University students for the 1964 rag week. This folk song about the Wizard of Dribble starts: "You've heard of Greaves and Puskas, and Pelé from Brazil / But Stanley Matthews from the Potts is the greatest of them all." Dodgy rhyme, but the second verse is better: "Last night I had a curious dream I've never dreamed before / Stan Matthews on the wing for Stoke at the age of 84."

Glenn and Chris forget the Hoddle and Waddle bit – and their dignity

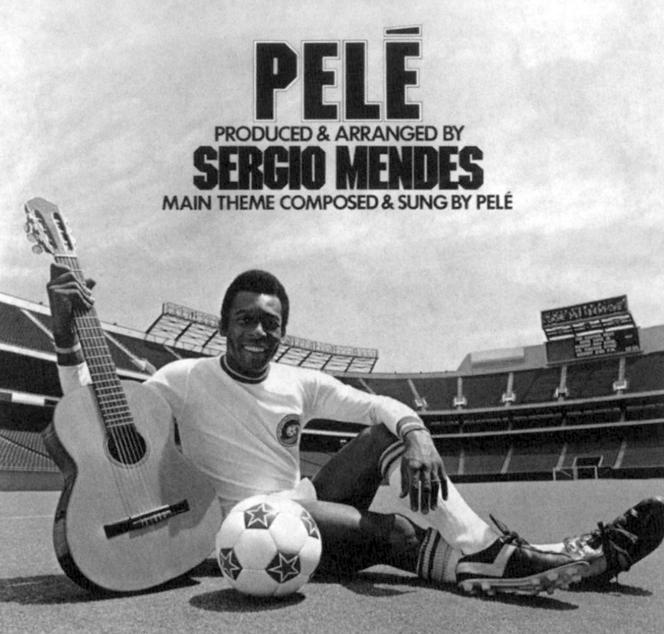

Pelé stars in his own musical masterpiece, a 1960s jazz collaboration

Throughout the 1960s, more and more teams made records (or 45s as they were called back then) but it wasn't until 1970 and *Back Home* that the national side made it onto *Top Of The Pops.* Even **Lonnie Donegan**'s 1966 theme *World Cup Willie* missed the charts completely. The success of *Back Home* spawned a host of imitators and something even worse – the spin-off album. As Phelan explains: "One of the pioneers in this area was Larry Page. He managed The Troggs and ran a record company called Page One. He was looking for a way to exploit the Larry Page Orchestra and so he went to Liverpool, Manchester United and Chelsea, and did these singalong records."

Invariably this meant professional footballers, who should have known better, performing ghastly early 1970s schlock and doing it very badly. The *Back Home* album contained such treasures as **Bobby Moore** and **Francis Lee** singing *Sugar Sugar*; **Geoff Hurst**, **Jeff Astle** and **Peter Bonetti** warbling *Lily The Pink*;

and the whole England team attempting to croon their way through *Puppet On A String*, and *Ob-la-di Ob-la-da*. You have to hear it to believe it.

But who on earth actually bought this stuff? "Mums and grandmas were probably responsible," says Phelan. "They saw these things in shops, said 'That's just right for little Johnny, he likes football', and they bought them as birthday and Christmas presents." As Mari Wilson might say, "just what I always wanted." First on the bandwagon were **Chelsea**. A bunch of blokes called Stamford Bridge had a No.47 hit (if there's such a thing) with *Chelsea* in May 1970. It was the first FA Cup final promotional hit record and seemed to do the trick as the London club beat **Leeds United** 2-1 in the replay. This was just a trial run for 1972 when Chelsea and the Larry Page Orchestra produced the ever-popular *Blue Is The Colour*. The album spin-off featured **Peter Osgood** singing *Chirpy-Chirpy Cheep Cheep*, an act of musical homicide.

The one exception to this trend in the early 1970s was **Don Fardon**'s *Belfast Boy*, a remarkably prescient warning to **George Best**. "Just play the way the ball bounces / And bounce the way the ball plays," it starts mysteriously. "Cos you won't have long in the limelight / No you won't have many days / Georgie, Georgie, they call you the Belfast joy." This entered what your parents still embarrassingly referred to as the "hit parade" the same week as *Back Home*, but never soared higher than No.32.

> ***" 'Arry Cripps is his name / Right up to the last minute / He always gets stuck in it"***
>
> *From Millwall's* The Ballad Of Harry Cripps, *1972*

But the die was cast. It was possible to have a hit record with a football song, even one sung by footballers, and everyone had to have a go. Some songs were specifically written (generally by someone's agent on the back of an envelope) but many used new words grafted on to familiar pop themes. While most are utterly unmemorable, a few do stand out. **Millwall**'s 1972 *The Ballad Of Harry Cripps*, a tribute to their hard-tackling left-back, contains some of the best lyrics. "Divisions Four, Three, Two and One, 'Arry has played in every one / He is a man who time will never age / 'Arry Cripps is his name / Right up to the last minute / He always gets stuck in it."

However, that's nothing compared to the poetry of **Wealdstone**'s *We Are The Stones*, which contains the following imperishable lines: "We go to places as far away as Barrow / One place we always try to win and that's Harrow / If you like a drink go to the players' bar / Oh no, let me think, we haven't built it so far." They don't write them like that any more.

The big football hit of 1973 was *Nice One, Cyril* by **The Cockerel Chorus**, which took the punchline from a TV commercial for bread and applied it to

A compilation album of football hit singles

SONG	ARTISTS	YEAR	HIGHEST POSITION	WKS IN CHART
Back Home	England World Cup Squad	1970	1	16
Please Don't Go	KWS	1992	1	16*
Three Lions	Baddiel and Skinner and The Lightning Seeds	1996	1	15
Come On You Reds	Manchester United	1994	1	15
World In Motion	England/New Order	1990	1	12
Nessun Dorma	Luciano Pavarotti	1990	2	11
Fog On The Tyne	Gazza/Lindisfarne	1990	2	9
Anfield Rap	Liverpool FC	1988	3	6
Ole Ola	Scotland World Cup Squad	1978	4	6
We Have A Dream	Scotland World Cup Squad	1982	5	9
Blue Is The Colour	Chelsea FC	1972	5	12
Ossie's Dream	Tottenham FA Cup Final Squad	1981	5	8
Hot Stuff	Arsenal FC	1998	9	5
Leeds United	Leeds United FC	1972	10	10
Diamond Lights	Glenn And Chris	1987	12	8
Here We Go	Everton FC	1985	14	5
Don't Come Home Too Soon	Del Amitri	1998	15	4
We've Got The Whole World In Our Hands	Nottingham Forest with Paper Lace	1978	24	6
Black & White Army	Black And White Army	1998	26	2**
Head Over Heels	Kevin Keegan	1979	31	6

Spurs full-back **Cyril Knowles**. It reached No.14. The spin-off album spun off.

The Scotland World Cup squad's *Easy Easy* was a No.20 hit in 1974, while **Manchester United** had their first hit in 1976 with, oddly, *Manchester United*. It wasn't until 1979 that anything vaguely different emerged. In October that year **B A Robertson** produced the No.8 hit *Knocked It Off*. "I knocked it off, yeah I knocked it off / I was standing in the corner when the ball came across / I thought I'd had another go / But I never thought I'd put it away," he explained. Robertson revealed his football-loving credentials with various contributions to Scotland World Cup records alongside other such Tartan titans as the Bay City Rollers and Lulu. Incidentally, until you've heard **Denis Law** accompanying Rod Stewart on Jimi Hendrix's *Angel* you can't claim to have lived a full life.

The other big football hit of the year was **Kevin Keegan**'s *Head Over Heels In Love* which plateaued at No.31. The follow-up, *It Ain't Easy*, was much less

SONG	ARTISTS	YEAR	HIGHEST POSITION	WKS IN CHART
I'm Forever Blowing Bubbles	West Ham FC	1975	31	2
We'll Be With You	The Potters	1972	34	2***
Do The Right Thing	Ian Wright	1993	43	2
Let's Dance	Middlesbrough FC	1997	44	1****
Viva El Fulham	Tony Rees And The Cottagers	1975	46	1
Glad All Over/ Where Eagles Fly	Crystal Palace	1990	50	2
Nine In A Row	Rangers FC	1997	54	2
Niall Quinn's Disco Pants	A Love Supreme	1999	59	2
Go For It!	Coventry City Cup Final Squad	1987	61	2
The Boys In The Old Brighton Blue	Brighton & Hove Albion FC	1983	65	2
Outstanding	Andy Cole	1999	68	1*****

**Please Don't Go* was Nottingham band KWS's desperate plea to Forest and England centre-back Des Walker not to go to Sampdoria. The song was a No.1 smash but failed to persuade Des to stay, though he has since returned to the City Ground.
**Newcastle United fan vocalists
***The Potters were also known as "Stoke City Football Supporters' Vocal Group"
****With Chris Rea and Bob Mortimer
*****An Amazon customer review of this single, by "a music fan from Paris" says: "My advice to you – don your leather jacket and gold jewellery and choose *Outstanding* as your soundtrack to a night's cruisin' around town"

successful but much funnier, revealing just how hard life was for the soccer superstar. "But I come home too tired for loving / Something a girl finds hard to understand / Believe me, it ain't easy to live this life with me."

Keegan was not the first player to heed bad advice about the quality of his voice and be lured into the studio. **John Charles** teamed up with the William Galassini Orchestra while in Italy and recorded Welsh/Italian hybrid ballads. **Franz Beckenbauer** has been recorded whispering his way – Julio Iglesias style – through *1-0 Für Deine Liebe* (*1-0 For Your Love*). Even worse are **Terry Venables**' Frank Sinatra impersonation as he murders Cole Porter's *I've Got You Under My Skin* and his Cockney knees-up rendition of *Bye-Bye Blackbird.*

By the early 1980s, the traditional football song was on its way out. Scotland, with comic actor **John Gordon Sinclair** fronting the squad, tried to inject some humour into *We Have A Dream.* England, though, having been out of the

World Cup for 12 years, were completely unhip and produced *This Time*, a stereotypically jaunty effort which went all the way to No.2. Again it's the album, produced by K-Tel – buy-one-and-get-the-warehouse-free – that takes the breath away. Not only do you get **Glenn Hoddle** shrieking his way through Queen's *We Are The Champions*, but there's also an instrumental rendition of *This Time* performed by the **Leyland Vehicles Brass Band**. In addition to the K-Tel klassic, there was another 1982 England album, the "Officially Approved Souvenir LP" with the sleeve bearing a strangely ominous "Football Association Approved" stamp. What's strange about this record is that it's a rip-off of the K-Tel disc, featuring many of the same songs performed by completely different people, including members of the 1966 squad.

By far the best football songs of 1982 were on *The Revolution Starts At Closing Time*, the debut (and probably the only) album of a London band called **Serious Drinking**. Their *Spirit Of 1966* made the same mistake as *This Time* with a cheerful chorus – "We're gonna win the World Cup in Spain / We're gonna hoist that World Cup again" – but the verses consisted of the names of the 1966 players yelled at top volume. A surreal touch was added by referring to England's left back as Leonard (not George) Cohen throughout. Also on the album was a reflection on 1970's off-pitch shenanigans entitled *Bobby Moore Is Innocent*.

Before all that we'd had the familiar fare. Nottingham Forest teaming up with

England players ill-at-ease on a very 1970s *Top Of The Pops*

Paper (*Billy Don't Be A Hero*) Lace for *We've Got The Whole World At Our Feet*, and Spurs with Chas'n'Dave for *Ossie's Dream* and that truly dreadful trembly-Wembley rhyme. The **Nolan Sisters** had recorded *Blackpool, Blackpool*, and 10CC (under the pseudonym Tristar Airbus) had made *Willy Morgan On The Wing*, but the big hits were drying up. Brighton's *The Boys In The Old Brighton Blue* peaked at No.65 in 1983, although Manchester United's *Glory, Glory Man Utd* reached No.13 the same year.

It took footballers of quality and vision to break the mould: **Hoddle** and **Waddle**. Despite suffering a sense of humour bypass that prompted them to use their first names, they had a No.12 hit in 1987 with the smoochy ballad *Diamond Lights*, the first for singing footballers (rather than a squad press-ganged into the studio) since Keegan. Their follow-up, *It's Goodbye*, flopped. Hoddle didn't hit the charts again until Chelsea's *No-one Can Stop Us Now* in 1993.

In fact, the only British footballer to have more than one chart hit is, almost unbelievably, Gazza. Having played a significant part in the ground-breaking *World In Motion* World Cup song (the biggest football hit since *Back Home*, and unlike all the others, one that almost bears repeated listening), Gascoigne reached No.2 in 1990 with a funked-up *Fog On The Tyne*. The follow-up, *Geordie Boys (Gazza Rap)* hovered just outside the Top 30.

Rap seemed the only way forward. **Ian Wright** made a brief appearance (two weeks, No. 43) in the charts in August 1993, rapping out *Do The Right Thing*, which was better than Vinnie Jones' spirited rendering of *Woolly Bully*. **Andy Cole** was perhaps ill-advised to title his solitary foray into music *Outstanding*, as it was anything but. Enter Baddiel, Skinner and Ian Broudie (the bloke from Lightning Seeds who looks like a long-lost Baddiel sibling) with the omnipresent *Three Lions* – a pleasant singalong which tends nonetheless to induce psychotic rage on repeated listening. The tune emerged for Euro '96 and was resurrected by popular demand for the World Cup two years later (Scotland opted for the Del Amitri-backed *Don't Come Home Too Soon*. They did). In the absence of any other presentable song – Bell & Spurling's *Sven Sven Sven* in 2002 was a particular low – don't rule out a reappearance.

For the aficionado, the best music in this genre is probably by **Half Man Half Biscuit** who aside from penning songs with such inspired titles as **I Was A Teenage Honved Fan** and All I Want For Christmas Is A Dukla Prague Away Kit also gave us the immortal spoof of Abba's Dancing Queen: "Friday night and the gates are low..." Just as exhilarating, in its way, is **Música De Futebol** (on the Mr Bongo label), a CD of the best Brazilian music inspired by football, interspersed with commentaries highlighting the great moments in the game's history in Brazil. If your idea of a perfect start to the day is a burst of commentary describing the Carlos Alberto goal against Italy in 1970, this is for you.

"YOU FILL UP MY SENSES, LIKE A GREASY CHIP BUTTIE"

Ever since football started (long before John Denver's hit *Annie's Song* was adapted by **Sheffield United** fans), fans have sung. The oldest known football song still used today is Norwich City's *On The Ball, City*, written by Albert T Smith, a City director, around 1890 as a music hall song. A **Blackburn Rovers** song sung at the FA Cup final against Old Etonians in 1882 shows that the words may change but the sentiments remain the same. "All hail, ye gallant Rover Lads, Etonians thought you were cads, they've found a football game their dads, By meeting Blackburn Rovers." Rovers lost 1-0.

The **West Ham United** classic *I'm Forever Bowing Bubbles* is also getting on a bit. It was first heard in 1923 at the White Horse final at Wembley which West Ham lost. In 1975 it was released as a single and got to No.31 in the charts. The team did rather better that year, winning their second FA Cup.

The wit and speed with which new songs and chants are unfurled would put Ben Elton to shame: Manchester United fans' rendition of the *Flintstones* theme at a recent Charity Shield being just one example. And who invented the "Ooh, aah, [Cantona]!" chant anyway? Arsenal fans claim to be one of the first to sing

it when Anders Limpar made his debut for Arsenal in Sweden in 1990. Unfortunately, Anders did not react in quite the way the Gunners fans had hoped. They were as bewildered at his expressions as he was by their chant – until a Swedish fan pointed out that "Ooh aah" means "Who is" in Swedish.

Paul McGrath claims to have been the first target of such affectionate chants. And there are many more. Songs have incredible power sometimes: you just need to listen to a **Barça** fan singing of Catalan blood. Or Liverpool supporters away from home singing *Poor Scouser Tommy*. Home fans are often stunned into silence, as their initial attempts to drown out the words are thwarted by the sheer determination of the Reds to finish the whole bloody song.

The passing of the terraces may mean an end to some of the wit and wisdom as it becomes harder to get chants and songs taken up. But then songs didn't always come into being via the gallows humour of the terraces; sometimes they came through less obvious routes. Jimmy Hill, for example, was responsible for two songs still heard today. When manager of **Coventry City** in the 1960s he and chairman Derrick Robins thought they should devise a club song for the terraces to sing. "I sat down one Sunday night with John Camkin – a board member and commentator for Anglia TV – and we had a few gins, well we had a whole bottle actually, and he'd heard the *Eton Boating Song* on the radio and said 'Why don't we build it around that?'"

Hill then came up with the words for the *Sky Blue Song* and somehow persuaded Ted Heath (the bandleader, not the former prime minister) to record an "upbeat" version of the song which sold "quite well," in parts of Coventry anyway. The Sky Blues were 2-0 up in a match against **Barnsley** when fog descended and the match was temporarily abandoned. Hill and Robins, who had sung in amateur opera, seized their chance for stardom: Robins on the mike and Hill conducting the crowd through the mist. To ensure all the Coventry fans sang, the words were printed in the programme.

The other song Hill wrote was when he was Head of Sport at LWT. In 1971, the big match was Arsenal against Liverpool in the FA Cup final and Hill asked TV viewers to write a song for Arsenal to the tune of *Land Of Hope And Glory*. However the Elgar Society, which owned the copyright to the tune, complained about the trivialisation of one of England's greatest anthems and Hill was left with the embarrassment of having to change his tune (all good practice for *Match Of The Day* reporting).

In a flash of inspiration befitting one who had been the first-ever manager to face the *Match Of The Day* cameras at half-time, Hill asked **Bertie Mee**, Arsenal's manager, if he would accept *Rule Britannia*, with Hill's words, as Arsenal's song for the Cup final. Mee accepted, the band played it at the next home match and the Gunners' favourite *Good Old Arsenal* was born. "I still get royalties for that song," says The Chin. "It's a long way from Phil Collins, but it's still nice."

LOOK AND LISTEN

The first match to be broadcast on British television was Arsenal v Everton on 29th August, 1936, so the traditional cry of "not Arsenal again!" is older than you thought. Football on television has come a long way since then, although as late as the 1950s it largely amounted to friendlies involving **Wolves** against "crack" continental opposition. It wasn't until 1964 that *Match Of The Day* was launched on the new minority-interest TV channel BBC2, with Kenneth Wolstenholme journeying to Beatleville to commentate on Liverpool against, yes, Arsenal. The programme was not supposed to run and run: it was really a dry run for the BBC's 1966 World Cup coverage.

The fact that lots of people actually wanted to watch football on TV evidently took the academics at the Beeb by surprise, but *Match Of The Day*'s continuing success saw it moved to BBC1 in 1966. David "**One-nil!**" Coleman took over as commentator-in-chief three years later.

By then ITV had launched *The Big Match* on LWT in 1968, introducing revolutionary new devices like the slow-motion replay under the stewardship of **Brian Moore** and **Jimmy Hill**. The duo also headed up ITV's innovative pundit panel for Mexico '70, with Malcolm Allison, **Derek Dougan** et al opinionating in a kaleidoscope of lurid shirts, kipper ties and cravats. By now most ITV regions were running their own Sunday afternoon highlights package, but Hill, it was said, was lured to the nationwide stage of the BBC in 1973 because he'd outgrown performing only to the London gallery and was tired of northern cabbies asking him what he was up to.

Meanwhile the battlefront had extended to Saturday lunchtimes. **Sam Leitch** and later **Bob Wilson** fronted the Beeb's *Football Focus* (title devised by Motty, fact fans), while Brian Moore hosted ITV's *On The Ball*, and the two sides entered into head-to-head competition every FA Cup final Saturday. The natural order was shattered in 1978, however, when in a "**Snatch Of The Day**," ITV bought up exclusive coverage of the Football League. The BBC complained to the Office of Fair Trading and got their rights back, but had to cede the Saturday night slot to ITV every other season. Jimmy Hill over the roast spuds was just all wrong.

> ***"I've always supported the Lilywhites. Do they still call them the Lilywhites?"***
>
> *Bruce Forsyth, Cup Final Saturday*

Ratings then went into decline, and by 1985 things were in such a mess that when contract talks broke down, television walked away, leaving the screens football-free for months – much to the delight of wives and girlfriends everywhere.

Their joy was shortlived, however, as normal service was resumed in time for Mexico '86. In 1988, upstart satellite newcomers BSB tried to poke their nose in but were beaten to the Football League contract by ITV. With the accent now on live matches, ITV's "live and exclusive" coverage (now fronted by the oleaginous **Elton Welsby**, who makes Jim Rosenthal look like Des Lynam) concentrated firmly on the Big Five (unlikely as it may seem, younger readers, Everton and Spurs were the other two). The first campaign ended in a breathtaking climax, Arsenal beating Liverpool in the final seconds of the season.

The looming threat of satellite intervention finally materialised in 1992, when the rights for the new Premiership were bought up by the riches of **Rupert Murdoch**'s Sky Sports, who had already eaten up BSB. Their "revolution" promised a Whole New Ball Game of wall-to-wall coverage, Monday night matches, cheerleaders, **Andy Gray**'s incisive analysis and imperfect mastery of the video machine, and Richard Keys' blazers (furnished by Yves St Laurent). A deal was also done to allow the return of *MOTD* on terrestrial TV, now with Des

Statto, creation of presenter/Eurosport commentating legend Angus Loughran

Lynam behind the desk. Euro '96 indicated that football was a primetime attraction once more, and the cost escalated to a price the BBC couldn't pay. In 1999, the unthinkable happened: Lynam defected to ITV, and the Premiership highlights followed. The BBC consoled themselves with the FA Cup and the emergence of **Gary Lineker** as anchorman, while OnDigital (later ITV Digital) bought the Nationwide League rights for a fee that would bankrupt the network. Along with the failure of ITV's Saturday evening highlights Premiership package in 2001, it hinted that the football boom was about to go bust.

Honourable mention must also go to Channel 4's **Gazzetta Football Italia**, especially to the Sunday when, due to the vagaries of the Italian weather and broadcasting technology, a long pass soared into the air in one stadium to land in another 50 miles away. Commentator Peter Brackley was, as ever, unflappable.

Football drama has been less of a success. *Those Glory, Glory Days*, about a girl's obsession with Spurs' Double-winning side of 1960-61, was made by Channel 4 in 1983 and had a limited cinema release. Tyne Tees made *The World Cup – A Captain's Tale*, based on the true story of a team of Durham miners who represented England in the first ever "World Cup", played in 1910, and won it, beating **Juventus** in the final. Dennis Waterman played **Bob Jones**, the West Auckland centre-half and captain. The whole project was Waterman's idea. He stumbled across the story while reading a book about football on the loo.

The theme of women breaking into the board and changing rooms has been explored with Cherie Lunghi in *The Manageress*, and in the BBC play *Born Kicking*. Both tackled wider issues (sexism, racism, violence etc) but were let down by their action scenes. *In Born Kicking*, the ponytailed Roxy scores a remarkable number of headed goals without a challenge in sight. The highlight of the action is her Vinny Jones-inspired gonad grab on a rather-too-close marking defender, but the play fails to avoid the cliché of Roxy coming off the bench to score the winning penalty in the dying seconds.

The single best television programme about football still has to be the fly-on-the-wall Graham Taylor documentary, available on video as Do I Not Like That. Among the many classic moments are Nigel Clough struggling to understand Taylor's instructions when he comes on as sub, Gazza shaming Taylor's amateurish training by showing the manager how to plot a set piece, and the famous badgering of the officials: "He's cost me my job…" As Taylor himself said many times during this Channel 4 programme, "what sort of thing is happening here?" You tell us, Graham. It certainly wasn't football.

Television has undoubtedly had a profound effect on the sport it is covering. In the Premiership, the huge sums from screening rights have brought about spiralling wage demands from imported (and domestic) star attractions, to say nothing of fixtures disruption for the non-armchair fan. At a lower level, however, the failure of ITV Digital imperilled the future of several Nationwide League clubs who were supposed to be benefiting from its income and spent the money before it came in. But in an era when a mini-dish can bring you action from around the planet 24 hours a day, and has delivered such innovations (or irritations) as pick-your-own camera angles, tactics trucks and Peter Drury, it seems impossible now to conceive of professional football without it.

Before vision, there was only sound. The first match to be broadcast on the radio was the 1926 Cup final between **Bolton** and **Manchester City**, which was relayed back to Manchester to be heard in large public halls. The BBC broadcast the Arsenal-Sheffield United game at Highbury a year later, introducing a unique system in which the pitch was printed in the *Radio Times*, divided into eight numbered squares. While the commentary went on, an announcer in the background called out the squares' numbers as the ball passed them, thereby allowing listeners to visualise where the action was taking place and giving rise to the phrase "back to square one". The system died out after the war.

Radio commentaries were massively popular, but the Football League took a dim view, fearing attendances would plummet. A ban on broadcasting live matches was imposed in 1951, but rescinded later in the decade.

The arrival of Radio 5 in the 1990s was a Sky-style revolution, but wall-to-wall coverage on the box is slowly killing the medium, with inane banter of the my-team's-better-than-yours variety now standard fare for an entire station (former *Sun* editor Kelvin MacKenzie's Talk Sport). And that's without even mentioning David Mellor or Jonathan Pearce, whose breathless account of Eric Cantona's kung fu attack ("And I care not one jot for his talent...") is a classic of its kind and was circulated as a promotional tool by Capital Gold. It's a rare privilege to hear a man almost have an aneurysm live on air.

SIX GREAT CUP FINAL SATURDAY FEATURES

1 CUP FINAL ON THE BUSES

No, not a special edition of the unroadworthy Reg Varney sitcom, but the annual tradition of reporting live from the teams' coaches as they depart their Buckinghamshire hideaway and head for the stadium. Introduced by ITV with **Sunderland** in 1973, it invariably features at least one player doing an impression of Frank Spencer on the coach. In 1983, the BBC used a helicopter to shadow the **Brighton** team bus as it made its way through the Home Counties to face Manchester United at Wembley, and the following year it stuck a camera on a train full of **Everton** fans.

2 CUP FINAL SWAP SHOP

It's 1978, Saturday mornings are the domain of Noel Edmonds on a trimphone and the Cup final isn't going to get in the way of that. So Cheggers was dispatched to Highbury to follow Arsenal's preparations, but controversially, *Swap Shop* resident chef and lifelong Norwich City fan Delia Smith reported from Portman Road, allegedly wearing an **Ipswich** scarf. We'd like to see the video evidence, please (offers: Scalextric, Hazel O'Connor LP).

3 CUP FINAL TARBY AND FRIENDS

"Ho ho!" That was his catchphrase. No Cup final was complete in the 1980s without Jimmy Tarbuck on ITV, wearing a Pringle sweater, manning a fake bar and cracking jokes about Kenny Dalglish's golf handicap with an assortment of celebs of the calibre of Kenny Lynch. Not forgetting Bruce Forsyth's appearance on *Cup Final Grandstand* in 1991. "Oh yes, I've always supported the Lilywhites – do they still call them the Lilywhites?" No. See also Arsenal devotee Kevin Costner in 1998 and Tony Blair in 1999 for more Cup final bandwagoneering.

4 CUP FINAL PUNCHLINES

"Remember what you heard, and where you heard it!" In 1981, ITV's build-up included a commemorative edition of the **Lennie Bennett** quiz show, in which

C-list "personalities" in little boxes a la *Celebrity Squares* told jokes (remember the great bit where they all had to change places?).

5 CUP FINAL ALF GARNETT

In 1975, *Grandstand* recruited **Warren Mitchell** to stand in front of a fake graffiti wall and deliver some quips about "yer actual Hammers", while in the 1980s it was the turn of Mel Smith and Griff Rhys Jones ("Everton, Everton, Everton – it's a genuinely musical city, isn't it?"). In 1984, the BBC dispatched Michael Barrymore and Freddie Starr to the team camps for some "morale boosting". Starr had reduced **Dickie Davies** to tears several years earlier on ITV when checking the Wembley goalnets for Humphreys (you know, the 1970s milk-snaffling, er, straws) while dressed as a Nazi.

6 CUP FINAL SNOOKER

Jimmy White and Alex Higgins were roped in by the BBC to perform some trick shots prior to the 1982 final, while in 1986, **Mark Lawrenson** and Gary Lineker – he's a friend of Willie Thorne, you know – faced off across the green baize in a pan-Merseyside snooker showdown in shiny waistcoats. Lineker won. And we're not about to forget 1987's celebrity football match between Tarby's Sky Blues and the Tottenham (David) Frostspurs in a hurry.

FIVE GREAT ITV REGIONAL COMMENTATORS

1 HUGH JOHNS (Star Soccer/ATV)

"Here's Hurst, can he make it three? He has! He has!" Johns was ITV's commentator on the 1966 World Cup final, but his finest hour remains forever in the shadow of Wolstenholme's "They think it's all over" for the BBC. The operatic Johns described the mud-spattered Midlands deeds of the likes of **Terry Hennessey** and **Tony "Bomber" Brown** for decades before moving to HTV Wales in 1982. "What a whacker!"

2 GERALD SINSTADT (The Kick-Off Match/Granada)

The debonair, bespectacled Sinstadt joined Granada in 1969 as commentator and presenter of the north-west's Friday night magazine programme *Kick-Off*. Earned the Kop's everlasting enmity after introducing a smug musical montage of Liverpool's exit from the European Cup to the tune of *The Party's Over*. Joined *Match Of The Day* in the 1980s. Has commentated on rowing.

3 GERRY HARRISON (Match Of The Week/Anglia)

"Mills. Wark. Whymark!" Harrison was the voice of Anglia football for 20 years,

Ron Atkinson, a man who's taken commentary to a whole new level

chronicling all the region's big names: Norwich, Ipswich and, well, that's it. So closely affiliated with the successful Ipswich team of the 1970s, it's amazing he wasn't offered a plum role in *Escape To Victory*.

4 BRIAN MOORE (The Big Match/LWT)

Frontman and commentator of the English capital's "glamour" football programme, Mooro's unrestrained earlier incarnation could be heard every Sunday screaming over some goal-packed thriller from swinging Stamford Bridge or homely Craven Cottage, before chatting to guests like – yes, it's him again – Freddie Starr and Elton John, introducing his Fun Spot (usually an Irish goalkeeper swinging on a crossbar and breaking it) and answering Australian viewers' letters.

5 ARTHUR MONTFORD (Scotsport/STV)

Best remembered for his "distinctive" loud checked sports jacket and polo neck combination, his dulcet tones and beaming grin as he introduced his beloved **Morton** clinching promotion against **Airdrie**. In sharp, painful contrast, he also had to commentate on Scotland's many and various World Cup calamities (his "Disaster for Scotland!" has passed into common Scots parlance). Montford fronted no fewer than 2,000 editions of *Scotsport*. "What a stramash!"

 "Junior Des", Lawro and Jocky prepare for some easy-going banter

FIVE GREAT FOOTBALL SITCOM MOMENTS

1 WHATEVER HAPPENED TO THE LIKELY LADS?

Bulgaria v England, "it's on the box tonight," "Malcolm McDonald uses the same conditioner as me," **Brian Glover**, "people don't go around saying nil-two," heavy pitch, "Koreans - not to be trusted… Danes – pornographic!," "the crowd will have streamed back to their collective farms," "the gospel according to Sir Alf," "England… flooded out!"

2 PORRIDGE

The episode where Spurs fan Fletch hoodwinks Norris, a fellow HMP Slade inmate due for release, into buying a treasure map, only to dig for the hidden contraband in the middle of Elland Road.

3 STEPTOE AND SON

In the episode *Divided We Stand*, Harold and Albert end up partitioning their bijou Oildrum Lane abode, a decision which extends to dividing the TV set in half, only for father and son to argue over whether to watch ballet or the European Cup. "Was that a goal?" "No, he saved it!" "Oh gawd!"

4 RISING DAMP

Leeds United fan and sleazy landlord Rigsby recalls the 1975 European Cup final. "When Bayern Munich scored that second goal, I thought they were going to break out into the goosestep…"

5 FATHER TED

Father Ted tests his managerial skills in the annual All-Priests Over-75s Five-a-Side challenge match – except that his best player is dead, Father Jack has overdosed on Dreamy Sleepy Nighty Snoozy Snooze, and rival Father Dick Byrne has signed a crack Italian star (Dougal: "The Italians know about football all right. And fashion. Ted, do you remember that fella that was so good at fashion they had to shoot him?") Alas, Ted's plan to snatch victory using rubber arms and an electric wheelchair is thwarted.

FIVE BEST FOOTBALL PROGRAMMES

1 SOCCER AM Sky Sports

Sky's Saturday morning pre-match fry-up, masterminded by preening Chelsea boy **Tim Lovejoy** assisted by fire-eating Torquay überfan **Helen Chamberlain**, plus highly attractive women in replica shirts and rock stars shakily professing their love of football. Essentially three hours of *Tiswas*-but-with-football, it's given the world the majestic Third Eye (amusing happenings at matches caught on camera), not to mention the virus-like cult of the Save Chip banner.

2 SOCCER SATURDAY Sky Sports

Then, if you want to waste your Saturday completely, spend the next five-and-a-half-hours in front of this compelling non-stop football chat and results programme, anchored by the unruffled cult hero **Jeff Stelling**. **Rodney Marsh**, **George Best**, **Frank McLintock** et al sit behind a desk watching matches on television and describe the action in their own unique style – in McLintock's case, this involves praising Arsenal unquestionably and often becoming so animated he forgets that viewers can't actually see what he's seeing ("Frank... what's happening…? Frank, what's actually happening?").

3 SGORIO S4C

Years before James Richardson ordered his first cappuccino and skimmed through the latest *Gazzetta Dello Sport*, Welsh-language channel S4C presented the finest action from Serie A and La Liga every Monday night. The programme acquired cult status on Merseyside, where S4C transmissions could be picked up.

 Footballers mixed with celebrities with mixed results on the half-decent *Soccer AM*

4 FANTASY FOOTBALL LEAGUE BBC2/ITV

David Baddiel and Frank Skinner sit on a battered sofa, bung on funny football clips old and new, natter with guest "managers" (Peter Cook, Bob Mortimer and Basil Brush to name three), abuse Angus "Statto" Loughran, appear in vaguely satirical sketches ("Saint And Greavsie Talk About The Endsleigh League As If It's Important"), recreate classic moments in someone's back garden in Phoenix From The Flames ("Play David Coleman!") and Jeff Astle sings. Badly. Fantastic stuff in its pomp, less so for the live France '98 revival on ITV, but we'd open the door to them again any time soon.

5 KICK-OFF Granada

Essential viewing for any north-west fan in the 1970s, this Friday-teatime preview was fronted by Gerald Sinstadt, who would sometimes take an unusually uncompromising line ("We'll be asking Lawrie McMenemy why his **Southampton** team were so boring at Old Trafford last week"). Light relief came in the form of the Who's My Daddy quiz, where viewers had to guess the identity of a famed footballer from his offspring's clues, more original than the mystery sportsman on *A Question Of Sport* and, to be fair, more naff. Brilliant theme tune as well. Briefly revived in the late 1980s with the omnipresent Elton Welsby.

FIVE WORST FOOTBALL PROGRAMMES

1 POLAND V ENGLAND 1997 (Channel Five)

Perhaps a contender for the worst programme of all time, full stop. The nascent C5 bought up the World Cup qualifier to raise its profile, but for some inexplicable reason they hired racing commentator **Brough Scott** (in a plaid jacket that sent the cameras funny), professionally unfunny Scot Dominik Diamond and page-three stunna **Gail McKenna** to present three interminable hours of "build-up" from a noisy "football café" peopled by ex-Gladiators and the "stars" of lacklustre soap *Family Affairs*, before **Jonathan Pearce** bawled his TV debut in the commentary box. Tragic.

2 THE MATCH (ITV)

Live and exclusive, only on ITV! Sunday afternoons around the start of the 1990s meant **Elton Welsby** and co presenting a live match, although as someone once pointed out, ITV's season started in November and ended halfway through a Howard Wilkinson interview. The two highlights were Arsenal's *Fever Pitch*-inspiring last-gasp clincher in 1989, and live coverage from **Lee Chapman**'s front room in 1992 as Leeds United discovered they were champions after rivals Manchester United slipped up.

3 JIMMY HILL'S SUNDAY SUPPLEMENT (Sky Sports)

Jim is assisted by Brian "The Bison" Woolnough and two other hacks, who convene in a fake MFI kitchen in Isleworth. They chew the fat, mull over the back pages and settle old scores while Jimmy attempts in vain to convince viewers that the set is real ("I'm just off to baste the meat").

4 THE PREMIERSHIP (ITV)

ITV's bid to make football highlights a Saturday evening attraction rapidly became the biggest TV prime-time failure in recent years, thanks to such misguided innovations as the Tactics Truck (inside which **Andy Townsend** helpfully explained to a nonplussed **Ugo Ehiogu** why his team had lost) and ProZone, a load of numbers on a computer screen which Terry Venables attempted to get enthusiastic about. Tel, Des and **Ally McCoist** bantered for all they were worth, but the programme was soon shunted back to 10.30pm.

5 MONDAY NIGHT FOOTBALL (Sky Sports)

It's all very respectable these days, but in the early days of *Monday Night Football*, pre-match entertainment was provided by the Sky Strikers dancing troupe, who were intended to bring a bit of all-American razzmatazz to Boundary Park or Carrow Road on a damp November night. Memorably, they once danced out of a huge Christmas cracker before a festive fixture at Ayresome Park. Other notable moments included "half-time musical guests" technopop outfit The Shamen being greeted by the North Bank with a full-throated "Oo the f***in' 'ell are you?"

FIVE FICTIONAL TV FOOTBALL FOLK

1 GABRIELLA BENSON

Played by Cherie Lunghi (the kind of actress always described as "delectable"), Benson was **The Manageress** in C4's 1989 series about professional football's first female boss. Despite the decried "it'll never happen" premise, it was a decent stab at a realistic football drama, with Warren Clarke as the dodgy chairman and a team featuring Stephen Tompkinson and Mark McGann. Lunghi soon legged it to run some coffee company, mind.

2 JOSSIE BLAIR

Written by **Sid Waddell**, the drinking man's Alan Bennett, *Jossie's Giants* (BBC1, 1986) depicted the travails of former Newcastle United star Joswell "Jossie" Blair, aka Jim Barclay, in his comic attempts to coach a hopeless kids team, the Glipton Grasshoppers. The theme song claimed that football was just a branch of science, but Jossie's coaching methods suggested that the writers were simply desperate to find a rhyme for "giants".

3 MAC MURPHY

In slightly grittier vein, ITV's *Murphy's Mob* (1985) followed the adventures of Dunmore United's junior supporters' club. Mac Murphy, portrayed by Ken Hutchinson, was the team's phlegmatic Scottish manager, while the club chairman was former rock star Rasputin Jones. Appropriately enough, the series was filmed at Vicarage Road for a time.

4 DARREN MATTHEWS

The hero of ITV's *All In The Game*, a 1993 drama about a top English striker who makes a big-money move to Barcelona. Clearly a scenario which must have taxed the imagination of co-creator Gary Lineker, who naturally popped up to deliver an MDF cameo offering Matthews some sage advice before his transfer ("Don't forget rule number one – score some goals, you dope!"). Lineker also inspired *An Evening With Gary Lineker* which, as football comedies go, was quite funny and only slightly smug.

John Motson, sheepskin-wearer and master of the statistic

5 FRANNY SCULLY

The creation of Alan Bleasdale, who invented the Liverpool-obsessed teen idler to entertain pupils when he was a teacher. His stories later became a Radio Merseyside series and a BBC play, before C4's 1984 adaptation. The titles depicted Scully (Andrew Schofield) running out in front of the Kop in his daydreams to the strains of "There's only one Franny Scully!" The series boasted a great theme tune from Elvis Costello and cameos from Kenny Dalglish.

TEN GREAT TV COMMENTARY MOMENTS

1 "Rivelino... watch Pelé now – what a beautiful goal from Pelé – El Rai Pele!"

In a career that spanned Molineux and the Maracanã, Hugh Johns' erupts as Pelé leaps like John West's finest to put Brazil ahead in the 1970 World Cup final.

2 "Pelé, out to Carlos Alberto on the right... and it's four! Oh, that was sheer delightful football!"

Never mind all that overexposed stuff from 1966, Ken Wolstenholme never bettered his description of the climax four years on. They seemed to take it in turns to give an exhibition.

3 "And the goal by Astle... and Leeds will go mad! And they've every right to go mad!"

Referee Ray Tinkler waves offside **West Brom** on, Jeff Astle scores, Albion win 2-1, fans spill on to the pitch, Leeds lose the 1971 title by a point (don't laugh – oh, all right then, if you must), **Barry Davies** almost seems to encourage a riot.

4 "...Radford again... oh, what a goal!" Radford the scorer, Ronnie Radford! And the crowd are invading the pitch!"

Easily the most repeated clip after 1966, but one you never tire of seeing. Non-leaguers **Hereford** slay the Mags in 1972 as a youthful John Motson gets his big break. Small boys, parkas for goalposts, enduring image, isn't it?

5 "Lee... interesting... very interesting! Look at his face... just LOOK at his face!"

Two great lines in one. **Derby**'s **Frannie Lee** belts a screamer into the **Man City** net in 1974. Barry Davies gets all ecstatic, and a little Aled Jones halfway through.

6 "Goals pay the rent, and Keegan does his share!"

David Coleman raves over Liverpool's 1974 FA Cup final triumph, exclaiming at one point that "Newcastle were undressed!" conjuring a terrifying image of **Frank Clark** and **Bob Moncur**. Keegan two, Heighway one, Liverpool three, Newcastle none!

7 "Thomas, charging through the midfield... it's up for grabs now!"

It's just after 10pm on Friday 26th May, 1989, and Brian Moore is on the mic as **Michael Thomas** wins the title for the Gunners in injury time. Recounted to Mooro by Arsenal-supporting cabbies until his dying day.

8 "Barnes, Rush, Barnes... still John Barnes... Collymore closing iiiiiinnn! Liverpool lead in stoppage time!"

Martin Tyler gives the Sky Sports lip-mic a real bashing as Stan The Man seals an extraordinary last-gasp 4-3 victory for Liverpool over Newcastle in 1996. Kevin Keegan slumps over a Carlsberg hoarding. He didn't love it.

9 "Can Manchester United score? They always score..."

Uttered by Clive Tyldesley spookily just before **Sheringham**'s equaliser ("Name on the trophy!") in the 1999 Champions League final in the Nou Camp, before

Ole Gunnar put the ball in the Bayern net seconds later ("and Solskjaer has won it!") Mercifully, Clive has rarely referred to that night in the Nou Camp since.

10 "And Urzaiz is there, and here's a chance for the goal. And it's in! It's Alfonsoooooo! It… it's unbelievable!"
The European Championships always seem to bring out something special from Motty – like his throaty "Tigana! Platini! In the last minute!" in 1984 and "It's dramatic, it's delightful, it's Denmark!" in 1992. Here, Spain come back from 3-2 down in injury time to win 4-3 during Euro 2000, sending Motson into orbit.

FOOTBALL ON THE WEB

Given the way the Internet has fundamentally changed the nature of buying, say, music, you might have thought football had escaped the digital revolution largely unscathed. You'd be wrong. Although it'll probably be quite a while before players are bought and sold on eBay (which hasn't stopped some sarcastic fans from trying), the Internet has fundamentally changed the way that clubs communicate with their fans. It allows immediate dissemination of official information, which then travels at the speed of light across the net via message boards and mailing lists. Supporters, too, have organised mass protests and launched campaigns online.

Today, every professional club must have its own site, yet for some that's a relatively new development. When the net was in its infancy during the mid-to-late 1990s, fans' sites ruled the roost, trading in gossip and often highly critical of clubs. **Chelsea** liked one fan site so much they gave its webmaster a full-time job. Slowly but surely, however, clubs woke up to the pressing commercial need for an online presence, and by the height of the dotcom boom, the Premiership was awash with official sites.

Fulham's, at one point, was valued at several million pounds, although the number of hits (and hence its value) was distorted by fans desperate for news about their club's uncertain future. There was even a spot of dotcom fever, with start-up news site Soccernet sold to US giant ESPN for around £80 million.

Most official sites are now run by a handful of companies and tend to offer fairly standard information and added extras, the latest of which is goals and highlights packages. It all comes at a premium, however (you often have to register for no obvious reason and registering often doesn't work, for no obvious reason) and may lead to all club sites becoming subscription-only – which would, in turn, fuel a revival for fans' sites. The net isn't yet revolutionising the way the game works, but it has its uses: FA coach Les Reed, for example, researches England's opponents by surfing. Email has also allowed rumours to spread like wildfire, even forcing Arsène Wenger to officially deny one baseless allegation. The **League Managers Association** gave top managers laptops so they could email each other to transfer players, swap gossip about referees and complain about how slimy they feel after being "interviewed" by Garth Crooks.

BEST FOOTBALL SITES

Football 365 www.football365.com
Combines admirable irreverence with selected news coverage of the British game and entertaining fans' feedback.

Soccerbase www.soccerbase.com
An online football encyclopedia to rival the mighty Rothmans – details of every player and every match can be found here.

Planet Football www.planetfootball.com
Regularly updates news and reports – this site is particularly good for finding out about European and overseas football news.

E-soccer www.e-soccer.com
The best repository of links, covering every UK club and more general sites.

Footballtransfers.net www.footballtransfers.net
Does what it says on the tin: a repository of information about transfers, records and rumours. Not the most up-to-date site, but we love the speculation section – divided into confirmed and unconfirmed. Unconfirmed speculation?

Rivals www.rivals.net
Collection of organised, competent fan-run sites covering all professional teams; a great way to catch up on rumours and off-the-wall happenings.

The Rec.Sport.Soccer Statistics Foundation www.rsssf.com
Statto's heaven – a massive archive of international and domestic football scores and scorers, rankings, various trivia and the odd argument about the merits of South American versus European football. Not a site to be visited if you have to get somewhere in a hurry.

Collect Soccer www.collectsoccer.com

The self-proclaimed "world's largest football memorabilia megastore." Get your programmes, posters, pennants and more.

ODDEST FOOTBALL SITES

The Famous Football Supporters' Page

www.railwayinn.freeserve.co.uk/famous.htm

Lee from Steps supports **Everton**, Peter Sissons favours **Liverpool**, while Wendy James of Transvision Vamp follows **QPR**. Plus many, many more…

AskGreaves www.askgreaves.com

The current whereabouts of every past great player – possibly the best way to while away an afternoon at work online.

The Football Quotes Page

www.geocities.com/SouthBeach/Palms/6687/quotesmain.html

Includes managers, commentators – plus Kevin Keegan: see "Young Gareth Barry – he's young" and "You're not just getting international football, you're getting world football." Often imitated, but this huge repository is never bettered.

The Referee's Alphabet

comedy.allinfoabout.com/ref.html

Audio-visual representation of the hilarious Half Man, Half Biscuit anthem: "The Referee's Alphabet." "T is for twenty-one man brawl..."

Bob and 1970-71 Footballers

http://dspace.dial.pipex.com/bob.dunning/boband.htm

Bob likes the 1970-71 season, so here's a site about it – which scarily omits any mention of any other season or event. Where nostalgia turns freaky.

BOOKS

Blame **Billy Wright**. Merchandising and off-field activities were rare among footballers in the sedate 1950s, so the then-captain of England hit on a nice little earner by writing about his life and career in such tomes as *Football Is My*

A WHOLE NEW BALL GAME

There's nothing in the rules of the game to say that you have to wear shorts. It's a loophole that Brazilian team Roza FC are particularly grateful for. Roza are Brazil's leading – and possibly only – transvestite football team. Based on a dirt pitch just outside Rio, Roza play their derby game every year against a local team of married men. Why the other team should all be married isn't made entirely clear, but when their opposition consists of drag queens and the referee is dressed in red PVC, it'd obviously be churlish to ask.

It's taken Brazilian journalist Alex Bellos' description of the side in his book, *Futebol: The Brazilian Way Of Life,* to bring Roza to a wider audience. Naming the referee as "Laura de Vision… a 20-stone silicone-enhanced club performer whose star trick usually involves lollipops, not whistles," Bellos describes some of de Vision's more dubious decisions, including the award of a penalty for "chatting up the centre-forward." Even if his book also includes what must be the most surreal action photograph ever, depicting a svelte player in a blue mini-skirt dribbling past a significantly less svelte figure squeezed into an unforgiving sequinned dress, Bellos does have the good grace to take Roza seriously. Team captain Kaika Sabatela, a 36-year-old in a shocking pink catsuit, tells Bellos: "We work, we pay our taxes and we like watching football – why shouldn't we be allowed to play the game?"

Passport, *Captain Of England* and *One Hundred Caps And All That.* Wright's writings – and those of fellow stars like **Neil Franklin** and **Bert Trautmann** – were acceptable enough and sold well. Unfortunately, this gave rise to the regrettable idea that all players could, and should, put pen to paper. Some of these autobiographies even proved prophetic. Maybe the FA should have looked at Don Revie's autobiography as a player and wondered why it was called **The Happy Wanderer** before they gave him the England job and before he happily wandered off to the Middle East. **Malcolm McDonald**'s effort **Not Afraid To Miss** is worth noting just for the honesty of the title; presumably Vladimir Smicer's memoirs would be called **Afraid To Shoot**.

The nadir was probably reached around 1998 with the publication of *My Story So Far* by **Alan Shearer**, a tome so devoid of character you could almost see it turning back into plant life. Chillingly, it's also available on audio cassette, read by Shearer lookalike Robson Green. Sample anecdote: "I was paying my extras bill at the hotel before we left for Highfield Road when a woman asked for my signature. I asked her if she would give me a minute while I settled my account. There was a query on the bill so it took a little longer than I expected. By the time I had finished, I had completely forgotten about the autograph-hunter and I left the hotel lobby without signing her book." Riveting stuff.

But if the old pros were bland, their books at least offered fans a glimpse into a private world rarely explored by the media. Tales of dressing-room camaraderie, lists of favourite opponents and such startling revelations as "I can't complain really, it's a smashing way to make a living" were what the public wanted.

Special mention should go to Fred Eyre, whose autobiography *Kicked Into Touch* (1981) became a surprise best-seller by virtue of its glamour-free grittiness. Eyre was a lower-division and non-league journeyman whose career was characterised by under-achievement, yet his very persistence and good humour endeared him to readers (although the two follow-ups detailing his career as a radio pundit and after-dinner speaker may have been pushing it a bit). Len Shackleton also entertained, entitling a chapter of his autobiography *What your average club director knows about football.* The next page was blank.

Come the 1990s, however, newspapers had woken up to the fact that autobiographies were potentially a rich source of scandal, particularly among players coming to the end of their careers. A serialisation became almost as important to publishers as sales of the book itself, and revelations came thick and fast. In *Rock Bottom* (1996), Paul Merson confessed the extent of his addictions, as did Tony Adams in the aptly named *Addicted* (1999).

> ***"I have had the finger of blame pointed at me when the toes have been cut out of socks"***
>
> *Laugh-a-minute Alan Shearer*

Others have trashed managers or fellow pros, or even both (see *Vinnie: The Autobiography*). Some really overstepped the mark – Glenn Hoddle's notorious 1998 World Cup diary and David O'Leary's *Leeds United On Trial* were ill-advised, badly timed and almost certainly contributed to both men losing their jobs.

When real writers have done the writing and left the footballers to the, er, footballing, however, things have turned out rather better. The surge in middle-class interest in the game created a range of coffee table titles of dubious quality but has also contributed some modern classics to add to a burgeoning library.

FOOTBALL BOOKS – THE TOP 10

1 All Played Out, *Pete Davies* (Jonathan Cape, 1990)

Davies' journey to the World Cup in Italy saw him follow, and interview, the England team, pondering the nature of football, the savagery of the media and the pointlessness of John Barnes. He also came closer than any other author to pinpointing what makes being a fan so important. Davies' compelling prose betrays his love for the game, yet he also places it, subtly, in a wider sociological context, mingling with supporters as they run the gauntlet of the Italian police and experiencing the lows of semi-final defeat.

2 The Glory Game, ***Hunter Davies*** **(Weidenfeld & Nicholson, 1972)**
Much of what we know (or think we know) about the inner workings of football comes from Davies' masterpiece – which is why it is still a fascinating piece of work even though the players and era (Tottenham's 1971-72 team) are now long gone. The journalist was allowed unparalleled access to players and staff, and told the story of how a typical club functions over the course of a season in simple, yet revealing, style. The passages on the players' hopes, views and lifestyles are a charming highlight.

3 Only A Game? ***Eamon Dunphy*** **(Penguin, 1973)**
Reaching the end of his career and desperate for a first taste of genuine glory, Irish-born journeyman Dunphy charted a season with **Millwall** and the personalities, issues and disappointments that ensued. It could have been standard fare, but it became a classic, with Dunphy's ruminations on the nature of the game giving the average professional footballer an articulate voice for perhaps the first time.

4 Football In Sun And Shadow, ***Eduardo Galeano*** **(Fourth Estate, 1997)**
Uruguayan author Galeano's work has become a coffee-table favourite, a gross injustice to the majesty of his prose. Though the style and premise of *Football In Sun And Shadow* border on the pretentious, there isn't a whiff of Nick Hornby here, just a football lover's genuine affection. Galeano recounts great players and moments from the game's history (albeit with a South American bent) in bite-size vignettes with, at times, tearful nostalgia and a heartfelt optimism for a sport now driven more by greed than passion.

5 The Story of the World Cup, ***Brian Glanville*** **(Faber & Faber, 2001)**
Glanville is rightly revered as one of Britain's finest football journalists, and his regularly updated history is a chronicle of all that's right in the game, balancing an eye for detail with magical descriptions of stars and teams. Best bit: calling former Tory sports minister Colin Moynihan "small but imperfectly informed" His *Football Memories* ain't bad either – if you skip all the bits about his own literary efforts.

6 Hand Of God, ***Jimmy Burns*** **(Bloomsbury, 1996)**
To many, Diego Maradona was a finer talent than Pelé. He was also a cheating, drug-taking hothead whose bizarre off-field circus often overshadowed his gifts. Burns achieves the rare feat of celebrating a God-given talent while investigating and castigating the influences which ruined it. While he is arguably too harsh on the star himself, this portrayal of a world of unyielding pressure explains much of the madness Maradona came to represent.

7 Full Time: The Secret Life of Tony Cascarino, *Paul Kimmage* (Scribner, 2000)
A ghosted autobiography of beanpole striker Tony Cascarino should have been pretty uninspiring stuff, but the result was astonishing. The former Millwall journeyman reveals his failings as a husband, friend and footballer (despite winning 60 caps for Ireland, he wasn't Irish) with such candid detail that it's often almost too much to bear. Yet he also recounts the vices that stalk the game with a real intelligence and eloquence.

8 Manchester Unlimited, *Mihir Bose* (Texere, 1999)
Telegraph journalist Bose has a nose for the cloudy world of football finance, and here he tells of the in-fighting and behind-the-scenes intrigue surrounding Manchester United's rise from mid-table mediocrity to richest club in the world. The best bit, however, deals with United lawyer Maurice Watkins' handling of Eric Cantona's FA disciplinary hearing following his infamous kung-fu kick: "Watkins heard Cantona, after apologising to the FA, his fans, his team-mates and the club, say 'And I want to apologise to the prostitute who shared my bed last evening.' Maurice turned, his mouth fell open and he almost fell off his chair. Gordon McKeag, one of the three-man tribunal, turned to Geoff Thomson, the FA chairman and said 'What did he say? He prostrates himself before the FA?' 'Yes,' said Thomson, eager to get away from the subject."

9 Left Foot Forward, *Garry Nelson* (Headline, 1995)
As with Messrs Cascarino and Dunphy, jobbing lower-division striker Nelson transcends the format of the autobiography with his candid diary, which pays admirable attention to detail. Anyone who's ever wondered what day-to-day life is like for the average professional will find the answer here.

10 The Rothmans Football Yearbook (Headline, 2003)
Not a novel, nor a warts-and-all autobiography, but the football fan's Bible (or, more accurately, their answer to *Wisden*). Since 1969, this fat volume has been compiling statistics, results, player details and fixtures from every echelon of the British game in a way that slimmer, less prestigious rivals could only dream of. A Great British institution. Now called Sky Sports Football Yearbook. Shame.

FIVE OF THE WORST

1 David Beckham: My Story/My World (1998/2001, Hodder & Stoughton)
Ah yes, the snipers are already saying, but young David is a footballer, not an author, so leave him alone. In which case, the reply must come, don't write books

then. These two volumes reduce every high and low in the footballing oeuvre to the most bland and easily digestible of emotions. When Glenn Hoddle has lambasted our hero in the World Cup, for example, he tells us: "You just have to get on with it," while winning the title is "great". Most of the dust-jacket quotes praise the photos without mentioning the prose – wonder why?

2 Sweeper!/Striker!/Defender!, *Steve Bruce* (Paragon Press)
While on holiday during his brief tenure as **Huddersfield Town** boss, Bruce put pen to paper to create the first of three seminal tales of intrigue and mystery at, ahem, Leddersfield Town. In them, manager Steve Barnes (formerly of Mulcaster United) must clear up a calamitous series of deaths and disasters, while also writing alarmingly short sentences: "A shiver ran down the length of my spine. And I'll tell you what. It wasn't because of the influenza virus." Sadly, Bruce is too busy keeping **Birmingham City** in the Premiership to pen the follow-ups, *Midfielder!*, *Winger!* and *Utility Man!* Still, literature's loss is football's gain.

3 The Hazell Books/They Used To Play On Grass, *Terry Venables* (Penguin)
Not so much bad as amusing – Venables' collaborations with Gordon Williams spawned five books (including the Hazell series of detective novels) and a hit TV series, yet never earned him the respect of an uncaring public.

4 My Story So Far, *Alan Shearer* (Hodder & Stoughton, 1998)
Let's just remind ourselves again: "I have been described as England's Captain Clean but I hate the public image that I am too good to be true. My team-mates will tell you I love a laugh and a joke the same as everyone. I've been known to take part in a few dressing-room pranks. I have had the finger of blame pointed at me when the toes have been cut out of team-mates' socks."

5 Any book on football violence
One of the worst excesses of the rise in football "literature" was the money suddenly thrown at reformed hooligans to tell all about their time on the wrong side of the law. Dougie and Eddy Brimson, who have now stretched their collective oeuvre to over a dozen titles, are the worst, but they're far from being the only offenders.

LITERARY CLASSICS WITH A FOOTBALL TWIST

The great football novel is yet to be written. How do we know this? Because every few years some mildly talented author publishes a book which carries on the back the blurb "the great football novel has now been written", usually credited to *The*

Auctermuchty Bugle. Those who have tried and failed include, predictably, Brian Glanville whose *Goalkeepers Are Crazy* is at least better than Steve Bruce's efforts. So, while we're waiting for the great football novel, we'll leave you with these variations on familiar fictional themes.

The Trial by *Franz Kafka*

"Someone had been telling lies about Josef K: he'd never said the gaffer thought tactics were a kind of mint." Josef K is a Czech winger who has signed for the all-powerful Liverpool football club and its imperious manager but, for reasons that are never made clear to us or him, is banished from the first team and left to languish in reserves "like a miserable dog."

Herzog by *Saul Bellow*

The American novelist's acknowledged masterpiece is a fine comic tale of the rise and falling over of Austrian footballer Andreas Herzog, a legendary figure whose pace, vision and finally sense of balance betray him.

Adam One Afternoon by *Italo Calvino*

A sparkling comic fantasy in which the protagonist, a Peter Mandelson lookalike called simply Adam, fondly imagines that he is in charge of the beautiful game. Calvino subtly raises the stakes and clouds the issue so that, by the end of this novella, the reader isn't sure if Adam's fantasies aren't real after all.

The Postman Always Rings Twice by *James M Cain*

Classic pulp novel in which postie (and former England and Chelsea goalkeeper) Peter Bonetti only rings the doorbell twice before leaving the package on the front step because he's tired of being asked why he let in West Germany's third goal in the 1970 World Cup quarter-final. Another variation on this theme is Charles Bukowski's *Post Office*, a picaresque romp in which each chapter tells the fictional stories of footballers who've become men of letters: Kevin Hector, Bonetti, Neil Webb, etc etc.

Oblomov by *Ivan Gonharov*

Seminal Russian novel about a lazy, overweight, oafish Spartak Moscow striker who refuses to get out of bed, even though he's due to report for pre-season training that morning. By the end, Oblomov's agent has managed to coax his client out of bed and into the armchair to pore over old scrapbooks.

The Mayor Of Casterbridge by *Thomas Hardy*

A moving, cautionary tale about the mayor of a small Dorset town whose dreams of turning Casterbridge United into a Premiership side founder on corruption, dodgy players and the mayor's decision to acquire a trophy wife.

1984 by *George Orwell*

Winston Smith is a promising defender who has just signed for a famous west London football club run by an omnipotent dictator known only as Big Brother, who is in a permanent state of war with the rest of the football world. The club is the capital of a totalitarian nightmare of a kingdom known only as "the Village" while Smith is struggling to find his true form before the controversial trainer O'Brien, who has been known to use small rodents in training, arrives.

FANZINES, MAGAZINES, STUFF LIKE THAT

Ever since the first footballing pioneers started kicking a pig's bladder around, fans have had an overwhelming urge to read about the thrilling heroics of their idols. The earliest publication in the British Library's football collection is *The Goal: The Chronicle Of Football*, from 1873, which lasted just 22 issues. For the next 75 years or so, titles came and went, like 1882's imaginatively named *Football*, which managed 28 editions before being merged with the equally excitingly titled *Pastime*, as well as *Football Bits* in 1919 and *The Football Favourite* in 1920.

But football magazines didn't really take off until after the World War II, and the arrival on the bookstands of Charles Buchan's *Football Monthly*, master-minded by the eponymous former England international-turned-journalist. The first issue in September 1951 cost 1/6 and featured a hand-tinted Stanley Matthews on the cover. At its peak, in the early 1960s, the magazine was selling 130,000 copies a month.

By the turn of the decade, however, the magazine, with its whiff of liniment and baggy-shorted ethos, suddenly found itself up against tricky new rivals more in tune with the era of George Best and the King's Road. *Goal* launched in August 1968, promising pages of colour, personalities and revealing, hard-hitting exclusives ("No, I'll Never Start Playing Like A Fairy, Says **Tommy Smith**"). And decades before *Footballers' Wives*, *Goal* trained the spotlight on our heroes' other halves in a series of weekly portraits ("Life can be hectic for a soccer star but that doesn't worry Marilyn, 20-year-old wife of **Billy Bonds**").

Shoot! hit the newsagents in 1969, yours for one shilling, with founding columnist Bobby Moore starring on the first cover. That premiere issue featured the debut of a perennial *Shoot!* free gift, the League Ladders – a cardboard ready-reckoner enabling fans to keep track of the league ups and downs via the medium of fiddly cardboard tabs. Inside, *Shoot!*'s big attractions were the star columnists. Back then, you knew you'd really made it when you were snapped up to put your name to a ghosted *Shoot!* column. Sales leaped 50,000 when George Best signed on the line, and Keegan, Dalglish, Shilton, Gray, Rush, Nicholas, Barnes and Gascoigne, among others, followed in his wake. Meanwhile, You Are The Ref tested readers' grasp of the laws of the game ("or c: an indirect free-kick?").

And there was the legendary Focus page, probing the likes and dislikes of the stars, and prompting a generation of impressionable young fans to yearn for the footballer's lager-and-lime lifestyle of *The Sweeney*, scampi, George Benson and Bo Derek. Frank Worthington declared his Most Difficult Opponent to be "my ex-wife" while the person Uli Stielike most wanted to meet was "the late President Sadat of Egypt". Oh, and commiserations to self-confessed *Daily Star* reader Gary Lineker, who never quite fulfiled his post-career ambition to be "a bookmaker, hopefully".

Other titles from the 1960s and 1970s included *World Soccer*, launched in 1960 and still frighteningly comprehensive today, the dour *Soccer Star*, Jimmy Hill's *Football Weekly*, *Inside Football* and *Striker*. *Football Monthly* responded to the competition by dropping the Buchan name from the cover and campaigning for Champagne Soccer, rewarding teams who scored six goals with a magnum of bubbly for the supporters' club – not much incentive for the players, surely? In 1974, the magazine adopted a *Reader's Digest*-style A5 look, but the game was up, although the title managed to limp into the 1990s under a succession of titles, owners and formats.

The late 1970s brought the Marshall Cavendish partwork *Football Handbook*, edited by Martin Tyler with "consultant" Graham Taylor and building up over 63 weeks into a big pile of magazines. In 1979, *Shoot!* gained a rival in the shape of clone *Match Weekly*, but the football recession of the 1980s meant that there were few launches, save for the weighty-but-pretentious *Soccer International*, and *Football Today* for the parka and Thermos brigade. But in the wake of Heysel, Hillsborough and the spectre of membership cards, the rise of the fanzine at last gave supporters a more readable alternative to the glossies.

The first fanzine was probably *Foul*, a sort of footballing *Private Eye* published by Cambridge undergraduates between 1972 and 1976. The torch was rekindled in the mid-80s by the Midlands-based *Off The Ball*, *The Absolute Game* in Scotland

> **"He's nice, who's he? David Beckham? I'll go up to Manchester then, we can have dinner afterwards"**
>
> *Victoria Beckham opens her heart to* 90 Minutes *magazine*

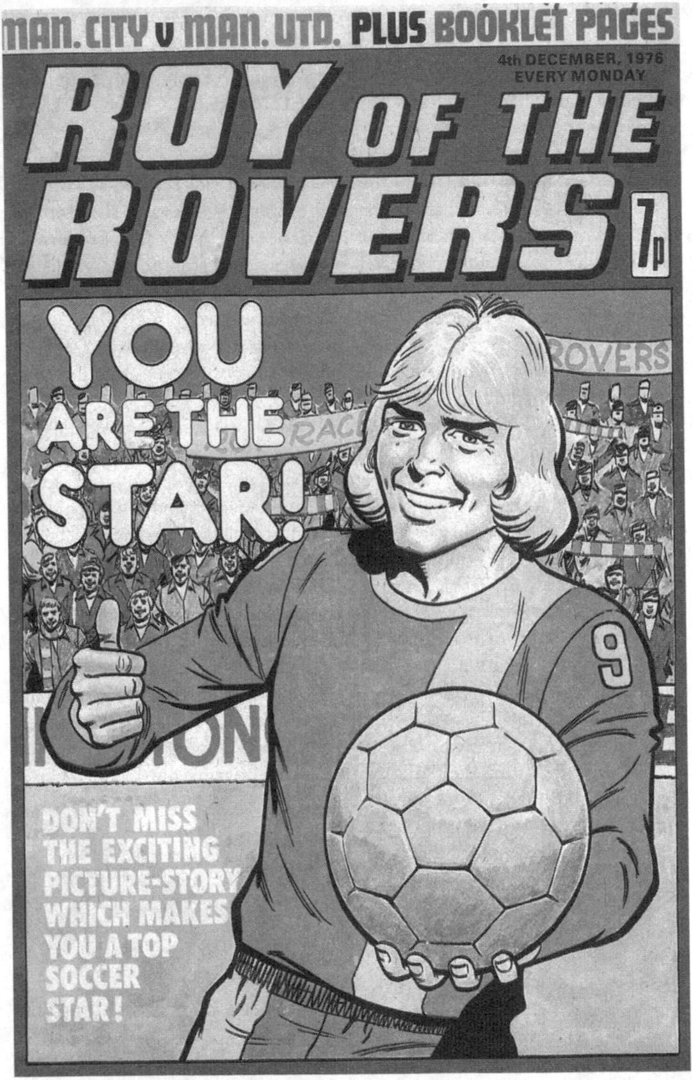

MAN. CITY v MAN. UTD. PLUS BOOKLET PAGES

4th DECEMBER, 1976
EVERY MONDAY

ROY OF THE ROVERS 7p

YOU ARE THE STAR!

ROVERS

DON'T MISS THE EXCITING PICTURE-STORY WHICH MAKES YOU A TOP SOCCER STAR!

and the best-known of the lot, *When Saturday Comes*. In their wake came an avalanche of inky bedroom-published 'zines devoted to clubs from top flight to non-league, spearheaded by **Bradford City**'s *City Gent*.

Even if the content wasn't always particularly original, it was passionate, and at its height the movement boasted a magnificent array of titles: **Gillingham's** *Brian Moore's Head Looks Uncannily Like The London Planetarium*, **Crewe's** *Super Dario Land*, **WBA's** *Grorty Dick*, **Blackburn's** *Four Thousand Holes* and the *Leyton Orienteer*. The influence of the fanzines inevitably filtered into the mainstream, exemplified by *90 Minutes*, launched a few weeks before Italia '90 and finding a niche as a sort of fanzine-equivalent of *Shoot!* that kids and *NME* readers alike could read. Highlights included a prescient Gordon Grenville interview with the Spice Girls. (Victoria: "Ooh, he's nice, who's he? David Beckham? Oh, I'll go up to Manchester then, we can go out for dinner afterwards!")

FourFourTwo arrived in 1994, somehow surviving showing Jimmy Hill in a football kit on the cover, followed the following year by *Total Football* and a relaunched *Goal* from the *90 Minutes* stable, and in 1997 the BBC weighed in with *Match Of The Day* magazine. But even though football was more popular than ever, the rise of the Internet, wall-to-wall TV coverage and countless newspaper supplements sated the appetite of potential readers, and all the adult titles bar *FourFourTwo* went to the wall. Even *Shoot!* ceased popping through the letterbox as a weekly in 2001, lingering on only as a monthly.

COMICS

"Oh I say... that is Schoolboy's Own stuff!" Barry Davies had it right when he exploded with delight at Paul Gascoigne's extraordinary free-kick for Spurs in the 1991 FA Cup semi-final. But for the best part of five decades, improbable feats like Gazza's were performed week in, week out in the pages of the comics, in an alternative footballing universe where scrap metal dealers kept goal, magic boots made kids play like Johan Cruyff and Melchester Rovers never, ever lost...

ROY OF THE ROVERS (TIGER/ROY OF THE ROVERS)

Far and away the most celebrated football strip ever, *Roy Of The Rovers* was conceived for the launch of *Tiger* in 1954 as a more down-to-earth hero than Dan Dare, star of *Tiger's* sister comic *Eagle.* Devised by Frank Pepper, the story originally focused on the teenage Roy Race's battle to make the big time. Established in the Melchester Rovers front line alongside Blackie Gray, Roy set about winning everything in the game, invariably bringing him into conflict with nasty cheating foreigners and the odd jealous team-mate.

The late 1970s and 1980s brought a touch more realism, with Roy no longer scoring a hat-trick with his left-foot rocket every week. He even married secretary Penny in 1976, the year Roy's own comic was launched. In 1981 Rovers were relegated, and Roy was shot by actor Elton Blake. Two years later, a restless Roy resigned to manage Walford Rovers, but returned within months. Bizarrely, in 1985 **Martin Kemp** and **Steve Norman** of Spandau Ballet were briefly recruited to the Rovers squad after impressing in a charity match, a move which coincided with the beginning of the end. Despite (or perhaps because of) storylines which included half the team being blown up by terrorists, the comic's popularity waned; it closed in 1993 as Roy lost his left foot in a helicopter crash. In four decades, Roy had won the League 10 times, the FA Cup six times, the European Cup three times, scored 436 goals and even briefly managed England.

BILLY'S BOOTS (SCORCHER/TIGER/ROY OF THE ROVERS)

"Is this me or is this Dead Shot Keen?" was the catchphrase of Billy Dane as he bore down on goal – a fact noted by Half Man Half Biscuit on the album *MacIntyre, Treadmore and Davitt* (named after Michael Palin's Barnstoneworth United team in Ripping Yarns, natch). Dane had somehow acquired the boots that had belonged to 1920s hotshot Keen, which magically enabled the otherwise-talentless adolescent to play like him. Naturally the boots were discarded with frustrating regularity by Billy's gran (like all comic teens, he was an orphan) who kept giving them to jumble sales or tossing them onto bonfires. The inspiration for rubbish footyflick *There's Only One Jimmy Grimble.*

GORGEOUS GUS (WIZARD/VICTOR)

Our aristocratic hero in this 1960s strip was the, er, Earl Of Boote, who bought the ailing Redburn Rovers after they failed to score in their first four games of the season. He was christened Gorgeous Gus by the fans because of his distaste for tackling and running – he simply expected his team-mates to set him up with chances which he'd blast into the net. Once Rovers had established a commanding lead, Gus would retire to a special area on the touchline, where he would be attended to by his butler Jenkins.

THE HARD MAN (ROY OF THE ROVERS)

This told tough-tackling tales of Johnny Dexter, a sort of Terry Butcher figure forever in trouble with the footballing authorities and blessed with the ability to perform perfect headlong diving headers, as only comic footballers can. Dexter's gaffer at Danefield United was Viktor Boskovic, an Eastern European of uncertain origin who predated the current vogue for foreign coaches by at least a decade and looked a bit like Fred Elliott off *Corrie*. Dexter later spun off into a new story, Dexter's Dozen, before winding up at the mighty Melchester Rovers.

HOT SHOT HAMISH (TIGER/ROY OF THE ROVERS)

Hamish Balfour, a Herculean striker with an blond mullet, was brought from a tiny Hebridean island to play for Princes Park in the Scottish League by manager Mr McWhacker. He had a pet sheep called McMutton. In later seasons, when *Tiger* merged with *Roy Of The Rovers*, he teamed up in a Butch-and-Sundance-style double act with rotund footballing hospital porter Mighty Mouse.

IRON BARR (SPIKE/CHAMP)

The star of this was giant Charlie "Iron" Barr who, you'll be amazed to learn, worked as a scrap metal dealer when he wasn't playing in goal for Darbury Rangers for free (he preferred to remain amateur for some bizarre reason). He once scored from his own line, and on another occasion dribbled the length of the field to put the ball in the net. Later handily signed for United when Spike merged with Champ. He also had his own column, Iron Barr's Sports Round-up.

JACK OF UNITED AND JIMMY OF CITY (SCORE AND ROAR/SCORCHER)

The adventures of two brothers playing for rival clubs in the same city provides the storyline here. The square-jawed Jack was the more reliable Bobby Charlton figure of the two, while Jimmy was the glamourous maverick Stan Bowles type. Each had their own strip every week, with a neat "crossover" element.

LIMP ALONG LESLIE (WIZARD/HOTSPUR)

Talented youngster Leslie Thomson was involved in a car accident as a child which, naturally, killed both his parents, and rendered his left leg shorter than the right. Now he lived on Low Dyke Farm with his Aunt Lucy and Uncle Arnold, and was torn between his two ambitions – to play for the mighty Darbury Rangers or to train his sheepdog Pal into a champion. Scored brilliant curling free-kicks.

MIKE'S MINI MEN (ROY OF THE ROVERS)

Teenager Mike Dailey owns a Subbuteo team called Redstone Rovers. Er, that's it. On the *Billy's Boots* principle, they got nicked or lost every three weeks.

MI££IONAIRE VILLA (ROY OF THE ROVERS)

This one's a bit of a rip-off of *Gorgeous Gus*, with millionaire David Bradley giving Division One club Selby Villa £2million on condition he plays in the first team. Possibly the inspiration for Michael Knighton's takeover bid and keepy-uppy exploits at Old Trafford.

NIPPER (SCORCHER/TIGER/ROY OF THE ROVERS)

The enduring story of Nipper Lawrence – you've guessed it, a young orphan who played for Blackport Rovers – outlasted the rest because Nipper was just that bit more human than his rivals, cursed as he had a quick temper. Had a dog called Stumpy.

THE SAFEST HANDS IN SOCCER/GOALKEEPER (ROY OF THE ROVERS)

For five years Safest Hands, beautifully drawn by Osvaldo Torta, followed the daring deeds of ace No.1 Gordon Stewart, who played for Tynefield City and Longford Forest before being killed in a car accident. Twelve months later, *Goalkeeper* picked up the story of his talented teenage son Rick, and his attempts to emulate his dad at rival clubs Tynefield United and Oakhampton.

TOMMY'S TROUBLES (ROY OF THE ROVERS)

Tommy Barnes and his trusty best pal Ginger Collins were just mad about football. But guess what: they only play rugby at Crowhurst Road School! Realising this might result in a somewhat truncated football story, Tommy sets about assembling his own extracurricular soccer team, Barnes United. Lasted a good 10 years, this one.

WE ARE UNITED (CHAMP/VICTOR)

This was an excellent attempt at putting a more realistic spin on the *Roy Of The Rovers* formula. Manager Joe Pearson was the man attempting to revive sleeping giants United, aided and abetted by Mohicaned punk winger Hedgehog Jones, mercurial Welsh striker Terry Evans and later, that man Charlie Barr. The story neatly followed the season's actual fixture list, whereas it seemed to take Melchester a month to complete one game. Pretty good, all told, even once dabbling with a hooliganism storyline, when a bunch of Pringled-up casuals affixed themselves to the club.

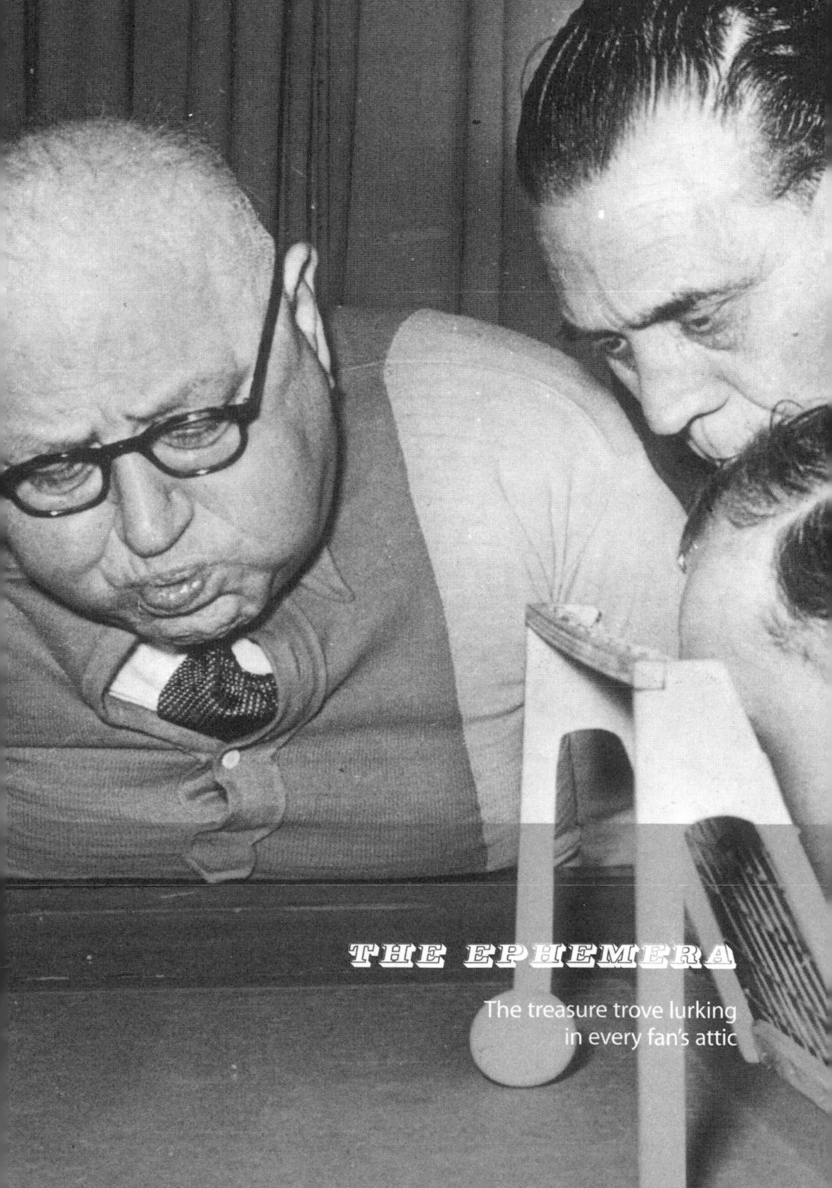

THE EPHEMERA

The treasure trove lurking in every fan's attic

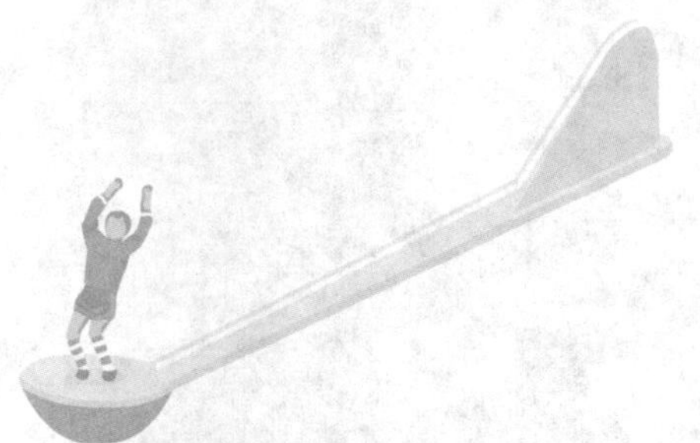

Early efforts at blow football needed some fine-tuning

"For sure, continuations of negative campaigns may well see the club relegated, and one would have thought that nobody or no groups of people would be as futile, self-centred or indignant enough to place themselves in a position where they consider they are more important than the well-being of the establishment"

(Brief) extract from the programme notes of Colin Murphy, former Lincoln boss

Before football clubs took memorabilia to the extreme with the mandatory club shops and new strips every few months, ticket stubs, programmes and playing kit were the stuff of the most avid fans' collections. The British are without doubt the biggest spenders on memorabilia. While the French and Italians stick to competition medals and team badges, the Brits are often unconcerned whether they're buying sought-after collectables or simply junk.

Programmes were once the core memorabilia items. Age and scarcity tend to add to market value, though the passing years are unlikely to add greatly to the desirability of that **Raith Rovers** vs **Brechin City** programme you kept from that far-off childhood holiday. Ticket stubs, meanwhile, have recently increased in value. Anyone who went to the 2002 World Cup is advised to put their tickets in a safe place if they want to secure a large payout.

The value of signed items varies widely. An autographed pair of boots used by Beckham or Owen sounds like a dream purchase to a **Manchester United** or **Liverpool** fan. Unfortunately, unless they were used in a prestigious event, you're unlikely to reap much in the way of monetary rewards, simply because both are still playing and the market could be flooded with similar items.

Finally, aim for originality when you're putting together your collection. Official mascot postcards issued for the 1966 World Cup, for example, fetch up to £50 today, collectors viewing them as unusual and prestigious enough to warrant that kind of money.

MOST VALUABLE MEMORABILIA

1. Yellow Brazil shirt worn by Pelé in the 1970 World Cup final
The hammer finally fell at £157,750, a record for a football shirt at an auction
2. Gordon Banks' World Cup winner's medal
Fetched £124,000 in 2001
3. Red England shirt worn by Geoff Hurst in the 1966 World Cup final
Sold for £91,750 in 2000
4. England World Cup 1966 international cap
Sold at Christies for £37,600 in 2000
5. "Match card" giving the line-up for England v Ireland in 1897
Predicted to fetch around £1,500 but went for £4,600

MOST SOUGHT-AFTER FOOTBALL PROGRAMMES

A 1999 survey claimed that football fans across Britain were hoarding £15 million worth of memorabilia, a figure that would reach over £30 million by 2003. Much of that money was tied up in programmes, for years the preserve of anorak-clad ground-hoppers but more recently the plaything of the richer fan, willing to pay handsomely for that rare collectible, with anything involving Manchester United worth considerably more than average.

The first known programme was produced for a **Preston North End** v **Derby County** fixture in 1893, but no copies remain. As a rule, pre-war programmes are collectors' items, worth the extra expense as an investment. A 1966 World Cup final programme could set you back around £400 and will continue to increase in value, partly because not enough copies were printed and partly because England don't look like repeating that success.

The 1966 programme costs over £300

Programmes from the past 20 years are usually worth little more than the cover price, and often less, but those in the know advise that it's always worth looking out for anything slightly unusual. Last-minute postponements are a particular favourite – if a game is called off with just hours to go, the programmes will already have been printed but rarely go into circulation.

1. Tottenham Hotspur v Sheffield United, FA Cup final, 1901
At £14,400, it's the dearest programme ever sold at an auction – commanding five times its reserve price
2. Scotland v England, 1897
The oldest international match to come to auction, fetching £6,000
3. Manchester United v Wolverhampton Wanderers, 1958
The match that was never played due to the Munich air disaster. Although the programme was printed and then pulped, a few copies got into the hands of fans and now fetch around £1,000
4. Any pre-war FA Cup final £500 –£2,000
5. 1966 World Cup final programme £300-£500

WORST PIECES OF OFFICIAL MERCHANDISE

In the pre-*Fever Pitch* days, it was considered shameless corporate exploitation to try and flog your fans a training top. But then football clubs started floating on the Stock Exchange and club directors slowly realised the potential income to be squeezed from the loyal supporter. Car stickers, mugs and pens became pyjamas, slippers and bedspreads. Manchester United opened an Old Trafford Megastore which made Harrods look like a corner shop. They also became one of the first clubs to introduce a branded credit card, so that even the money you spent on the club was owned by the club. Still, it's hard to argue that a nodding-head Ryan Giggs isn't the sort of item any self-respecting car owner wouldn't treasure.

Manchester United mortgage
Your home may be at risk if you don't keep up repayments, but you do get a free subscription to MUTV
Arsenal dog collar £7.50
Make Fido's misery complete with a Gunners-themed restraint
Liverpool FC tax disc holder £1.50
Insert your own joke about car ownership and scousers
Celtic calculator £40
Handy for those championship run-in home games against Kilmarnock when the goal count gets confusing
Aston Villa earmuffs £8
For when it just all gets too much in the cauldron-like atmosphere of Villa Park
Fulham baby bibs £5
Until surprisingly recently, the Fulham club shop sold infant items with a graphic of a smiling house and the embarrassing motto "I'm A Little Cottager"…

GAMES

"So he'd send his doting mother up the stairs
To get Subbuteo out of the loft
He had all the accessories required for that big match atmosphere
The crowd and the dugout and the floodlights too
You'd always get palmed off with a headless centre forward
And a goalkeeper with no arms and a face like his
And he'd managed to get hold of a Dukla Prague away kit
'Cos his uncle owned a sports shop and he'd kept it to one side"

So runs *All I Want For Christmas Is A Dukla Prague Away Kit*, a nostalgic tribute to **Subbuteo** by Wirral punks Half Man Half Biscuit that will strike a chord with anyone who grew up in the 1970s or 1980s. Young boys have always followed football obsessively, so it's no wonder that board games manufacturers fought tooth and nail to capture a potentially lucrative market.

Striker was a smaller, five-a-side version of Subbuteo where you pressed players on the head to activate a kicking mechanism. **Cup Final** consisted of two teams with three players – a goalkeeper who could throw (and score, if you were well-practiced), a "chipper" with shovel-style feet, and a "shooter", who kicked along the ground. There was also the inexplicable dice game **Wembley**, and **Supercup Football**, with ice-hockey-style twisting players controlled by dials. This led on to standard table football, which has recently enjoyed a renaissance (perhaps due to its urban-cool factor after appearing in the TV *Friends* apartment), but strangely remains more popular in French bars than here.

For the more cerebral, there were basic management games. Terry Venables invented and endorsed his game **The Manager**, a management exercise "for all ages and two to four players". In true El Tel style, the player making the most money – rather than winning the most honours – won. Other efforts like Emlyn Hughes' **Team Tactix** came and went.

But conquering the lot for playability, value for money, a realistic looking set-up and teams to collect and keep, was Subbuteo.

The pitch, either original baize or **Luton Town**-style astroturf, would be laid out on a carpet, or if you were lucky, the kitchen table. Under Subbuteo's surprisingly strict rules, only the nail part of the finger was

> ***"As a boy in the 1960s, Subbuteo was all you had. That and* Barbarella *... and here, with a* Barbarella*-style haircut, comes Ray Parlour"***
>
> *Jonathan Pearce in full flow, 2002*

Sir Alex Ferguson lets loose his Subbuteo Roy Keane

permitted to make contact for "the flick", but various methods of cheating soon became apparent, from melting down and stretching the goalkeeper's arms to furniture-polishing player bases for extra glide. At least one player would inevitably be trodden or knelt on during every game, and the throw-in men rarely functioned properly, but Subbuteo still became an obsession for many, who would log results in their schoolbooks with incredible dedication, even staging Subbuteo versions of major tournaments in bedrooms across the land.

Some people never grew out of the fascination, and Subbuteo is now a highly collectable alternative for grown men who would really like a train set but are too afraid to ask their partner. One of the best aspects of Subbuteo was the massive range of accessories – from stadiums to floodlights, from ball-boys to miniature trophies – that were entirely surperfluous to the actual game itself. Having crowd trouble? Simply deploy a policeman, or install crowd control barriers. There was a cameraman in the stands to catch it all, and at the end even a mini-Her Majesty the Queen to present the tiny FA Cup. The possibilities were endless.

Then there were goalkeepers on plastic control rods, number transfers so you could identify players individually, linesmen, corner flags, athletics tracks to help create a European feel and different tournament balls. One enthusiast even went as far as to manufacture streakers for use in competitions. Don't laugh – if a streaker was on the pitch, play would stop until your opponent flicked a policeman close enough to make an arrest. You could waste vital seconds.

That's even before you get to the different teams. Fancy a crack outfit in the 1970 Haiti kit? It's available – at a price. How about the **Boston Minutemen**? **Landskrona**, **Antwerp**, **Hartford Bicentennials**, **Admira Wacker**, **Wisla Krakow**, the **Port Vale** away kit… they're all here, and you'll never own the lot, even if you visit car boot sales daily for the rest of your life. Three black players were belatedly added to all English sides in 1987 to reflect their proliferation in the real-life game (the French national side had boasted coloured stars as early as the 1970s); in 1992, there was a bold, but ultimately unsuccessful, attempt to have Subbuteo made an Olympic sport.

Unsurprisingly, there's a big internet community devoted to Subbuteo, and even a magazine called *The Flicker* for the real devotee. The manufacturers branched out into snooker, rugby, baseball, speedway, hockey and – at a particular nadir – even angling, but nothing can top the original and best game. It has seen off many rivals, and remains popular even in the era of PlayStation, X-Box and Nintendo, even though it's no longer being manufactured and exists merely as memorabilia. Up to the loft, mother…

COMPUTER GAMES

In April 2003, **Championship Manager 4** shattered all videogame sales records by shifting 124,627 copies in its first week alone. The extraordinary popularity of *CM*, a game so addictive it has been cited in three divorce cases, highlights just how far getting your football fix via keyboard or joystick has come since the 1970s, when prehistoric monochrome *Pong*-style TV games were as good as it got.

The 1980s saw the rise of Atari, promoted by **Trevor Brooking** with the help of Morecambe and Wise, and a tidal wave of affordable home computers like the Spectrum and Commodore 64 washed up a surfeit of soccer games. Footballers and their agents weren't slow to recognise the lucrative potential of a superstar's signature on the box, although for every **Emlyn Hughes' International Soccer**, there was a **Peter Shilton's Handball Maradona** or a **Gary Lineker's Super Skills**, which involved Leicester's favourite son performing press-ups, weightlifting and squat thrusts. Oh, and let's not forget **Jack Charlton's Fishing**.

In the 1990s, football gaming became a huge industry, with games such as

Kevin O'Callaghan and Eric Gates get to grips with a particularly early Pong

Fifa and *International Superstar Soccer* battling for dominance on the new generation of consoles, led by the PlayStation. It wasn't always this way, though..

FOOTBALL MANAGER

It sold a million and made a cult hero of creator Kevin Toms, the bearded boffin who appeared on the box. In this godfather of the management genre, you played the sheepskin-clad boss of a Division Four team, wheeling and dealing your way to the top of the league. It might look primitive now, with its animated matchstick highlights, but its gripping gameplay and the inclusion of authentic teams, cups and players was a revelation in 1982, even if the price tags might have been a touch unrealistic (Kevin Keegan for £5,000?) **FM2** followed in 1988, with a World Cup Edition in 1990.

MATCH DAY

The first really successful attempt at an arcade-style football sim, *Match Day* hit the shelves in 1985 and sold by the shedload. It offered a 3D view of the pitch, smooth animation and maximum playability, although you couldn't foul the opposition, much to the frustration of armchair Terry Butchers everywhere. And it played the *Match Of The Day* theme at the start. **Match Day 2** arrived in 1988 and managed to be even better.

PETER SHILTON'S HANDBALL MARADONA

File under blatant rip-off. Funnily enough, this appalling game featured neither Peter Shilton nor Diego Maradona. In effect, it was a goalkeeping sim, of all things, and thus proved to be the videogame equivalent of the hopeless kid who always had go between the sticks down the rec every Saturday morning. No cups, no leagues – all you had to do was save four shots in a row to move up a skill level. It was simply dire. See also the official Mexico '86 title, *World Cup Carnival*, which managed the impressive feat of scoring zero in some reviews.

EMLYN HUGHES' INTERNATIONAL SOCCER

It's 1988 and with *A Question Of Sport* in its pomp, even Princess Anne can't escape the bejumpered clutches of the permachuckling Crazy Horse. Perfect fodder for a timely cash-in, then, except this one was actually quite good. Neatly combining management and arcade genres, *International Soccer* enabled you to fine-tune your team on the practice pitch before taking on the computer or your mates. There was also the inevitable *Question Of Sport* tie-in, allowing you to enjoy "you'll find these three sportsmen at the beach!" fun in your living room.

FOOTBALLER OF THE YEAR

Neither a management game nor an action sim, this 1986 release and its sequel allowed you to work your way up from a 17-year-old apprentice in the nether regions of the league to become the country's best striker and, well, Footballer Of The Year. You did this by memorising tactics and hence scoring goals, answering trivia questions and – here's the realistic bit – gambling cash. Not bad, all told.

BRIAN CLOUGH'S FOOTBALL FORTUNES

A predictably idiosyncratic effort, this managerial challenge was a bizarre hybrid of computer and board game. Team-building involved the usual ducking and diving, with added obstacles thrown up by the toss of the dice. Fun enough, even if scenarios like your two star strikers being killed in a car crash seemed a little unnecessary. Green sweatshirt optional.

SUBBUTEO

Exactly what the point was, nobody's quite sure, but in 1991 a computer adaptation of the flick-to-kick tabletop perennial was released. Sure, it meant that your precious Dukla Prague star striker no longer faced being flicked under the settee, but the interminable take-it-in-turns gameplay (translated faithfully from the original) undermined the big match atmosphere somewhat. Even The Undertones' cousin Kevin would have turned up his nose at this.

Championship Manager – a phenomenon even in the divorce courts

SENSIBLE SOCCER

Sensi, as its devotees called it, seized the crown from *Match Day 2* in 1992, despite competition from the popular **Kick-Off** and its sequels. Both incorporated a bird's eye view of the pitch, but while *Kick-Off* might have allowed you to put bend on passes and shots, *Sensi* was the first arcade release to boast those all-important real teams and be fully customisable. More improvements and tweaks throughout the 1990s, including the addition of ear-bashing commentary from Jonathan Pearce, extended its reign.

FIFA

The first *Fifa* game appeared in 1994, and since then the series has undergone a succession of facelifts and taken on a battalion of rival titles like **Actua Soccer** and the **International Superstar Soccer/Pro Evolution** dynasty. The rise of the PC and the PlayStation in the 1990s enabled programmers to take the action game to new levels in terms of graphics and realism, even if *Fifa*'s commentary team of Des, Motty and Andy Gray wasn't quite authentic. Blur's *Song 2* blaring out of *Fifa '98* was pretty cool, mind. In the wake of *Fifa*'s success, there was a scramble to produce official Uefa and Premiership games but pleasingly, they didn't sell, because despite the brands, they weren't much cop.

CHAMPIONSHIP MANAGER

The *CM* series is nothing short of a phenomenon. Devised over five years by brothers Paul and Oliver Collyer, the first edition of "*Champo*" was released in 1992, with 2003's *CM4* smashing all sales records. Extraordinarily realistic and vast in its scope, it's based around a database of hundreds of thousands of real players from around the world rated by fans themselves. Star devotees include **Ole-Gunnar Solskjaer** and **Rangers**' **Michael Ball**, who had to sell himself because he was asking for too much money. Managers have even used it to assess foreign players before signing them, although *CM* superstars like Everton's **Ibrahim Bakayoko** sometimes prove less successful in reality.

FASHION

"I was the first man in Britain," declares **Frank Worthington** in his candid autobiography *One Hump Or Two?*, "to own a tank top." The wayward striker's bold claim speaks volumes about the long, shameful relationship between footballers and fashion. Handsomely paid, and with too much time on their hands, players have always had the chance to model the latest threads.

While the results can be impressive, they usually aren't. Serial offenders are numerous, but first into the fashion police's cells would be the likes of **Barry Venison** (leather cowboy ties, chessboard jackets, completely straight face) and **John Barnes**, who has sported a variety of garish monstrosities that even *Soooooo* Graham Norton would reject as too outlandish.

It all started, inevitably, in the 1960s. As television made national stars out of local heroes, the more flamboyant footballers found themselves lining up alongside pop groups as fashion icons. **George Best** led the way, opening a boutique in Manchester and modelling roll-necks, flares and suits with his fifth-Beatle looks. Best's main rival in the fashion stakes was **Peter Osgood**, the Chelsea forward and Kings Road dandy. The dapper forward always had the latest tailoring, and his style even attracted actress and sex symbol Raquel Welch. "Osgood epitomised swinging London as much as David Bailey or Paul McCartney," reckoned Chelsea chairman Brian Mears.

Mike Summerbee managed to run a high-quality bespoke tailors (with Michael Caine and, later, Sylvester Stallone, as clients), but others had less success, notably **Malcolm MacDonald**'s Newcastle store – called Malcolm MacDonald – and **Kenny Dalglish**'s menswear shop, Dalglish. Terry Venables invested, too, but the 1970s and 1980s were pretty much a write-off fashion-wise, summed up by dodgy perms, tracksuits and Kevin Keegan's massive collars (it was perhaps inadvisable for Kev to start his own range, but he did anyway).

You'd have thought a suit would help avoid derision, but even this wardrobe staple (usually kept handy for court appearances) can go wrong. Liverpool's hideous cream Armani '96 Cup final outfit confirmed the side's reputation as the "Spice Boys", a triumph of appearance (though certainly not style) over substance. Several players had modelling as well as football contracts – **David James**' Armani gig just topping **Jason McAteer**'s work for Head & Shoulders. Even a tie can cause offence – **Wayne Rooney**'s skew-whiff kipper at the BBC Sports Personality of the Year awards led to uproar from Middle England.

Then there's the omnipresent **David Beckham**: a one-man ongoing fashion revolution, with triumphs sitting equally alongside terrible disasters. Highlights to date include wearing a sarong, nail varnish and his wife's underwear;

John Barnes cuts a dash at one of Liverpool's infamous "fancy dress" parties

Hull City's turn-of-the-nineties stripes: what were they thinking?

endorsing Brylcreem and then immediately shaving his head; and inspiring a generation to get mohican, spiked and plaited haircuts. And that's before you get to his huge contracts with Police sunglasses and Adidas, not to mention some football club called Real Madrid. He's even been credited with putting men in touch with their feminine, grooming-friendly sides.

It's unlikely ever to end. As Robbie Savage contemplates his next Armani tattoo, Vinnie Jones is about to launch a range of menswear on the unsuspecting public. The days when footballers had simple tastes – for snooker, *Minder* and tank tops – seem long gone, and nobody can predict quite what will be beckoned in next. One thing is for sure, though: it's unlikely to be tasteful.

THE WORST FOOTBALL KITS OF ALL TIME

Hull City 1992-93

Hull City are nicknamed the Tigers, and their marketing department – who presumably didn't really understand this new-fangled football thing – decided a tiger-striped shirt was therefore in order. The result was universally mocked – and ultimately disappointing, as touching the shirt revealed it to be made of cotton rather than fur.

Coventry City 1978-81

Brown is a colour synonymous with the 1970s, when it principally adorned sofas, lampshades and wallpaper, but was still rarely seen on football shirts. **Coventry City** broke the mould and committed a double faux-pas by including double white stripes which ran up the shorts and onto the shirts.

Brighton & Hove Albion 1987-90

Brighton's blue-and-white striped kit has always had the overall air of the Tesco carrier bag, as many opposing fans have noted to their amusement. The 1987-era kit was particularly cheap-looking and bag-like, and saw the indignity completed by the inclusion of the sponsors' name – stationery firm NOBO. Some fans took self-deprecation to new heights by actually donning a Tesco bag with holes cut in for arms. Attempting to make amends, the daring 1991-92 away shirt was a memorable red-and-white combo which, as fans pointed out with a by-now weary disdain, resembled a Chewits wrapper.

Norwich City 1993-94

The Norfolk side's yellow-and-green ensemble had worked well for decades, but tradition counts for nothing when madmen are let loose with the colours, and the result in the 1993-94 season was a yellow background with loud, random green splodges. So keen were the club to avoid a similar disaster that in 1997 they had designer Bruce Oldfield come up with something a tad more refined.

Arsenal 1990-91

Accurately compared to a bruised banana, the infamous black splodges on Arsenal's yellow change shirt must have seemed like a novel idea at the time, but it struck about as much fear into the opposition as Everton's salmon pink change shirts a few years later.

... AND THE BEST

Peru 1970

A diagonal red stripe on a white shirt with white shorts, it seemed to symbolise the attacking football played by **Teofilo Cubillas** and masterminded by their coach, the Brazilian great **Didi**. It was later adopted, to less effect, by Crystal Palace, when the club, with such alumni as **Vince Hilaire** on their books, tried to become the Team of the Eighties. There's still the 2080s...

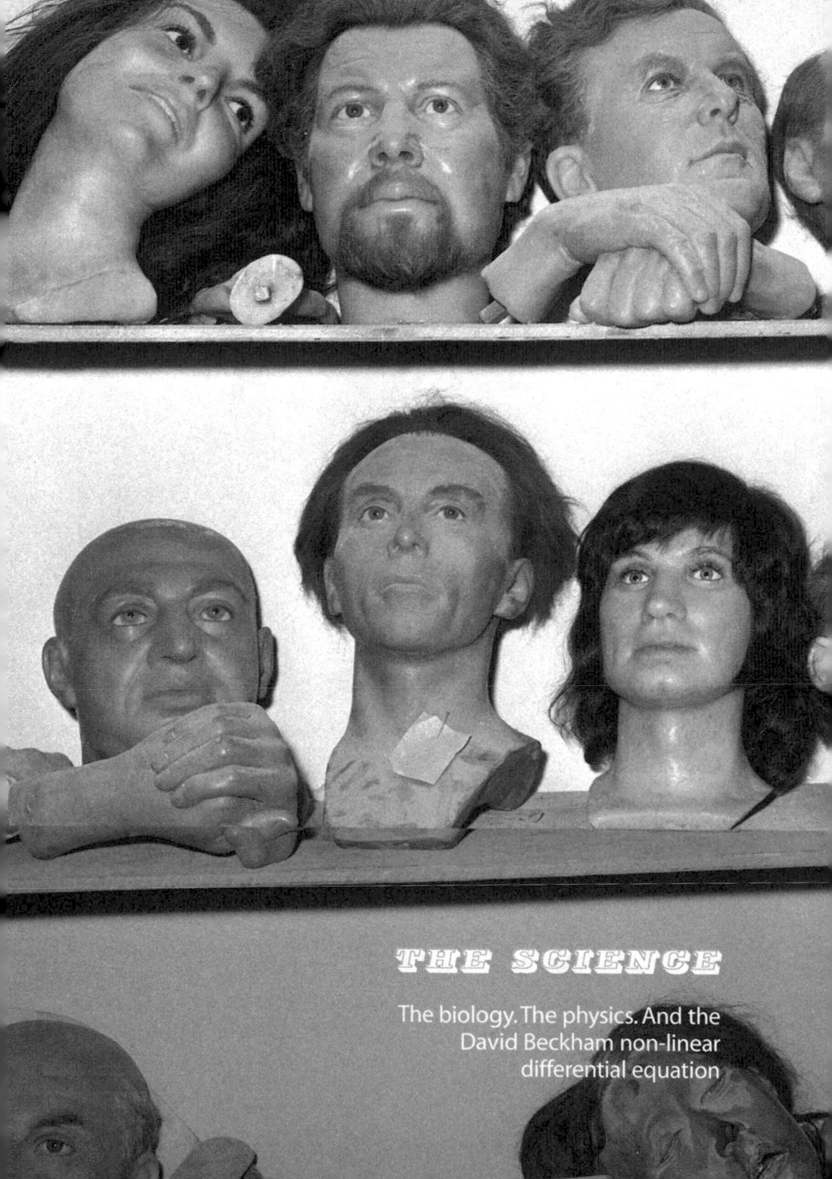

THE SCIENCE

The biology. The physics. And the David Beckham non-linear differential equation

That's George Best on the middle row. Not Valerie Singleton.

F = 1.5 x D3 x f x V newtons where D is the diameter of the ball in metres, f the spin frequency of the ball, and V its velocity

The mathematical formula behind the perfect David Beckham curling free kick

BORN NOT MADE?

As our miserable poet laureate Philip Larkin almost said, they really screw you up, your mum and dad. One of the hitherto unremarked-upon ways they foul things up is by not being footballing geniuses. As naive eight-year-olds kicking the ball around the back garden, we all dreamed of scoring that winning goal in an FA Cup final but, sadly, for many of us it was already too late. There is a growing body of statistical and scientific evidence to suggest that, as the Finnish sports scientist Per-Olof Astrand says, if you want to be a sporting legend, you have to pick your parents wisely.

This is not to say that you should give up just because your mum didn't play for **Doncaster Belles** and your dad's idea of fancy footwork is kicking the cat. It's just that if your family could put the gene into footballing genius, the odds are slightly more likely to be in your favour.

It's at this point that you're probably stifling a yawn thinking that the clichéd story of the **Charlton** dynasty is about to rear its head once again. The Charlton/Milburn story is probably the greatest conspicuous example of footballing talent (nine league players in the same branch of the family, three of whom became full England internationals and one an England B international) but the point is perhaps as convincingly illustrated by looking at the beautiful game's most beautiful team: **Felix**, **Carlos Alberto**, **Brito**, **Piazza**, **Everaldo**, **Gerson**, **Clodoaldo**, **Rivelino**, **Jairzinho**, **Tostao** and **Pelé**.

The Brazilian team of 1970 was so ludicrously talented, it seems impertinent to try and trace the roots of their footballing genius. Pelé, particularly, seemed one of a kind. But he only became a footballer despite his mother's opposition; she regarded his chosen profession as "somewhere beneath bank robbery". She didn't want him to fail like his father, Dodinho. After starring in the local football team in the town of Tres Coracoes, Dodinho signed for the Belo Horizonte club **Atletico Mineiro** only to tear his knee ligaments on his debut. He returned to his hometown club and extended his playing career by the dangerous expedient of packing his knee with ice between matches. His son still loyally says of him: "He was my first coach. He taught me how to trap the ball with either foot. He would have been a great player but for the injury." It is doubtful if even paternal pride would enable Pelé to say the same about his own son **Edinho**, recently jailed for murder, who kept goal for **Santos** for two years.

Although Tostao, aka the White Pelé, came from a comfortable middle-class background, his father played amateur football for a Belo Horizonte club so it was no great surprise when Tostao and his four brothers all played for local youth sides. Roberto Rivelino's father, Nicolino Rivelino was, in his son's loving words, "full of shit. He says he was a great player, but they called him The Horse." Rivelino Snr insists this nickname was a compliment and that he turned down a deal with a big club because the money they offered wasn't as good as his salary at the telephone company. Gerson, the side's playmaker (who even in the Mexican heat always lit a fag at half-time), had a father and an uncle who played professionally for clubs in Rio, while two of Carlos Alberto's brothers struggled in the lower echelons of the Brazilian game.

The more biographies of famous players you examine, the more family ties to the game you find. **Michel Platini** was a second-generation footballing genius (his dad Aldo was captain of the local side **AS Jouef** in which junior made his debut), **Uwe Seeler**'s father played for Hamburg, as did his elder brother Dieter, **Mathias Sammer**'s dad Klaus won 21 caps for the GDR and **Ruud Gullit**'s dad George played international football for Surinam. You can add to this vaguely contemporary pan-European list the **Cruyffs**, the **Maldinis**, the **Inzaghis**, the **de Boers** and the **Laudrups**.

Michael and Brian Laudrup are of particular note because their childhood was dominated by spherical objects. Father Finn was a Danish international in the 1970s and their mum Lone was a professional handball player, while Michael's son Andreas joined Amsterdam side **AFC** a few years back. (Among the other players whose family history includes other sporting skills are **Ryan Giggs**, whose father Danny Wilson played rugby union for Wales and **Gustavo Poyet**, whose dad was a basketball professional.)

But is there anything beyond a pile of anecdotal evidence? The obvious way to solve this argument – compulsory DNA tests for all PFA members – seems a tad unrealistic. But an analysis of the professional footballers in a recent PFA handbook found 37 famous sons, 40 famous brothers, six famous cousins and one famous great-grandson. The pick of the bunch is not **Gary** and **Phil Neville** (even if they were the 20th set of brothers to play for England) but **West Ham United**'s goalkeeper **Stephen Bywater**. Signed as a teenager for up to £2.3m from **Rochdale**, young Steve is the fourth generation of Bywaters to keep goal.

His great-grandfather plied his trade for **Aston Villa**, his grandfather Leslie for **Huddersfield** and Rochdale and his dad, David, for **Halifax**. Yet taken together, these dynasties only represent about four per cent of the talent registered to the PFA and besides, scientists will say, even if 72 Charltons had played for England this wouldn't prove footballing skill was inherited.

It wouldn't because geneticists still argue how much of what we are is down to nature or nurture. There is also the undeniable fact that having, say, **Frank Lampard** as your dad gives you a head start. "By the time Frank and **Jamie** [**Redknapp**, Frank's cousin] were six or seven, you could see they had good touch on the ball and the fact they came from a football environment meant they picked up things quickly," said Lampard Snr. "As a father you want them to improve and as a coach you're more aware of what they should be doing."

The state of the current debate is summed up by Professor Dave Collins, head of sport at Edinburgh University, who says: "All of these things only mean that people have the potential to go on. You also have to consider opportunity and tradition." Scientists have begun to identify specific genes which may influence sporting behaviour but each new study needs to be treated with caution as many headline claims for various genes have soon been rubbished. A growing band of psychologists are also redefining human intelligence in ways that might lead them to trace skills like spatial awareness to certain parts of the brain.

The all-conquering Brazil 1970 side was packed with footballing pedigree

Michael (right) and Brian Laudrup; born to excel with spherical objects

If football is a game of gene rummy, not everyone gets a winning hand. Imagine how poor old Joel Cantona feels looking at brother Eric's career and thinking: "Hey, there but for a tiny bit of genetic code go I." Other famous sons have ended up looking as if they're a few links down the football evolutionary chain from their dad. The saddest case (yes, sadder even than Sam Shilton or Jordi Cruyff) is probably **Stefan Beckenbauer**. When Stefan was a kid, his dad's mate Helmut Schoen came around one day and watched him kick the ball around. "You see Franz," said the German national coach, "the boy is football crazy. What a pity you weren't that crazy about football when you were a boy." Unfortunately, Stefan's rare combination of football craziness and the most famous surname in German football couldn't hide the fact that his career never really got any better after he'd signed on for **Bayern Munich** as a trainee. Father Franz did the decent thing and paid for his boy to join newly-promoted **Saarbrucken** in 1992, but after two years which saw the club relegated again, Stefan rode off into German football's equivalent of a Western movie sunset.

THE MAGNUS FORCE

No doubt about it: **David Beckham** is a master of non-linear differential equations. Just think about that curling free kick he sent past the Greek defence from 30 yards out in the World Cup qualifying match in June 2001. While the rest of us were making paper darts and playing hangman in maths class, Beckham, D. was getting to grips with the finer points of Reynolds Numbers, Magnus Forces and drag coefficients (and no, before you ask, that's got nothing to do with being persuaded to wear your wife's underwear).

Of course, like all geniuses, Beckham didn't do his swotting in something as conventional as a classroom. He picked up his equation-solving tricks by booting a ball a few million times. For while any smart-aleck physicist can write down the equations governing the dynamics of the Curling Kick, actually getting them to work during a real match is another matter. Like all the great dead-ball players of our time – Carlos, Figo, Zola, Zidane – Beckham wisely eschewed hours in theoretical physics classes in favour of years of trial and error on the pitch.

For those of us who'd be glad just to get a ball to travel in a straight line, there's still some advantage in mugging up on the physics behind such amazing shots, as it gives an even greater appreciation of the skill of these players. What they're doing is little short of miraculous, optimising three different forces, two of which change constantly while the ball is in flight.

The first force is the most familiar: gravity. Nothing too complicated there, as it stays constant. The second is much trickier to deal with. Known as the Magnus

Force (after HG Magnus, a German physicist who first investigated its properties about 150 years ago), this is the force directly responsible for curling the ball off its normal trajectory. Unless a ball is kicked dead-centre, it always spins slightly as it flies through the air. As one side of the spinning ball is thus moving in the direction of flight while the other side turns away, there's a difference in the relative speed of the air on either side of the ball. That, in turn, creates a pressure difference which forces the ball to curl as it flies. The rule is: kick right-of-centre to give the ball an anticlockwise spin, and it will curl to the left.

It sounds simple, except that getting the ball to curl isn't enough: it must curl by precisely the right amount, and that depends not only on the spin-rate, but also on the speed of the ball through the air. The force of the kick has to be perfectly judged, so that it optimises both speed and spin-rate.

With a bit of practice, even your average Sunday clogger has some chance of getting a ball to curl past a keeper every now and again. The real skill comes when there's a defensive wall to beat as well. Then the maestros show their mastery of the third force involved in the curling kick: aerodynamic drag. Like the Magnus Force, the drag force changes with the speed of travel. The trouble is, it does so in a much more complex way, making it harder to control. Worse still, its strength critically affects the size of the Magnus Force, and thus the way the ball curls.

The obvious way to cut through all this is just to hit the ball with the same force every time, and focus on getting the spin-rate right. But to a dead-ball genius confronted by a defensive wall, the drag force offers a handy way of fooling both the defenders and the goalkeeper at the same time.

Struck off-centre and hard – say, over 70 mph – the ball starts off flying wide of the wall, with little drag and no obvious hope of going in the net. The defenders relax and the keeper rolls his eyes in contempt. But as the ball slows, the drag increases rapidly, which in turn boosts the Magnus Force, making the ball curl ever more swiftly. All of a sudden the keeper finds the ball curling in towards him, then towards the far post; and before he can get anywhere near it, it's gone in.

Back-of-the-envelope calculations

ON THEIR KNEES

The next time you hear of a star player being sidelined by unspecified "knee problems", a call to the *News Of The World* may be in order. A London medical student identified sexually acquired reactive arthritis (SARA) as being widespread among footballers – and because diagnosis is difficult, it often ends careers. The virus which causes the condition is sexually transmitted and is far more prevalent among sportsmen than ordinary members of the public, with footballers the worst culprits. This isn't particularly surprising – one club doctor reports that when asked if they have had sex recently, most players take this to mean "in the past couple of hours".

David Beckham curls in a free kick and becomes a mathematical genius

show that the swing from 25 yards out can exceed five yards, well over half the width of the goal-mouth. It has to be seen to be believed, and Beckham's impressive effort was far from the most extraordinary demonstration of the effect. That accolade belongs to **Roberto Carlos** of Brazil in the pre-World Cup Tournoi match against France in June 1997.

Slicing the ball with the outside of his left foot from 35 yards out, Carlos sent the ball spinning at 85mph to the right of the defensive wall. It seemed so far off-target that the ball-boy standing to the side of the goal ducked. But as the ball slowed, the magic of the Magnus Force revealed itself. Spinning anticlockwise, the ball curled left at an ever-faster rate and shot into the net.

THE OFFSIDE CONUNDRUM

You can always spot real football aficionados: they're the ones who can spot a dodgy offside decision faster than Motty. For while even maiden aunts can tell the difference between a foul and a dive, only true fans get into a lather over the geometrical relationship between three blokes and a ball.

They have much to get into a lather about: recent research suggests that assistant referees make errors in as many as one in five offside decisions. That's a pretty high failure rate for something that can affect the outcome of a multi-million pound event like a Premiership fixture. But before you fire off a note to the FA querying its policy of hiring the illegitimate and visually-impaired to act as assistant referees, grab a couple of pens and try the following little experiment.

Hold a pen upright in each hand, and line the pens up at arm's length, so that one is hidden behind the other. Now, imagine that hidden pen is **Michael Owen** on a run from left to right, and the pen closer to you is **Sol Campbell**, playing the offside trap. Clearly, from where you're looking at them now, they're right in line, and so Owen is onside. But keeping the two pens dead still, just move your head slightly to the right. As you now see it, Owen appears to be to the right of Campbell – that is, closer to the goal-line. Of course, he's really still in line with Campbell, yet he appears to be just offside. In other words, only an assistant referee who's exactly in line with the players involved in an offside decision can call it reliably. If he's closer to the goal-line and therefore looking backwards at the action, he's more likely to get it wrong.

In a study published in 2000 in the prestigious science journal *Nature*, Raoul Oudejans and his colleagues at the Free University of Amsterdam showed that assistant referees were indeed slightly ahead and looking backwards at the key players in 90 per cent of offside decisions. They weren't out of line with the players by very much – just a yard or so – but experiments proved it was still enough to lead to the flag being raised far too often.

There's more. Using video analysis of real matches, the researchers also found that when the action was taking place close to the assistant referee, a striker attempting an outside run against a defender was more likely to get the benefit of the doubt. Again, the pen experiment shows why. Line the pens up close to your eyes, this time with the defender hidden behind the striker. Keeping the pens still, move your head right, towards the goal-line. The defender now appears to the right of the striker and thus closer to the goal-line. That means the striker can be quite a way forward of the defender before he'll seem obviously offside.

This shows quite clearly that strikers should try to make their runs along paths that put them closer to the assistant referee than the defenders. That way, they'll be able to exploit the optical effect found by the scientists, and, in theory at least, get the benefit of the doubt from the assistant referee.

THE TWILIGHT ZONE

Where Joseph Stalin rubs shoulders with Johnny Giles as the Honey Monster looks on

French players experiment with moto-foot in 1958

"Football – it's an old, funny game"

Gianluca Vialli reinvents the cliché

TOP FOOTBALLING GHOSTS

Ghost Lady Elizabeth Hoby
Ground haunted England's HQ, Bisham Abbey

This lass is said to slip out of her portrait (which hangs in the great hall) and go off for a walk whenever it takes her fancy. She died in 1609 and her ghost is believed to be constantly washing her hands, perhaps in **David Beckham**'s bathroom – well, if you had a choice of basins… Anyway, many of the England squad say they have seen her or felt her presence. The Sunday tabloids have yet to run a kiss-a-ghost-and-tell so maybe she's keeping a few stories up her medieval sleeves for when she needs some quick cash. She's permanently sorrowful, which some say is because one of her six children died after she locked him in a tiny room and forgot about him.

Ghost Fred
Ground haunted Boundary Park, Oldham

Legend, or at least word, has it that a loyal fan, perhaps called Fred, who always stood in the same place and died during the 1960s, does stuff that freaks people out. Or maybe he just gets in the way – after all, there's not much room between seats in the stands these days and he must wonder where he's meant to go.

Ghost John Thomson
Ground haunted Celtic Park

Thomson was a goalie who died in a collision with a **Rangers** forward in 1931. He may be a figurative rather than a literal ghost, but he is celebrated for his bravery by the Celtic faithful in his own song – "Between your posts there stands a ghost."

Ghost Anonymous
Ground haunted Priestfield Stadium, Gillingham

A displaced gipsy cursed the ground and although the curse was exorcised,

Gillingham fans still conveniently believe it may have contributed to any game in which their team were rubbish.

Ghost **The White Horse**
Ground haunted **Highbury**

A horse died during the construction of Arsenal's North Bank – builders these days, they're all cowboys – and apparently he neighs during crucial games. Perhaps it's something to do with donkeys on the pitch…

Ghost **Herbert Chapman**
Ground haunted **Highbury**

Apparently his footsteps can be heard walking through the marble halls. How anybody knows they're his footsteps remains undisclosed, but opinion says they're not Patrick Vieira's, because a) he's still alive; and b) halfway along the halls he'd have thrown himself to the floor, and people would have heard him collapse in a heap, twist around a bit, then yell for the referee.

Ghost **Lord Nelson**
Ground haunted **Bloomfield Road, Blackpool**

The admiral haunts **Blackpool**'s boardroom. Not because he was a Blackpool fan who was aggrieved at a transfer, but because the panels in the room were apparently constructed from wood from one of his flagships. The club labrador occasionally goes all funny and barks at the walls, as dogs do when ghosts are present.

Herbert Chapman: ghostly presence

Ghost **Anonymous**
Ground haunted **The Old Show Ground, Scunthorpe**

The ground vacated by **Scunthorpe United** in 1988, in favour of their new purpose-built accommodation at Glanford Park, is said to reverberate at night to the sound of the thud of leather on leather and rustling goal nets. Anyone know any of the Iron squad of 1988 who haven't been seen for a while…?

WHAT ASTROLOGY CAN TEACH US

ARIES **March 21-April 20**

Teddy Sheringham and Robbie Fowler are both Aries. Both have a desire to conquer. They are aggressive, strong, highly sexed, positive and energetic. They can also be rude, jealous, combative, destructive (well, Robbie did once cut up Razor Ruddock's new shoes) and obstinate, but they're also known for being dynamic and quick to respond.

TAURUS **April 21-May 21**

David Beckham is a Taurus and they're a careless bunch, which might account for his funny eyebrow a couple of seasons ago – perhaps he over-tweezed. They're also overly romantic (we know he's a big softie when it comes to his missus), tactful (which Becks has mastered the art of), gentle and friendly.

GEMINI **May 22-June 21**

Frank Lampard is a Gemini but he's not joined to a twin when he's on the pitch (if he was he'd have to be pulled up by the referee; that would clearly be an unfair advantage). On the plus side he's adaptable (let's face it, at **Chelsea** you'd have to be), expressive (that's why he's in midfield) and bright (that'll be the Cockney kind of "bright", as in chirpy).

CANCER **June 22-July 22**

This is interesting – Patrick Vieira and Paolo Di Canio are both Cancerians. They're known to be moody (strike one), they like to worry (Paolo is a world-class worrier) and they get jealous, but they're sensitive (to the slightest touch in Patrick's case), romantic and maternal.

LEO **July 23-August 22**

Roy Keane and Alan Shearer are both Leos. They're egotistical and vain (face on front of autobiography?), extravagant (goes without saying), honourable (to club though arguably, in Roy's case, not country), creative (they've both written books for a start), controlling and impatient.

VIRGO **August 23-September 23**

David Seaman and Gareth Southgate both share the honour of being a Virgo. Critical, petty, self-centred and industrious, they're also humane and loving. It doesn't say anything about penalty saves or penalty misses, though, but the industry is perhaps represented by making adverts about them.

LIBRA September 24-October 23

Graeme Le Saux and **Robbie Savage** are apparently over-sensitive (they do over-react just a bit on occasions), snobbish (Le Saux does read broadsheets, which by his team-mates' estimation makes him stuck-up) and demanding.

SCORPIO October 24-November 22

Dwight Yorke and **Rio Ferdinand** are both Scorpios. They're domineering, fanatic, self-obsessed and likely to undertake a career in sport. Anytime soon?

SAGITTARIUS November 23-December 21

Michael Owen and **Joe Cole** have a lot in common. They're young, they're in the spotlight and they're both fairly dull. Neither of them are scoring enough goals at the moment either.

CAPRICORN December 22-January 20

Lee Bowyer is a Capricorn, which marks him out as cold, miserly, indifferent and rigid. There's allegedly a good sense of humour in there as well, along with self-discipline. His lucky colour is dark brown, the same colour as... a monk's habit. A change of career beckons.

AQUARIUS January 21-February 19

Francis Jeffers and little **Nicky Barmby** share the same traits, as well as the same ex-club in **Everton**. Aquarians are rebellious, erratic, eccentric and perverse. They're also resourceful, intuitive, inventive and stubborn.

PISCES February 20-March 20

James Beattie and **Nicolas Anelka** are Pisceans. Supposedly they're dishonest and indecisive, yet caring and sensitive. Indecision features in Anelka's football career – the will-he-won't-he stay or go at **Manchester City** saga (and that after the **Arsenal** debacle) dragging on longer than *Gone With The Wind*. Pisceans' lucky colour is sea green; Beattie lives in the marina in Southampton.

FOOTBALL AND RELIGION

"God's footballer hears the voices of angels above the choir at Molineux," sings folk-rocker Billy Bragg in *God's Footballer*, about the career change of footballer-cum-Jehovah's Witness **Peter Knowles**. In 1970, Knowles, aged 24 and on the verge of an England call-up, swapped scoring goals for **Wolves** for door-to-door soul-saving. Apparently he feared his temper would get the better of him and he'd put someone out of the game. Truly the Lord works in mysterious ways. Knowles is not alone in embracing religion having previously been fully immersed in the world of professional football (a fact that maybe says something about football's inherent insignificance in the great scheme of things).

For one there was **David Icke**. Former **Coventry** and **Hereford** keeper Icke worked as a journalist, TV presenter and a Green Party parliamentary candidate before famously appearing on the Terry Wogan chat show in 1991 to proclaim he was the Son of God and cataclysmic flooding and earthquakes were imminent. Icke seemed surprised that nobody took him seriously. His turquoise shellsuit didn't help. Nowadays he tours the globe, lecturing and selling books, the focal point of his theory being that the world is run by a shape-shifting reptilian elite.

Danish European Championship winner (1992) and **Luton Town** record signing (1989) **Lars Elstrup** quit football to join the Wild Goose Buddhist sect in 1993, changing his name to Darando (which translates as "the river that streams into the sea"). A little while afterwards he was arrested in Copenhagen for flashing. Elstrup attempted a football comeback and still plays in Danish amateur leagues, though "finding inner truths and to get more contact with Self and God," still takes up a serious amount of his time.

In 1999, **Carlos Roa** stunned **Real Mallorca** by announcing that, at 30, he was quitting football for God. He had become a Seventh Day Adventist Church pastor and the former Argentinian international retreated to a mountain farm to await the Apocalypse, scheduled for the new millennium. When the end of the world discourteously declined to show up, however, Roa reappeared on the football scene and went looking for a new club.

Taribo West is another who has put God before goals. During his career, the Nigerian has often suffered the wrath of managers angry at him for spending too much time at his Milanese church (like Roa, West is a pastor).

Football is full of people who believe in various gods – but not many players can boast that they are a religion. Step forward **Diego Maradona**, who has inspired a 100-member-strong church of "Diegorian Brothers" who hold his autobiography as their bible, celebrate Christmas on his birthday and have re-written the calendar – the year is in fact 42AD (After Diego).

DICTATORS

Football is said to be the opiate of the masses – and, as such, a pretty useful way to exert mass control over the proles. Throughout history, dictators have recognised the dark power of the beautiful game, though their forays into the sport haven't always entirely gone to plan.

ADOLF HITLER

The Führer was a fan of opera and film, but football held little allure because, some suggest, it was very difficult for him to control. This view is borne out by the only recorded instance of Hitler watching a game, the Germany v Norway clash in Berlin in 1936. The VIP box was a fearsome sight, with Goebbels, Goering and Hess accompanying the dictator. After six minutes, Norway took the lead and Goebbels noted: "The Führer is very agitated. I'm almost unable to control myself." Hitler upped and left when the motherland went 2-0 down.

FRANCO

The Spanish dictator abandoned his hometown club to seek glory as **Real Madrid**'s number one fan. Franco is frequently accused of bribing referees and opposition to ensure Real won, but in fact the only charge that really sticks is of using his influence to ensure the club had the pick of the best players available. Franco was also a pools obsessive, playing twice a week until his death.

MUSSOLINI

Glory-hunting wasn't in the Italian dictator's vocabulary. Mussolini shunned his country's bigger sides to pledge his allegiance to **Lazio**, then a small, underachieving suburban side from Rome. Though they won nothing during his lifetime, Mussolini's legacy can be seen in the Olympic Stadium he left behind for them, and the other grounds he funded as part of his bid to stage the 1934 World Cup. The well-known story about Il Duce's telegram to coach Vittorio Pozzo on the eve of the 1938 World Cup final ("win or die") is probably apocryphal.

JOSEPH STALIN

Stalin, it's fair to say, was not a football fan, but he tolerated the game to keep the crowds happy. In the 1936 gymnasts' parade, he arranged for the **Spartak Moscow** side to display their skills, but if he waved a white handkerchief they were to be removed from his sight. As one biographer recalled: "Stalin did not wave his handkerchief and the footballers interpreted this to mean they found favour. They were mistaken. The Boss was simply allowing these pathetic, puny creatures to amuse themselves. For the last time."

THE GADAFFIS

While the Libyan despot has shown little enthusiasm for the game himself, his family does own a 7.5 per cent stake in Juventus, which is looked after by his football-mad son **al-Saadi**. Saadi is widely regarded as one of the best players in his homeland, although owning the club he played for until summer 2003 (**Al Ittihad** in Tripoli) gave him quite an advantage. Saadi then surprised the

Lars Elstrup: used to play for Luton, but now he's on a higher plane football world by earning a spot on Perugia's Serie A roster, though he doesn't expect a regular first-team place. In the meantime, he hopes to garner support for hosting the 2010 World Cup in Libya; he'd be 37 by then, but it's fair to say Saadi would probably somehow find a way onto the team bus.

THE HUSSEINS

Saddam himself wasn't fussed about football, but eldest son Uday certainly took an interest – much to the disgust of the players. Named head of the Iraqi Football Federation at 21, Uday picked the team, screamed at players down a walkie-talkie and, it's alleged, beat the side savagely when they lost a World Cup qualifier to Kazakhstan in 1997. The allegations weren't proved when Fifa went to Baghdad to ask questions, although as one anti-Saddam campaigner pointed out: "That's like going to the streets of Chicago in the 1930s and asking the shop owners, 'Do you like Al Capone?'" The players' one consolation was Uday's own lack of talent in the game, although that didn't stop him summoning the country's best footballers to his palace at 2am because he fancied a kickaround.

RIDDLES

The football riddle has been around for ages, like the one about the thing that gets taken to the Cup final but never used – the answer being the losing team's ribbons (or **Malcolm MacDonald** if you're old enough to remember 1974). But

SUPERSTITION

Every team boasts at least one superstitious character – the sort who needs to be last out, first out or wearing the same boots they first put on in 1984. Some players, however, have taken the concept of the pre-match ritual to extremes. Alan Rough, the former Scotland goalkeeper, who carried half-a-dozen lucky items around with him (including an old tennis ball and a keyring), wore a number 11 shirt underneath his own, bounced the ball on the wall of the tunnel on the way out and blew his nose during games for good luck. Quite what all this did for Rough, who was widely regarded as one of the dodgiest of the suspect custodians from north of the border, is unclear. Like Rough, Ronnie Whelan only shaved on a matchday, while Gary Lineker refused to shoot in the warm-up. At the height of his managerial power, Don Revie wore the same blue suit on matchday for 10 years. King of superstition, however, was Argentinian keeper Sergio Goycochea, who relieved himself on the pitch prior to the penalty shoot-out with Italy in the semi-final of the 1990 World Cup; having won, the urination became a pre-penalty ritual. Barry Fry, as Birmingham boss, urinated in all four corners of St Andrews, in an unsuccessful attempt to lift an ancient gypsy curse.

in recent years the internet has seen a new virulent strain of riddle circulated round offices by email with the intensity of a mass spam campaign for Viagra. One was even supposedly devised by an Ibiza holidaymaker curious to see how far he could propagate a myth. The answer: a long way.

Like the quatrains of a latterday pub-Nostradamus, these riddles have been told, retold and often become garbled in the process, but here they are, for the first time, with some definitive answers – and some outright denials...

"Once you have done it, you can never do it again. Aston Villa did it at their first attempt, Chelsea did it in 1970 and Manchester United did it in 1992. Spurs, Wolves and Manchester City have also done it. West Ham have never done it, nor have Newcastle. Nobody can do it this season."

The daddy of football riddles. It's all about clubs who've completed the set of the championship, the FA Cup and League Cup. **Aston Villa** were the first winners of the League Cup in 1961, while Chelsea and Manchester United took a bit longer. It's been around a few seasons, so the line about "nobody can do it this season" tends to get left in even when someone can (for instance, prior to **Blackburn** doing it in 2002). **Leeds** are sometimes incorrectly fingered as a team who've never done it.

"Arsenal can't do it unless Arsène Wenger leaves, Manchester United have done it more times than any other British club, and Liverpool have done it once but not in the usual way. Everton, Oldham and Charlton have all done it once, but Wimbledon can never do it unless Crystal Palace go bankrupt. What is it?"

Everyone's heard this at some point, but the solution isn't that simple. The answer is supposedly "staging rugby league matches". It's rather shakily alleged that Wenger once turned down a request by the Rugby Football League to stage a match at Highbury as it would churn up the pitch. But several clubs share grounds with rugby league teams so United, despite the numerous internationals and Super League Grand Finals at Old Trafford, certainly haven't done it the most. Nobody quite knows how Liverpool, who have hosted more than one rugby league game, managed it in an "unusual" way. And there's always been a chance that Wimbledon could acquire a new ground and host rugby league, regardless of Palace's financial status. Rubbish, we say.

"Arsenal do it once every four years, Liverpool have done it the most, Manchester United have never done it and Everton did it once. As a player Rio Ferdinand has done it the most and Duncan Ferguson the least."

There are various suggestions for this one, such as losing the fewest derbies in the Premiership, receiving the fewest disciplinary points in a season, or even finishing above Alex Ferguson – the tenuous twist there being that it refers to

THEY DO RON, JOHN, DON...

Between 1971 and 1988, West Bromwich Albion undertook the most bizarre sequence of managerial names in history – Don, Johnny, Ronnie, Ron, Ronnie, Ron, Johnny, Ron, Ron. Here's how:

DON HOWE (1971-75)

If there was a world populated with great football coaches/not-so-good football managers, Don Howe would rule the continents. As coach he helped orchestrate Arsenal's march to the 1971 League and Cup double. As manager, he confused everybody with his revolutionary idea: drop the "West Bromwich", keep the "Albion" and thereby ensure the club would be top of the league between May and August. Howe's ultra-defensive football went hand-in-hand with relegation in 1973 and the failure to bounce back left him waving his P45 like a limp, white flag.

JOHNNY GILES (1975-77)

Having gone down the tried and tested route, Albion's board opted for the great unknown when they appointed the untried Johnny Giles. In doing so they helped to mould one of the first successful player-managers, clinching promotion in his first season. Giles then took the well-trodden path of Albion successes by creating a summer of discontent and resigning, citing board power and a lack of influence in club affairs. But supporter and player power changed his mind: he stayed on and the club finished seventh in 1977 – when he quit again.

RONNIE ALLEN (1977)

Blink and you may have missed him. Allen, a goalscoring hero for Albion and England in the 1950s, barely had time to warm the hot seat vacated by his predecessor before leaving it himself. The lure of sun, sand and silver was too much for Allen, who (presumably inspired by Don Revie) decided to quit the glamour of the Black Country to take charge of the Saudi Arabian national team.

RON ATKINSON (1978-1981)

Had Graham Taylor accepted Bert Millichip's offer to manage the club, you wouldn't be reading this now. But he didn't and Atkinson said yes. Having guided Albion to the FA Cup semi-final within three months of his arrival, the sun-tanned one made the first of many TV gaffes by allowing the BBC to film him walking out at Wembley on the morning of the clash against Ipswich. Albion lost 3-1 with Ipswich boss Bobby Robson later claiming no team-talk was needed.

RONNIE ALLEN (1981-82)

For those of you who dozed off for a few weeks of 1978, Allen was back. Bereft of Old Trafford-bound midfielders Remi Moses and Bryan Robson, Allen struggled to recapture Atkinson's exciting era. Semi-final defeats in the FA Cup and League Cup were followed by a flirtation with relegation. Amid reports of dressing room bust-ups, Allen was eventually asked to "go upstairs" to become general manager.

RON WYLIE (1982-84)

With Albion chairmen slowly working their way through the Rons, along came Mr Wylie. Or, "that bloke from Coventry" as he was known on the Birmingham Road End. His inglorious and largely anonymous spell at The Hawthorns was punctuated by the retirement of Brendon Batson, as well as poor defeats on the pitch.

JOHNNY GILES (1984-85)

Johnny Giles, Nobby Stiles and Norman Hunter arrived in 1984 as Albion's three musketeers, but were more *Z Cars* than *A-Team*. Giles upset the fans by growing an unnecessary perm, sending hero Cyrille Regis to Coventry City and guiding Albion to an astonishing nine defeats in the opening 10 games of 1985-86.

RON SAUNDERS (1986-87)

Replacing caretaker-boss Nobby Stiles and having already more or less relegated Birmingham, Saunders was brought in to trim the club of its high-earners. Sam Fox couldn't have done a better job of stripping. Asset after asset was flung out of The Hawthorns' exit door, with future England cap Steve Bull being sold to Wolves for supposedly not being good enough.

RON ATKINSON (1987-88)

The saviour returns. Actually, Jesus was involved, but only as the man who ended up whisking Atkinson away after just 14 months of a stumbling second reign at The Hawthorns. This time he had to make do with journeymen players and those at the wrong end of their careers to keep Albion in Division Two. The big man lasted just 12 games of the 1988-89 season before Athletico Madrid's eccentric chairman Jesus Gil offered him an exciting (but ultimately short-lived) exit route to Spain, thus bringing Albion's "glorious" 17-year era to an end. It was to be followed by the less-thrilling Life of Brian (Talbot).

clubs finishing above United in the league, while Duncan Ferguson will never finish above Fergie in an alphabetical list of Premiership participants (Rio, on the other hand, always will). But none of these half-baked attempts are borne out by the statistics, so probably another red herring.

"What comes on to the pitch at half time, and doesn't leave until after the game on a Saturday, and not until the next day for a Wednesday game?"

Clearly the work of a sadist. One suggestion is that it's fork marks – groundsmen tend to fork the pitch at half time, the marks being removed by a roller straight after Saturday games, while the roller doesn't come out until the morning after midweek matches. Not a convincing answer, and nor are other suggestions like urine samples, shadows, floodlights or even referees, who apparently only stay in a hotel for midweek matches. Suspected to be another fake, from the evil mind of American TV commentator Lionel Bienvenu.

"Which current Premiership player survived the Munich Air Disaster?"

This was asked around five years ago, and the answer was allegedly former Arsenal and Leeds goalkeeper **John Lukic**, who was a foetus in his stewardess mother's stomach as the plane carrying the Manchester United team hit the tarmac. However, although there was a stewardess called Lukic on board she was unrelated to the Highbury custodian and her unborn child was a girl. Also, the disaster took place in 1958 and Lukic wasn't born until 1960, which would have made his the longest gestation in medical history.

"Who is the only person to have scored for Newcastle and played in goal for Manchester United?"

Now there is a genuine solution to this one... sort of. It's the **Honey Monster**, who scored a last-minute winner for **Newcastle** in a Sugar Puffs commercial made during the dying light of the **Kevin Keegan** era, before briefly donning **Peter Schmeichel**'s gloves in an advert a couple of seasons later. Keegan, bizarrely, first publicly discussed his resignation from St James' Park with the giant golden furball in one advert. The Honey Monster was last seen telling an enthralled **Dennis Wise** about the honey.

THE LISTS

Miscellaneous facts
that are sure to amaze
friends, family and foe

Gerd Müller doesn't subscribe to the "no ball in training" school of thought

"They're the second best team in the world and there's no higher praise than that"

Kevin Keegan

The only list that really counts in football is, of course, the league table, that unyielding final report on a team's performance. They say the table doesn't lie (although **Neil Warnock** is just the latest in a long line of managers to suggest that it maybe does distort the position a tad), but for **Minerul Aninoasa** of Romania's Divizia C in the early 1980s, the truth was hard to bear: they finished last in their 16-team league despite amassing just three points fewer than the second-placed team (see page 302).

There are other reasons, of course, why lists are important:

1. They enable us to forget the team nature of the game by ranking players and coaches on an unashamedly subjective basis. On such a basis, **Dave Bassett** is a finer manager than **Busby**, **Shankly** and **Ferguson** combined.

2. Some lists are finite, but others are endless: such as the list of reasons why **Graham Taylor** should never have been appointed England manager, Scottish World Cup disappointments or inexplicable refereeing decisions that went against your team.

3. You can always think of lists, as football magazines and broadsheet newspaper sports sections know only too well. Already done the World's Greatest Players or 10 Great FA Cup Upsets? No problem – how about 20 Great Players Who Aren't in the Premiership at the Moment but Were at One Point (playing fewer than 20 games)?

4. People like lists, and writers like making them. If you space them out nicely
like
this,
then you can take up lots of space with very few words, thus exerting less effort in the process. Not for nothing does the word "journalists" end as it does.

Top 10 teams in the history of the English Football League

1. **Liverpool**	98 seasons	5071 points
2. **Manchester United**	99 seasons	5037 points
3. **Arsenal**	98 seasons	4851 points
4. **Wolverhampton Wanderers**	103 seasons	4702 points
5. **Aston Villa**	103 seasons	4680 points
6. **Preston North End**	103 seasons	4669 points
7. **Sunderland**	101 seasons	4644 points
8. **Everton**	103 seasons	4633 points
9. **Blackburn Rovers**	103 seasons	4606 points
10. **Burnley**	103 seasons	4605 points

The league's most "yo-yoing" teams (between top two divisions)

1. **Leicester City/ Leicester Fosse**	Promoted 11 times	Relegated 10 times
= **Manchester City/Ardwick**	Promoted 11 times	Relegated 10 times
3. **Birmingham City/ Small Heath**	Promoted 10 times	Relegated 9 times
4. **Bolton Wanderers**	Promoted 9 times	Relegated 9 times
= **Sheffield Wednesday/ The Wednesday**	Promoted 9 times	Relegated 9 times
6. **Middlesbrough**	Promoted 8 times	Relegated 7 times
7. **Nottingham Forest**	Promoted 7 times	Relegated 7 times
= **Sunderland**	Promoted 7 times	Relegated 7 times
9. **Chelsea**	Promoted 7 times	Relegated 6 times
10. **Derby County**	Promoted 6 times	Relegated 7 times
= **West Bromwich Albion**	Promoted 6 times	Relegated 7 times
12. **Sheffield United**	Promoted 6 times	Relegated 6 times
13. **Leeds United**	Promoted 6 times	Relegated 5 times
= **Manchester United/ Newton Heath**	Promoted 6 times	Relegated 5 times
15. **Notts County**	Promoted 5 times	Relegated 6 times
= **Preston North End**	Promoted 5 times	Relegated 6 times
= **Stoke City**	Promoted 5 times	Relegated 6 times
18. **Crystal Palace**	Promoted 5 times	Relegated 5 times
= **West Ham United**	Promoted 5 times	Relegated 5 times
= **Wolverhampton Wanderers**	Promoted 5 times	Relegated 5 times

The five English League clubs whose names start and end with the same letter

Aston Villa
Charlton Athletic
Liverpool
Northampton Town
York City

Players who've appeared for more than one national team

John Hawley Edwards started the phenomenom in 1876, when he appeared for Wales despite having already played for England against Scotland two years previously. **Stan Mortensen** made his international debut for Wales against England at Wembley in 1943, despite being English; a half-time injury left the visitors short of players, so Mortensen turned out for them in the second half.

Ferenc Puskas and **Alfredo di Stefano** are the two most famous dual-country players. Both ended up playing for Spain at Franco's insistence, having begun their international careers with Hungary and Argentina respectively before moving to Real Madrid. Franco also persuaded **Ladislao Kubala** to turn out for Spain between 1953-6 after he'd already played for Czechoslovakia and Hungary.

Kubala aside, three other players are known to have performed for three different countries. Both **Yury Nikiforov** and **Akhrik Tsveiba** made their debuts for the C.I.S. before playing for both the Ukraine and Russia during the 1990s. **Josef Bican**, meanwhile, played for Austria and Czechoslovakia but also won one cap for Moravia, a Czech state "liberated" by the Germans in 1939.

The most-capped two-country player to date is **Victor Onopko**; the Real Oviedo defender has 107 caps for Russia. Onopko also won four caps at the start of his career for the C.I.S., but after the break-up of the Soviet Union he chose to play for Russia ahead of his native Ukraine.

Political changes have seen a huge rise in the number of dual-country caps: former East Germans to play for the German national team include **Ulf Kirsten** and **Mattias Sammer**; among former Yugoslavians to wear Croatian colours are **Robert Jarni** and **Robert Prosinecki**; and **Lubomir Moravcik** and **Dusan Tittel** switched from Czechoslovakia to Slovakia.

The only player to appear in two World Cup finals for different sides is **Luis Felipe Monti**, a loser with Argentina in 1930 who turned up again four years later as a 33-year-old with Italy, finally gaining himself a winner's medal as they beat Czechoslovakia 2-1.

Most frequent champions of Division One (formerly Division Two)

1.	**Manchester City**	7
2.	**Leicester City**	6
3.	**Sheffield Wednesday/ The Wednesday**	5
4.	**Small Heath/ Birmingham City**	4
=	**Liverpool**	4
=	**Derby County**	4
=	**Middlesbrough**	4
8.	**Notts County**	3
=	**Preston North End**	3
=	**Ipswich Town**	3
=	**Leeds United**	3
=	**Bolton Wanderers**	3
=	**Nottingham Forest**	3
=	**Sunderland**	3

The six double Golden Boot winners

1. **Eusebio**	1967-68	Benfica, 42 goals
	1972-73	Benfica, 40 goals
2. **Gerd Müller**	1969-70	Bayern Munich, 38 goals
	1971-72	Bayern Munich, 40 goals
3. **Dudu Georgescu**	1974-75	Dinamo Bucuresti, 33 goals
	1976-77	Dinamo Bucuresti, 47 goals
4. **Fernando Gomez**	1982-83	Porto, 36 goals
	1984-85	Porto, 39 goals
5. **Ally McCoist**	1991-92	Rangers, 34 goals
	1992-93	Rangers, 34 goals
6. **Mario Jardel**	1998-99	Porto, 36 goals
	2001-02	Sporting Lisbon, 42 goals

Most English Championship wins

1. **Liverpool**	18
2. **Manchester United**	15
3. **Arsenal**	12
4. **Everton**	9
5. **Aston Villa**	7
6. **Sunderland**	6
7. **Newcastle United**	4
= **Sheffield Wednesday/ The Wednesday**	4
9. **Huddersfield Town**	3
= **Wolverhampton Wanderers**	3
= **Leeds United**	3
= **Blackburn Rovers**	3

British teams who have gone an entire season unbeaten

1. **Linfield**	1892-93	10 games
	1894-95	6 games
	1903-04	14 games
	1917-18	10 games
	1921-22	10 games
2. **Belfast Celtic**	1926-27	22 games
	1928-29	26 games
3. **Shamrock Rovers**	1924-25	18 games
	1926-27	18 games
4. **Glentoran**	1916-17	10 games
	1980-81	22 games
5. **Preston North End**	1888-89	22 games
6. **Celtic**	1897-98	18 games
7. **Rangers**	1898-99	18 games

Biggest title-winning margins

18 points	Manchester United, Premiership, 2000
18 points	Bolton Wanderers, Division 1, 1997
18 points	Sunderland, Division 1, 1999
18 points	Swindon Town, (old) Division 4, 1986
17 points	Notts County, Division 3, 1998
16 points	York City, (old) Division 4, 1984
15 points	Middlesbrough, (old) Division 2, 1974
14 points	Fulham, Division 2, 1999
14 points	Wigan Athletic, Division 2, 2003
13 points	Everton, (old) Division 1, 1985

Stars who were turned down by clubs

Paul Gascoigne was turned down as a 14-year-old by Ipswich boss Bobby Robson after the youngster came down to Portman Road for a trial; apparently Robson was wary of taking a chance on the overweight teenager.

David Johnson, now at Nottingham Forest, was released by Manchester United because he was regarded as too short to make the grade.

Kevin Phillips only turned pro at 21, but having moved to Watford from non-league Baldock Town proved his goalscoring prowess and was soon on his way to Sunderland… and an England cap.

Alan Ball was turned down by Blackpool, who told him "you'd make a good little jockey."

Kevin Keegan, who grew up in Armthorpe, was a massive Doncaster Rovers fan but was rejected by the club for being too small – not something that seemed a problem as he took Liverpool (and then Newcastle) by storm, and was twice named European Footballer of the Year.

As a youngster **Roy Keane** wrote to English clubs for a trial, but didn't write to Manchester United. He didn't think he was good enough and was also led to believe he was too small – a problem he addressed by getting a job lifting beer barrels to increase his strength. He was 18 when Brian Clough invited him over from Ireland for a trial with Nottingham Forest.

Teams who took the title the year after winning promotion to the top flight

1. **Liverpool**	Promoted 1905	Champions 1906
2. **Everton**	Promoted 1931	Champions 1932
3. **Tottenham Hotspur**	Promoted 1950	Champions 1951
4. **Ipswich Town**	Promoted 1961	Champions 1962
5. **Nottingham Forest**	Promoted 1977	Champions 1978

Lowest League points tallies (post-war)

1.	**Stoke City***	Division 1, 1984-85	42 games	17pts
2.	**Leeds United**	Division 1, 1946-47	42 games	18pts
=	**Barnsley**	Division 2, 1952-53	42 games	18pts
=	**Queens Park Rangers**	Division 1, 1968-69	42 games	18pts
5.	**Sunderland***	Premiership, 2002-03	38 games	19pts
=	**Watford**	Division 2, 1971-72	42 games	19pts
=	**Workington**	Division 4, 1976-77	46 games	19pts
=	**Crystal Palace**	Division 1, 1980-81	42 games	19pts
9.	**Doncaster Rovers***	Division 3, 1997-98	46 games	20pts
=	**Chelsea**	Division 1, 1978-79	42 games	20pts

* Three points for a win

Players who've played for England while with overseas clubs

David Beckham	Real Madrid
Luther Blissett	AC Milan
Laurie Cunningham	Real Madrid
Trevor Francis	Sampdoria
Paul Gascoigne	Lazio
Owen Hargreaves	Bayern Munich
Mark Hateley	AC Milan and Monaco
Gerry Hitchens	Inter Milan
Gary Lineker	Barcelona
Steve McManaman	Real Madrid
David Platt	Bari, Juventus and Sampdoria
Trevor Steven	Marseille
Chris Waddle	Marseille
Des Walker	Sampdoria
Dave Watson	Werder Bremen
Ray Wilkins	AC Milan
Tony Woodcock	Cologne

Footballers who've been to jail

George Best – drink-driving, assaulting a policeman and jumping bail (1982)
Jamie Lawrence (Walsall) – armed robbery (1988)
Jan Molby – reckless driving (1988)
Tony Adams – drink-driving (1990)
Peter Storey – attempting to import pornography (1990)
Terry Fenwick – drink-driving (1991)
Mickey Thomas – passing forged bank notes (1993)
Duncan Ferguson – head-butting Raith Rovers' John McStay (1995)
Stig Tofting – assault (2002)

Diego Maradona has yet to serve the two-year sentence he received for shooting journalists with an air-powered pellet rifle in 1998.

Teams relegated after making it to both the League and FA Cup finals

1. **Chelsea** 1915*
2. **Manchester City** 1926
3. **Leicester City** 1969
4. **Brighton & Hove Albion** 1983
5. **Middlesbrough** 1997

*Were re-elected to the top division after the war without having to play in the Second Division

Top 10 FA Cup-winning teams

1.	**Manchester United**	10
2.	**Arsenal**	9
3.	**Tottenham Hotspur**	8
4.	**Aston Villa**	7
5.	**Blackburn Rovers**	6
=	**Newcastle United**	6
=	**Liverpool**	6
8.	**The Wanderers**	5
=	**West Bromwich Albion**	5
=	**Everton**	5

Eight players who've played in the Premiership, La Liga and Serie A

Winston Bogarde	AC Milan, Barcelona, Chelsea
Paulo Futre	Athletico Madrid, West Ham, AC Milan
Christian Karembeu	Sampdoria, Real Madrid, Middlesbrough
Darko Kovacevic	Sheffield Wednesday, Real Sociedad, Juventus
Savo Milosevic	Aston Villa, Real Sociedad, Juventus
Christian Panucci	AC Milan, Real Madrid, Chelsea
Florin Raducioiu	Espanyol, West Ham, AC Milan
Mario Stanic	Chelsea, Sporting Gijon, Parma

Boxing Day goal bonanza – the extraordinary 10 final scores in the First Division on 26 December, 1963

Blackpool	1-5	Chelsea
Burnley	6-1	Manchester United
Fulham	10-1	Ipswich Town
Leicester City	2-0	Everton
Liverpool	6-1	Stoke City
Nottingham Forest	3-3	Sheffield United
WBA	4-4	Tottenham Hotspur
Sheffield Wednesday	3-0	Bolton Wanderers
Wolves	3-3	Aston Villa
West Ham United	2-8	Blackburn Rovers

The Golden Boot winners who scored more than 40 goals

1. **Dudu Georgescu**	Dinamo Bucuresti (Romania)	47 goals	1976-77
2. **Hector Yazalde**	Sporting Lisbon (Portugal)	46 goals	1973-74
3. **Josip Skoblar**	Marseille (France)	44 goals	1970-71
= **Rodion Camataru**	Dinamo Bucuresti (Romania)	44 goals	1986-87
5. **Dorin Mateut**	Dinamo Bucuresti (Romania)	43 goals	1988-89
= **David Taylor**	Porthmadog FC (Wales)	43 goals	1993-94
7. **Mario Jardel**	Sporting Lisbon (Portugal)	42 goals	2001-02
= **Eusebio**	Benfica (Portugal)	42 goals	1967-68
9. **Hans Krankl**	Rapid Vienna (Austria)	41 goals	1977-78

Clubs named after people

Newell's Old Boys
Much-travelled Professor Don Isaac Newell, born in Kent, made such an impression on his ex-pupils that they decided to name the Argentinian town of Rosario's football club after him in 1903. Diego Maradona would later pull on the Newell's shirt.

Vasco da Gama
This Rio-based club, founded in 1898, were named after the Portuguese explorer who discovered the sea route from Europe to the East Indies. The city's Portuguese community still makes up the club's core support.

Deportivo Colo Colo

Based in Santiago, Chile's most successful side are named after the Mapuche native Indian chief, Colo Colo, who fought against European influence and the Chilean army for the freedom of his people.

Willem II
Founded in 1896, Tilberg's "royal" club adopted the name of the Netherlands' former ruler, who reigned from 1840-49 and had his military headquarters in the city.

FC Prince Louis
Burundi's 1981 League champions' moniker is a tribute to their former Tutsi Prince and Prime Minister Louis Rwagasore, who made major political reforms before being assassinated in 1961 – an act remembered annually on "Murder of the Hero Day."

Velez Sarsfield
Sarsfield (1801-1875) was the Argentinian patriot, lawyer, author and historian who helped write the Constitution for the State of Buenos Aires and the Argentine Code of Commerce. The Buenos Aires team named in his honour are one of the most successful in South America.

England's penalty shoot-out history

England v West Germany	1990	World Cup finals	Lost 4-3
England v Spain	1996	European Championships finals	Won 4-2
England v Germany	1996	European Championships finals	Lost 6-5
England v Belgium	1998	International Tournament	Lost 4-3
England v Argentina	1998	World Cup finals	Lost 4-3

England's biggest victories

1.	**England v Ireland**	(away)	1882	13-0
2.	**England v Ireland**	(home)	1899	13-2
3.	**England v Austria**	(a)	1908	11-1
4.	**England v Portugal**	(a)	1947	10-0
	England v USA	(a)	1964	10-0
6.	**England v Ireland**	(h)	1895	9-0
	England v Luxembourg	(a)	1960	9-0
	England v Luxembourg	(h)	1982	9-0
9.	**England v Ireland**	(a)	1890	9-1
	England v Wales	(a)	1896	9-1
	England v Belgium	(a)	1927	9-1

Footballers with staying power

Stanley Matthews	Oldest player in English top flight at 50 years 3 months
Roger Milla	Oldest player in World Cup history at 42
Jim Ryan	Oldest player to play for a senior professional club at 52
Dino Zoff	Oldest player to win the World Cup at 40
Leslie Compton	Oldest player to make his debut for England at 38
John Burridge	Oldest Premiership player at 43 years 5 months

Ten former professionals whose names alone should have made them famous

Frank Shufflebottom	Ipswich, Nottingham Forest, Bradford
Roy Proverbs	Coventry City, Gillingham
Tunji Banjo	Leyton Orient
Patrick Quartermain	Oxford United
Thomas Vansittart	Crystal Palace, Wrexham
Odysseus (Seth) Vafiadis	QPR, Millwall
Richard (Flip) Le Flem	Nottingham Forest, Wolves, Middlesbrough, Leyton Orient
Anthony Geidmintis	Workington, Watford, Northampton, Halifax
Rudolph Kaiser	Coventry City
David Hockaday	Blackpool, Swindon, Hull, Stoke, Shrewsbury

Five players who've scored for five different Premiership clubs

Stan Collymore	Nottingham Forest, Liverpool, Aston Villa, Leicester, Bradford
Ashley Ward	Norwich, Derby, Barnsley, Blackburn, Bradford
Mark Hughes	Manchester United, Chelsea, Southampton, Everton, Blackburn
Benito Carbone	Sheffield Wednesday, Aston Villa, Bradford, Derby, Middlesbrough
Nick Barmby	Tottenham, Middlesbrough, Liverpool, Everton, Leeds

Top freak injuries sustained by footballers

1. **Santiago Canizares, Valencia**
   The Spanish No 1 was ruled out of the 2002 World Cup after a shard of glass from a broken aftershave bottle severed a tendon in his foot.
2. **Alan Mullery, Tottenham**
   Was ruled out of England's 1964 tour of South Africa after cricking his back while shaving.
3. **Dave Beasant, Southampton**
   Damaged his foot trying to trap a bottle of salad cream that fell from a cupboard and was out for a couple of months.
4. **Richard Wright, Everton**
   On the sick list for a couple of months after falling out of the loft at his Suffolk home and damaging his shoulder, ruining his 2003 summer holidays.
5. **Celestine Babayaro, Chelsea**
   Launched into a somersault to celebrate someone else's goal in a pre-season match at Stevenage, and couldn't make his debut for the Blues until October.
6. **Alan McLoughlin, Portsmouth**
   Picked up his baby daughter and tore tendons in his arm; he was out for a month.
7. **Michael Stensgaard, Liverpool**
   Out for six months with a dislocated shoulder sustained trying to stop an ironing board from falling over.
8. **Alex Stepney, Manchester United**
   Dislocated his jaw shouting at his defence.
9. **Darren Barnard, Barnsley**
   Slipped on a puddle left by a puppy and was sidelined for several months with knee ligament damage.
10. **Kevin Keegan, Liverpool**
    Got a toe stuck in a bath tap; the injury ruled him out of several games.
11. **Rio Ferdinand, Leeds**
    Watching TV with his feet up on a coffee table left him with a damaged tendon.
12. **Steve Morrow, Arsenal**
    One of the most bizarre ends to a big match: Arsenal matchwinner Morrow left the Wembley pitch with a dislocated shoulder after being thrown backwards over skipper Tony Adams' shoulders during the over-exuberant celebrations that followed the 1993 League Cup final.
13. **Svein Grondalen, Norway**
    Had to withdraw from an international match after colliding with a moose while out jogging.
14. **Allan Nielsen, Tottenham**
    Missed several matches after his daughter prodded him in the eye.
15. **Charlie George, Southampton**
    Cut off his finger in a freak lawnmower accident.

Five Scottish clubs beginning and ending with the same letter

Celtic
Dundee United
East Fife
East Stirlingshire
Kilmarnock

Players who went into politics

Henry McLeish
On schoolboy forms at Leeds United, then played 108 times for East Fife. His political career peaked when he was made Scotland's (second) First Minister but resigned after just 378 days.
Lavrenty Beria
Left-back for a club in Georgia and head of KGB under Stalin.
Pelé
The world's best ever player became the Brazilian sports minister.
Zico
Another great Brazilian who had a brief foray in politics after retiring (he headed the Brazilian bid to host the 2006 World Cup, which was abandoned three days before the vote).
Biren Nongthombam
Played for Manipur, in eastern India, in the National Football Championship and took part in club tournaments in the late 1970s and early 1980s for the BSF, before becoming a member of the Manipur Legislative Assembly representing the Democratic People's Party.
Jamal Nasir
The former Malaysian footballer once made it as a Pahang assemblyman.
Willi Lemke (coach)
Coached Werder Bremen to the 1993 Bundesliga championship and is now a Social Democrat minister in the city-state government of Bremen.
H'Angus the Monkey (mascot)
Successfully elected mayor of Hartlepool… then took off his club mascot monkey suit and tried to be a serious politician.

England's most-capped players

1. **Peter Shilton**	125
2. **Bobby Moore**	107
3. **Bobby Charlton**	105
4. **Billy Wright**	104
5. **Bryan Robson**	90
6. **Kenny Sansom**	86
7. **Ray Wilkins**	84
8. **Gary Lineker**	80
9. **John Barnes**	78
10. **Stuart Pearce**	78

Not very local "local" derbies

1. **Perth Glory v Adelaide City Force**	Australia	1,700 miles (2,700km)
2. **Baltika Kaliningrad v Zenit**	Russia	600 miles (964km)
3. **Bodo Glimt v Tromso**	Norway	254 miles (410km)
4. **Marseille v Bastia**	"Med ports derby", France	205 miles (331km)
5. **Bordeaux v Toulouse**	"South west derby", France	132 miles (212km)
6. **Marseille v Nice**	"Med derby," France	97 miles (156km)

Footballers under assumed names

Pelé	Edson Arantes do Nascimento*
Pirri	Jose Martinez Sanchez
Zico	Artur Antunes Coimbra
Didi	Waldyr Pereira
Garrincha	Manoel Francisco dos Santos
Jairzhino	Jair Ventura Filho
Zizinho	Thomaz Soares da Silva
Ronaldinho	Ronaldo de Assis Moreira
A H Chequer	Morton Peto Betts (scored the only goal in the first FA Cup final, 1872)
Juninho	Oswaldo Giroldo Junior
Hamilton	Colin Veitch, Newcastle United 1899-1915**

*Pelé explains that at school, a boy called him Pelé for no apparent reason; he started a fight with him and received two days' suspension, but soon even his parents were using the new moniker
**As a trainee schoolteacher, he played under an assumed name due to the prejudice against professionalism at the time

The most successful managers to get the boot

Vicente Del Bosque, Real Madrid
Delivered Real Madrid's 29th league title and was rewarded with a sharp exit from the Bernabeu in 2003 when his contract was not renewed, presumably for failing to deliver a 10th European Cup.

Fabio Capello, Real Madrid
Spotted a pattern emerging yet? Del Bosque should have seen it coming given Real's disposal of Capello, now the Roma boss, despite him winning them La Liga. It was a decision that led to some serious backtracking by Real Madrid who, having dismissed Guus Hiddink, tried to woo Cappello back – unsuccessfully.

Bobby Robson, Barcelona
In 10 months in charge of the Catalan giants, Bobby Robson reeled in the Cup Winners' Cup, the Super Cup and the Spanish Cup. With all those distractions surely he could be forgiven for only steering Barca to second in La Liga? Well, no he couldn't.

Micky Adams, Fulham
Two words: Kevin Keegan. Impatient new Fulham owner Mohammed al Fayed was after a big-name gaffer. Keegan was his chosen one and Micky Adams never stood a chance, despite having saved the Cottagers from dropping into the Conference and subsequently building a side that played its way into Division Two.

Ruud Gullit, Chelsea
Ruud Gullit was brought in to steady the Chelsea ship after the departure of Glenn Hoddle to the England hot-seat, and the Dutch legend took the Blues to the quarter-finals of the Cup Winners' Cup and second in the table (and picked up the FA Cup along the way). He forgot to keep in with Ken Bates though, and in February 1998 was on his way.

Mike Newell, Hartlepool United
In six months at the Hartlepool helm, Mike Newell got the club promoted automatically to Division Two. But chairman Ken Hodcroft had wanted the 2002-03 Third Division title too; a late-season slump saw Rushden & Diamonds pip 'Pool to top slot and Newell's hopes of a new contract evaporated.

Ron Atkinson, Sheffield Wednesday
In November 1997 Sheffield Wednesday appealed to Big Ron to get them out of trouble. Ron duly obliged but come the following May, with Premiership status secured, he was out on his ear.

The record number of nationalities kicking off a Premiership game (Coventry v Chelsea, 4 January, 2000)

1. **England**	Telfer, Williams, Froggatt, Palmer, Wise
2. **France**	Desailly, Deschamps
3. **Italy**	Di Matteo, Zola
4. **Ireland**	Breen, Keane
5. **Morocco**	Chippo, Hadji
6. **Holland**	De Goey
7. **Spain**	Ferrer
8. **Nigeria**	Babayaro
9. **Uruguay**	Poyet
10. **Norway**	Flo
11. **Brazil**	Thome
12. **Sweden**	Hedman
13. **Scotland**	McAllister
14. **Belgium**	Roussel

The worst team ever?

The 2000-01 results for **Burton Brewers** of the West Midland Regional Women's Football League, Division One North (5th level):

Burton Brewers	0-6	Bescot
Burton Brewers	0-17	Shrewsbury Town Youth
Burton Brewers	0-18	Wolverhampton United
Burton Brewers	2-13	Crewe Vagrants
Burton Brewers	0-21	Darlaston
Burton Brewers	0-27	North Staffs
Burton Brewers	0-23	Willenhall Town
Crewe Vagrants	22-0	**Burton Brewers**
Burton Brewers	1-14	City of Stoke
Burton Brewers	0-16	Wem Raiders
Burton Brewers	0-57	Willenhall Town*

*(possibly a world record)

Clubs with the least-famous celebrity fans

Charlton Athletic	**Jim Davidson** and **Garry Bushell**
Bradford City	**Smokie**
Gillingham	**Rik Waller**
Rotherham United	**The Chuckle Brothers**
Wimbledon	**June Whitfield**
Cardiff City	**Neil Kinnock, Shakin' Stevens**
Huddersfield Town	**Nora Batty**
Luton Town	**Nick Owen**
Stockport County	**Mike Yarwood**
Rochdale	**Tommy Cannon** (but not Bobby Ball)

Brothers who have played for England

1. **Arthur, Edward** and **Ernest Bambridge** (the only instance of three brothers)
2. **Jack** and **Bobby Charlton**
3. **John** and **William Clegg**
4. **Bertie** and **Reginald Corbett**
5. **Arthur** and **Henry Cursham**
6. **Alfred** and **Charles Dobson**
7. **Frank** and **Frederick Forman**
8. **Frederick** and **John Hargreaves**
9. **Charles** and **George Heron**
10. **Alfred** and **Edward Lyttelton**
11. **Gary** and **Philip Neville**
12. **Frank** and **Reginald Osbourne**
13. **Charles** and **Thomas Perry**
14. **Herbert** and **William Rawson**
15. **Alfred** and **Charles Shelton**
16. **John** and **Septimus Smith**
17. **Clement** and **George Stephenson**
18. **Arthur** and **Robert Topham**
19. **Arthur** and **Percy Walters**
20. **Charles** and **Geoffrey Wilson**

Football clubs' original names

Dial Square	Arsenal
Small Heath Alliance	Birmingham
South Shore	Blackpool
Christ Church FC	Bolton
Boscombe St John's	Bournemouth
Black Arabs	Bristol Rovers
Abbey United	Cambridge United
Riverside	Cardiff City
Shaddongate United	Carlisle United
Singers FC	Coventry City
St Domingo FC	Everton
New Brompton	Gillingham
Glyn Cricket & Football Club	Leyton Orient
Ardwick FC	Manchester City
Newton Heath	Manchester United
Stanley	Newcastle United
Pine Villa	Oldham Athletic
Headington	Oxford United
St Jude's	Queens Park Rangers
Heaton Norris Rovers	Stockport County
Belmont AFC	Tranmere Rovers
Thames Iron Works	West Ham United
St Luke's	Wolverhampton Wanderers

The most radical changes to club colours

Leeds United
Changed from blue and gold to all-white by Don Revie when he took over as manager at Elland Road in 1961, to make the team seem as slick and modern as the all-white Real Madrid.
Albion Rovers
Changed from blue and white to the current yellow and red in 1961
Newton Heath
Changed colours from green and gold to white shirts and blue shorts in 1895, then to red shirts and white shorts in 1901-02 (the year they became Manchester United).
Burnley
Played in green until 1911 when they were persuaded that it was unlucky.
Newcastle United
Originally played in red and white stripes – the same as Sunderland; the switch to black and white came in 1904.
Everton
Early colours included black with a red sash, and salmon pink.
Gillingham
Changed their home shirts (which were originally black and white stripes) to blue to white.
Juventus
Played in pink shirts for the first six years before adopting the black and white stripes of Notts County.
Crystal Palace
Switched to red and blue from claret and blue (a result of initial kits being borrowed from Aston Villa) for the 1973 season, a change instigated by then-manager Malcolm Allison.
Arbroath
Now playing in predominantly maroon shirts and white shorts, Arbroath's original shirts were white with "black and spider stripes".
Tottenham
The White Hart Lane club's original colours were navy blue.

The 17 last names of Scottish League clubs

Academical
Albion
Athletic
City
County
Fife
Johnstone
Midlothian
Mirren
Morton
Park
Rangers
Rovers
South
Stirlingshire
Thistle
United

The 21 last names of English League clubs

Albion
Alexandra
Argyle
Athletic
City
County
Diamonds
End
Forest
Harriers
Hotspur
Orient
Palace
Rangers
Rovers
Town
United
Vale
Villa
Wanderers
Wednesday

Ten most unlikely England internationals

Tony Daley	Aston Villa
Gary Charles	Nottingham Forest
Chris Powell	Charlton Athletic
Mel Sterland	Leeds United
Paul Walsh	Luton Town
Steve Guppy	Leicester City
Mike Phelan	Manchester United
Brian Marwood	Arsenal
Eric Gates	Ipswich Town
Paul Stewart	Tottenham Hotspur

The alternative Maradonas

Gheorge Hagi	Romania	Maradona of the Carpathians
Ahmed Al Kass	Egypt	Maradona of the Nile
Saeed Owairan	Saudi Arabia	Maradona of the Desert
Emre Belozogle	Turkey	Maradona of the Bosphorous
Edvin Murati	Albania	Maradona of the Balkans
Georgi Kinkladze	Georgia	Maradona of the Caucasus
Gianfranco Zola	Italy	The Italian Maradona
Paul Gascoigne	England	The English Maradona
Joe Cole	England	The Maradona of the East End

Eleven cricketing footballers who aren't Denis Compton

Chris Balderstone
Carlisle United legend and Leicestershire all-rounder who, on September 15, 1975, finished a day's play 51 not out against Derbyshire and then played that evening for Doncaster Rovers against Brentford (in a 1-1 draw), before returning to complete his century the following day.
Keith Barker
Trainee at Blackburn Rovers' academy in 2003; fast bowler and batsman for England schoolboys.
Ian Botham
Finished his Test career with 383 wickets and 5,200 runs and, between 1979 and 1984, found time to make seven appearances for Scunthorpe United.
Leslie Compton
Brother of the more famous Denis, he made over 250 appearances for Arsenal as a right-back and centre-half between 1931 and 1951 while also keeping wicket for Middlesex. His place in the game's statistical history rests on the fact that he made his England debut (as a footballer) when he was 38 years and two months old, a record it's hard to see being beaten.
CB Fry
Never lost a Test as England captain, and also played for Southampton when they lost the 1901 FA Cup final and won one England cap (against Ireland) as a defender.
Edgar Lubbock
Played for Kent and England and won the FA Cup with Old Etonians in 1879. Master of the Blankney fox hunt and, later, a director of the Bank of England.
Harry Makepiece
Alongside his Lancashire team-mate Jack Sharp, Makepiece played for Everton in the 1906 and 1907 FA Cup finals, bagging a winner's medal in 1906.
Phil Neale
Lincoln City full-back, initially under Graham Taylor, from 1974 to 1984, and Worcestershire and England all-rounder.
Phil Neville
Like his elder brother Gary, Phil was forced to choose between cricket and football, representing England as a cricketer in the under-15 side.
Arnie Sidebottom
The only Manchester United central defender to have played in an Ashes Test (just the one, in 1985). His stats are not impressive: batting average 1, wickets taken 1, runs per wicket 65.
Jim Standen
The last of the 27 players who have won the FA Cup (as West Ham goalkeeper in 1964) and played county cricket, bowling for Worcestershire.

Ten most prolific goalscorers in international football

Ferenc Puskas	Hungary/Spain	1945-56	84
Ali Dael	Iran	1993-	77
Pelé	Brazil	1957-71	77
Sandor Kocsis	Hungary	1948-56	75
Gerd Müller	West Germany	1966-74	68
Majed Abdullah	Saudi Arabia	1978-94	67
Jassem Al-Houwaidi	Kuwait	1992-	63
Hossam Hassan	Egypt	1985-	61
Imre Schlosse	Hungary	1906-27	59
Kiatisuk Senamuang	Thailand	1993-	59

Players who've scored in the World Cup final – and won

1930	**Dorado**, **Cea**, **Iriarte**, **Castro** (Uruguay)
1934	**Orsi**, **Schiavio** (Italy)
1938	**Colaussi** 2, **Piola** 2 (Italy)
1950	**Schiaffino**, **Ghiggia** (Uruguay)
1954	**Morlock**, **Rahn** 2 (West Germany)
1958	**Vavá** 2, **Pelé** 2, **Zagalo** (Brazil)
1962	**Amarildo**, **Zito**, **Vavá** (Brazil)
1966	**Hurst** 3, **Peters** (England)
1970	**Pelé**, **Gerson**, **Jairzinho**, **Carlos Alberto** (Brazil)
1974	**Breitner**, **Müller** (West Germany)
1978	**Kempes** 2, **Bertoni** (Argentina)
1982	**Rossi**, **Tardelli**, **Altobelli** (Italy)
1986	**Brown**, **Valdano**, **Burruchaga** (Argentina)
1990	**Brehme** (West Germany)
1998	**Zidane** 2, **Petit** (France)
2002	**Ronaldo** (Brazil)

Players who've been champions in more than three countries

Marco Etcheverry	1991-98	Bolivia, Chile, US, Ecuador
Jose Manuel Moreno	1936-57	Argentina, Mexico, Chile, Colombia
Luis Artime	1967-73	Argentina, Uruguay, Brazil
Alfredo di Stefano	1947-64	Argentina, Colombia, Spain
Domingos da Guia	1933-43	Uruguay, Brazil, Argentina*
Elias Figueroa	1967-84	Uruguay, Brazil, Chile
Brian Laudrup	1987-97	Denmark, Italy, Scotland
Michael Laudrup	1986-98	Italy, Spain, Holland
Manga	1969-81	Brazil, Uruguay, Ecuador
Johan Neeskens	1970-82	Holland, Spain, US
Alfred Schaffer	1917-24	Hungary, Germany, Austria
Trevor Steven	1985-95	England, Scotland, France
Ulrich Stielike	1975-88	Germany, Spain, Switzerland

*Won three successive titles in three different countries between 1933 and 1935

Five teams who managed to defend the double at least four times in a row

Dinamo Tbilisi (Georgia)	1992-97	6
Djoliba AC (Mali)	1973-76, 1979	5*
Dinamo Tirane (Albania)	1950-53	4
Etoile Filante (Burkina Faso)	1990-93	4
Muharraq (Bahrain)	1961-64	4

* There was no League competition in Mali in 1977 and 1978.

Nissan in Japan, and South China in Hong Kong are the only clubs in the world to defend their domestic trebles. South China were the first side in world football to manage this feat in 1988 and Nissan followed suit in 1990.

Ten players labelled "the new Pelé"

Jason Euell (or so claimed Sam Hammam)
Abedi Pele
Ronaldinho
Michael Owen
Ronaldo
Nii Lamptey
Shaun Wright-Phillips
Wayne Rooney
Eusebio
Nicolas Anelka

Clubs who have gone beyond trebles

ACHIEVEMENT	CLUB	COUNTRY	SEASON	HONOURS WON
Sextuple	**Linfield**	N. Ireland	1921-22	League Champions, Irish Cup, Country Antrim Shield, Intermediate Cup, New Charity Cup, Gold Cup
Sextuple	**Valletta**	Malta	2000-01	League Champions, Rothmans Trophy, Super Cup, Lowenbrau Cup, Air Malta Centenary Cup, Super 5 Cup
Quintuple	**Celtic**	Scotland	1966-67	League Champions, European Cup, Scottish Cup, Scottish League Cup, Glasgow Cup
Quintuple	**Ajax**	Holland	1971-72	League Champions, European Cup, Dutch Cup, Intercontinental Cup, European Super Cup

Fourteen Scandinavian teams who were relegated the season after winning the league

B 71	Faroe Islands	1989 – champions; 1990 – relegated
Djurgårdens	Sweden	1959 – champions; 1960 – relegated
Fram	Norway	1950 – champions; 1951 – relegated
Freidrig	Norway	1948 – champions; 1949 – relegated
GAIS	Sweden	1954 – champions; 1955 – relegated
Haka Valkeakoski	Finland	1995 – champions; 1996 – relegated
Helsingborgs	Sweden	1934 – champions; 1935 – relegated
Herfølge BK	Denmark	2000 – champions; 2001 – relegated
Hvidovre	Denmark	1973 – champions; 1974 – relegated
IFK Goteborg	Sweden	1969 – champions; 1970 – relegated
Ilves-Kissat	Finland	1950 – champions; 1951 – relegated
KB	Denmark	1950 – champions; 1951 – relegated
SK Brann	Norway	1963 – champions; 1964 – relegated
TPV	Finland	1994 – champions; 1995 – relegated

The tightest-ever league

ROMANIA 1983-84, DIVIZIA C, SERIA A VIII-A

	P	W	D	L	F-A	Pts	
1. **Muresul Deva**	30	16	6	8	53-33	38	Promoted to Divizia B
2. **UMT Timisoara**	30	14	3	13	57-37	31	
3. **Mecanica Orastie**	30	15	1	14	49-53	31	
4. **Minerul Paroseni**	30	13	5	12	41-46	31	
5. **Minerul Moldova-Noua**	30	14	2	14	41-39	30	
6. **Minerul Stiinta Vulcan**	30	13	4	13	38-47	30	
7. **Metalul Bocsa**	30	13	3	14	40-32	29	
8. **Dacia Orastie**	30	11	7	12	58-50	29	
9. **Minerul Certej**	30	13	3	14	48-47	29	
10. **Metalul Otelu-Rosu**	30	14	1	15	38-40	29	
11. **Minerul Anina**	30	13	3	14	46-48	29	
12. **Victoria Calan**	30	13	3	14	35-37	29	
13. **Constructorul Timisoara**	30	13	3	14	57-62	29	
14. **Minerul Oravita**	30	13	3	14	39-45	29	
15. **Minerul Ghelar**	30	12	5	13	35-52	29	Relegated
16. **Minerul Aninoasa**	30	11	6	13	32-39	28	Relegated

This remarkable league table speaks for itself but it's worth noting that nine out of 16 teams in this division ended the season level on points. This is the only known case of an end-of-season table where two points separate the runners-up from the team which finished second-from-bottom. Fortunately, Divizia C didn't get much TV coverage – otherwise, the commentators could have come to grief as eight of the team's names begin with "Minerul" and two begin with "Metalul".

SK Brann's crazy yo-yo 1980s

1979 Relegated to second division
1980 Promoted to first division
1981 Relegated to second division
1982 Promoted to first division
1983 Relegated to second division
1984 Promoted to first division
1985 Relegated to second division
1986 Promoted to first division

If you thought Leicester City were forever bouncing between the top divisions, you haven't been to Bergen. Norway's second biggest city is home to SK Brann, who hold the unusual record of having spent more seasons than any other club being relegated and promoted between two leagues.

"Football is a game – the language, it don't matter as long as you run your bollocks off"

Danny Bergara, former Stockport manager